D0933879

LIFE WITH

Groucho

BY ARTHUR MARX

 1954

SIMON AND SCHUSTER

NEW YORK

Parts of this book have appeared in the Saturday Evening Post under the title My Old Man Groucho.

FIRST PRINTING
LIBRARY OF CONGRESS CATALOG CARD NUMBER: 54–9802
DEWEY DECIMAL CLASSIFICATION NUMBER: 92
MANUFACTURED IN THE UNITED STATES OF AMERICA
BY KINGSPORT PRESS, INC., KINGSPORT, TENN.

LIFE WITH

Groucho

CHAPTER 1

SOME YEARS BACK, on my twentieth birthday, I received the following communication from my father, Groucho Marx:

DEAR ART,

Twenty years ago today you stuck your head out into the world, and I hope you're doing the same sixty years from now. This will give you a total of eighty years, and when you get to my age you'll consider that plenty.

A lot has been written about my father in his lifetime, but I've never read anything that sums up his philosophy of life quite so poignantly as those few brief lines of his own.

He's a sentimentalist, but he'd rather be found dead than have you know it. And he's a dreamer, although he likes to pass himself off as a disillusioned realist.

Why he persists in this attitude is something only he can answer.*

He's lived a rich, full life, and he'll be the first to admit it. He started out at the bottom, the third son of an immigrant couple, and with his brothers—Harpo, Chico, Zeppo and Gummo—he worked his way to becoming one of the world's best-beloved comedians.

He's conquered every entertainment medium from vaudeville to

* And I'm not going to. My racket is asking questions, not answering them.
GROUCHO

television. He's had much success and very little failure, except in his early youth, and for a brief spell more recently when he ventured into the field of playwriting and producing. *Time for Elizabeth*, written in collaboration with Norman Krasna, folded after two days on Broadway. But that was more or less of an avocation, and besides, it was deductible.

On his climb up the ladder he has enjoyed life to the utmost. He has shaken hands with Presidents, danced cheek to cheek with Marlene Dietrich, played baseball with Lou Gehrig, traded backhands with Jack Kramer, strummed guitar duets with the great Segovia, and he's insulted nearly everyone worth insulting (including two of my employers, who promptly fired me).

He has owned expensive homes, eaten in the best restaurants, lived in the best hotels, had his clothes made by the best tailors, been seasick on the best liners and, until he went to work for the Chrysler Corporation, was master of a fleet of Cadillacs.

But unlike Edward Bellamy, he's not at all interested in looking backward. He claims the past is something he'd just as soon forget. That's why I'm writing this book, and not he.

"Besides," he's told me many times, "when a person starts writing his memoirs, that's a sure sign he's washed up!"

Being "washed up" is the one thing my father has always feared. No matter how well things are going, he's never been able to dispel the notion that it won't be very long (probably within the next day or two) before he'll be through in show business, completely destitute, and a burden to society, living out his life in a home for old actors.

Since he still has seven years of a ten-year contract with NBC to serve, there seems little likelihood that this will be his fate. But likely or not, the thought's disturbing enough to give him serious insomnia every night—and sometimes even in the afternoons, when it's his habit to stretch out on the couch in his study, with the radio going full blast, and take a short nap.

And he's been this way (worried, I mean; not on the couch) for as long as I can remember.

4

Back in the days before he and my mother were divorced, and my sister Miriam and I were still young enough to be living with our parents, the subject of "What's Going to Become of Father?" would frequently crop up at the dinner table. It would usually be the result of something that had happened to him at the studio that day—either an argument with one of the front-office executives about the script (generally culminating with my father's threatening to quit the movie business forever) or else something that had occurred on the set.

My father was never very happy when he was making a picture. The script was no good. The director was incompetent. The sound stage was drafty, and he was going to catch pneumonia. His brother Chico was too busy on the phone with a bookie to memorize his dialogue. And he himself was giving a very uninspired performance. ("How can they expect you to be funny at eight in the morning?" he'd groan repeatedly.)

Those were his standard complaints, and we learned not to pay much attention to them. But at least once during the shooting of every picture he'd come home even more downcast than usual; and still in his frock coat and painted black mustache (he was usually too tired to change), he'd take his place at the head of the table.

"I had a real shock today," he'd begin, in a tone so somber you'd think something calamitous had happened—like Harpo or Chico dropping dead on the set, or, at the very least, that he had run over a pedestrian on his way home from the studio.

We'd wait, breathlessly, for him to drop the bombshell which, for dramatic effect, he'd often hold in abeyance until after he had finished his tomato juice.

"A real shock!" he'd continue. "I met a fellow on the set today who used to be a big star. Now he works as an extra for fifteen bucks a day, and he's glad to get that."

We were always relieved to learn that it was only *that* again.

"Shows you what can happen if you don't save your money," Father would go on, usually with a slight shudder. "Here's a fellow who used to make ten thousand a week, and there wasn't even any income tax in those days. He had solid gold plumbing in his bathroom, and three swimming pools. Well, that's not going to happen to me."

"Why should it?" Miriam, who fancied herself a comic, would ask. "We don't even have one swimming pool."

"No, and we're not going to. If you want to go swimming, there's a very nice pool at the tennis club. That's the mistake all those fellows make. They get their expenses up so high that when they stop working they're sunk. They think this easy money out here's going to last forever."

The next day Father would run out and buy another annuity, and that night at the dinner table he'd proudly tell us about it.

"With this new policy, when I'm fifty years old, I'll have forty-five bucks a week for the rest of my life—even if I never work again."

"What makes you think you'll never work again?" Mother would ask, worried, probably thinking of the new car or fur coat she'd now be unable to talk him into getting her—at least for a couple of months.

"It happens to everyone," Father would predict glumly. "There comes a time in show business when they just don't want you any more. And even if they do want me, I'm not so sure I can keep this up forever. I'm getting too old for slapstick. I'm tired. I've been working since I was fourteen years old. And besides, supposing I should get sick and not be able to work? Then what?"

At the time he was in his mid-forties and in excellent health. But he was expecting the worst—almost welcoming it, it seemed —and he was going to be prepared for any eventuality.

Scenes of that nature would generally be followed by an economy wave that would sweep resolutely through the Marx household, destroying everything in its path, such as charge accounts at Saks' and Magnin's and the Westside Market; dinners at Romanoff's; extravagant plans for the future (new tennis rackets, bicycles, trips to Europe); and any contemplated raises in our allowances. And

6

there would also be mild bawlings-out if anyone left a room without turning off the lights, or left the tap water running in the basin, or had too many shirts in the laundry, or bought something without Father's consent, which he'd give readily if anyone bothered to ask for it.

But as a rule, these economy waves would spend their fury within a couple of days; the charge accounts would be reopened (along with a few new ones); and everything would return to normal until the next time Father tangled with the top brass at MGM or came across another destitute actor.

Since he went through this routine at least once during the making of every picture, and since each picture brought him that much closer to the termination of his contract, his anxiety about the future would increase proportionately.

Mother could never understand why he worried so. Whenever we were in the throes of a new economy wave and she'd have to curtail her spending, she'd always predict—and with quite some bitterness, now that I look back on it—that Groucho Marx would never be so washed up that he'd have to seek extra work. In fact, if he wanted her opinion (and in business matters, he most certainly did not), he'd probably always be an important star.

But even she couldn't forecast that a television quiz program called "You Bet Your Life" would eventually come along and springboard him to more fame and money than he had ever had before.

Of course, he's been considered one of America's top comedians ever since he and his brothers starred in three smash Broadway shows in a row—*I'll Say She Is, Cocoanuts,* and *Animal Crackers* —and appeared in two of the biggest-grossing comedies ever to come out of MGM—*A Night at the Opera* and *A Day at the Races.* But his name was never the household word it is today.

It's an ironic twist of fate—and a sad commentary on my father's judgment—that after he fortified his future with so many annuities he should be at the peak of his career at a time when the annuities are just reaching maturity.

But perhaps his almost pathological concern about the future is one of the reasons for his present popularity. Certainly it accounts for a good deal of it, for it has never allowed him to become complacent about his career or to take his ability for granted. And unlike so many comedians, he has never fallen into the trap of believing that what killed them at the Palace in '24 is going to get him a big Neilsen rating today.

Whatever the reason, he's still completely astonished by his present success. And if I didn't know he was enjoying it so much, I'd be inclined to believe that he's just a little disappointed that he hasn't had to fall back on his vaultful of annuities.

CHAPTER 2

IF I'VE GIVEN YOU the impression that Father is a miser, I'd like to correct that notion at once.* He isn't. On the contrary, he's one of the most generous men I've ever known.†

If he likes you, he'll spend any amount for a present for you. If you're in need, he'll help you over the rough spots and never ask for a penny of his money back. If you go out to dinner with him, he'll reach for the check, and unless you're a lot quicker and stronger than he is, he'll wind up with it. And the same applies to movie tickets, caddy fees, or even a thirty-five-cent tab at a parking lot.

For years he's been supporting a legion of impoverished relatives —some so distantly related that he doesn't even know them.

"And it's a good thing for them that I don't," he says. "If I knew them, I wouldn't send them a penny."

But along with his generosity, he has some very peculiar quirks about money—especially *his* money.

To begin with, he refuses to be pushed into buying anything against his will, even if it's an item that he secretly wants. He believes that since he earned the money, he has the absolute right to decide when and how it will be spent.

And secondly, he doesn't particularly mind how much he spends,

* You'd better, or I'll cut you off without a nickel. GROUCHO
† Now you're talking. GROUCHO

9

but it hurts him to waste money, no matter how small the amount involved, and he'll go to great extremes to avoid wasting it.

Not long ago, for example, he drove to Beverly Hills for a can of pipe tobacco. Beverly Hills, like a great many cities today, uses the parking-meter system. The rates run from a penny for twelve minutes up to a nickel for an hour. Father figured that it would take him no longer than twelve minutes to make his purchase, but after he parked in front of a meter he discovered that the only change he had in his pocket was a nickel. Now the average person making four thousand dollars a week and finding himself in a similar predicament might throw caution to the winds and put the nickel in the slot. But not Father. He walked a whole block in the broiling sun—we were having a heat wave at the time—to get the nickel changed, then walked back to the meter to put the penny in, and then walked another block to the tobacco store.

On the other hand, Father can be absurdly extravagant and never give it a thought. Several years ago, when he was making only three thousand a week, he paid eighteen hundred dollars to have an Inclinator installed in his house. An Inclinator is the electrically driven contraption that carries him up and down stairs when he doesn't feel like making the journey by foot, which is always, now that he has the Inclinator.

However, he'll only stand for extravagances if he is doing the spending. If someone else—like a wife or a housekeeper—is doing the buying for him, he'll expect that person to be as frugal as Scrooge and Silas Marner put together.

I can still remember an incident which took place during the lush days immediately prior to the 1929 market crash.

We were living in a beautiful home on Long Island at the time, and my father was starring in *Animal Crackers*. It was one of Broadway's biggest hits, and his take-home pay was about two thousand dollars a week. In addition to this, he was dabbling in the stock market on the side, and allegedly making a small fortune every day on Wall Street.

I was too young to play the market—I was eight—so Father decided to let me take horseback riding lessons instead. But horseback riding required riding pants, and I didn't have any. The result was that Father sent Mother to New York to buy me a pair.

Mother found a likely looking pair on sale at Macy's for nine dollars and sent them home C.O.D., confident that she had made a good buy and a substantial saving. But when the delivery man arrived with the pants and announced that it would take nine dollars to complete the transaction, Father looked at Mother aghast.

"Nine dollars for riding pants for a boy who hasn't been on a horse yet!" he exclaimed. "That's absurd. I won't pay it."

"They were the cheapest I could find," said Mother. "And it took me all day to find them, at that."

"Well, they're going right back," roared Father. "Nine dollars! I've never heard of such a thing. Why, when I was a boy you could buy a whole horse for nine dollars! Hereafter, let me do the shopping."

The next day he took me to Abercrombie and Fitch and bought me a riding outfit that came to forty-one dollars and thirty cents. On the way home he gave me a lecture on how women don't know the value of money.

When I pointed out to him that he had spent considerably more money than Mother had, he replied: "You're darn right I did, but these are better pants. They'll outlast that cheap pair your mother bought you by at least two years."

And as a matter of fact, they did last a long time, for he had bought them four sizes too large for me.

Father, of course, realizes that his spending habits are inconsistent. And he himself isn't sure why he is constantly vacillating between a you-can't-take-it-with-you philosophy and the opposite extreme.

But in his economies, he does feel that he's been greatly influenced by the improvident days of his childhood and early youth, when money was scarce and the possibility of his ever getting any seemed remote indeed.

Father was born in New York City late in the nineteenth century. (He doesn't know that I know what year it was, but I can tell you that on next October second he'll be old enough to be my father.)

Minnie, his mother, had come over to America from Dornum, Germany, when she was fifteen years old, and had taken a job in a straw-hat factory on Manhattan's upper East Side.

His father, Sam Marx, had also migrated to New York City from the old country. Sam was an Alsatian and a sterling patriot, who probably would have remained in his native country forever if he hadn't had to leave there abruptly to escape the French draft.

"He was only two years old at the time," claims Father, "but he was taking no chances."

Actually, Sam was about seventeen when he strode down the gangplank to take his first look at New York. And a dashing figure he was, in a green topcoat and a black stovepipe hat. But though he was sartorially perfect, there wasn't a man in New York more ill equipped than he to earn a living and eventually support five sons. His command of the English language left much to be desired; he couldn't speak a word of it. And his French wasn't much better.

In addition to his linguistic shortcomings, he had no trade. Undaunted, however, by what some might consider serious handicaps, Sam, after finding himself a rooming house, set out to conquer the world. He immediately got a job as an instructor at a dancing school right around the corner from the straw-hat factory in which Minnie had been toiling for about a year.

Finding themselves in a strange country, both Sam and Minnie knew very few people when they first came to America, and of course were extremely lonely. Although they didn't know each other at the time, both of them were whiling away their Sundays doing the same thing—riding the ferry boat to North Beach. On one of these Sunday excursions, Sam, who knew a pretty girl when he saw one, finally worked up the nerve to introduce himself to Minnie, who also seemed to be without friends or even an escort.

12

They got to talking, found that they had many things in common, and inside of a few months, decided to get married.

Shortly after the nuptials, Sam gave up being a dancing instructor and decided to go into business for himself. He and Minnie opened a tailor shop in a back room of their apartment.

Why Sam Marx decided to become a tailor no one to this day has been able to figure out.

"He'd had absolutely no training," Father told me. "And if you had ever seen one of his suits, you'd realize what an accurate statement that is. You see, Pop never used a tape measure. He didn't believe in it. He said he could just look at a man and tell his size, with the result that frequently he'd make a pair of pants with one trouser leg seven or eight inches longer than the other."

According to Father, Sam was a hard worker, but he never developed much aptitude for tailoring, and the shop did not flourish. But the family grew larger by the year.

Sam and Minnie's first child was named Leonard (Chico). About a year later they encored with one called Arthur (Harpo). And the third in line was my father. They named him Julius.

It was no capricious whim on their part to name him Julius. It was a shrewdly caculated move—a fact which my father substantiates in the following letter he once wrote to columnist Irving Hoffman:

Dear Irving:

"Late in the nineteenth century there was an Uncle Julius in our family. He was five feet one in his socks, holes and all. He had a brown spade beard, thick glasses, and a head topped off with a bald spot about the size of a buckwheat cake. My mother somehow got the notion that Uncle Julius was wealthy, and she told my father that it would be a brilliant piece of strategic flattery were they to make Uncle Julius my godfather.

At the moment I was being born, Uncle Julius was in the back room of a cigar store on Third Avenue, dealing them off the bottom. When word reached him that he had been made my god-father, he dropped everything, including two aces he had up his sleeve, and quickly rushed over to our flat.

In a speech so moist with emotion that he was blinded by his own eyeglasses, he said that he was overwhelmed by this sentimental gesture on our part and hinted that my future—a rosy one—was irrevocably linked with his. At the conclusion of his speech, still unable to see through his misty lenses, he kissed my father, handed my mother a cigar, and ran back to the pinochle game.

Two weeks later he moved in, paper suitcase and all. As time went by, my mother not only discovered that Uncle Julius seemed to be without funds but, what was even worse, that he owed my father thirty-four dollars.

My father volunteered to throw him out, but my mother thought that would be a mistake. She said she had read of many cases where rich men had lived miserly lives and then had left tremendous fortunes to their heirs when they died.

"Well, he remained with us until I got married. By this time, he had the best room in the house and owed my father eighty-four dollars. Shortly after my wedding, my mother finally admitted that Uncle Julius had been a hideous mistake and ordered my father to give him the bum's rush. But Uncle Julius solved everything by kicking off, leaving me his sole heir. His estate when probated consisted of a nine ball that he had stolen from a pool room, a box of liver pills, and a celluloid dickey.

One of the things that has constantly puzzled my father is how his folks managed to bring up the family on their pitifully small income. But it's obvious that it didn't worry them very much. At any rate, it didn't prevent them from having more children. Milton (Gummo) was born not too long after Father, and Herbert (Zeppo) followed a few years later. With five hungry boys to feed —to say nothing of Uncle Julius—it wasn't always easy to scrape together enough money to pay the landlord, especially when the family was squandering twenty-five cents a week on piano lessons for Chico. But fortunately Minnie was an accomplished charmer, and could always talk the landlord into letting them remain in the apartment, even though he knew, as well as she, that the prospect of his ever getting the rent was pretty dim.

"We never went hungry," relates Father. "At least not *too* hungry. But there was generally some kind of a brawl at the dinner table over who would get what. I distinctly remember one occasion when I almost lost an arm over a sweet roll.

"It was the last one on the platter and all through dinner, I had been eying it hungrily and trying to work up the nerve to reach for it. Finally, when I thought the other boys weren't looking, I stealthily slid my hand along the table and up onto the platter. But just as I did, Harpo picked up a meat cleaver, which he obviously had been saving for this purpose, and brought it down viciously in the general direction of my hand.

"I withdrew my hand just in time, but the platter was shattered into little pieces, and the cleaver went halfway through the table. What's worse, I didn't even get the roll. Uncle Julius wound up with it."

Although Father was usually not averse to a little good clean fun at the groaning family board, that incident left an indelible impression on him. Poverty was not for him, he decided—not if it meant risking his life and limbs for a stale sweet roll.

Of course, there was no immediate salvation at hand. He was only twelve years old and hadn't started to work yet. But he made up his mind at the time that if he ever did get any money he would not waste it. He'd live well, but he'd salt enough money away so that, no matter what happened, he'd never have to worry about where his next sweet roll was coming from.

He never has stopped worrying about it, however—even with a well-stocked deep freeze at his disposal.

CHAPTER 3

HOW FATHER became a comedian is a long story and one that I will touch upon just briefly, since I wasn't around to be an eyewitness in those days and can only take his word for it.

But I can see that his early youth could be likened to that of the young Abe Lincoln, the chief difference being that there weren't any rails to split in the vicinity of Ninety-third Street and Third Avenue.

"Just the third rail on the L," recalls Father, "and there wasn't much of a future in fooling around with that."

He was an avid reader. He had plowed through all the Frank Merriwell * and Horatio Alger stories by the time he was fourteen. Moreover, he did his reading under far more difficult conditions than Lincoln ever had to contend with.

"We didn't even have a fireplace that I could read by. I had to use a gas lamp."

Despite his fascination with the printed word, Father was not a born scholar. In fact, he wasn't any kind of a scholar, if his school record is any indication. He had a disdain for most of his teachers, and an unfortunate inability to solve problems in arithmetic. These things, coupled with the fact that my grandparents couldn't afford to support him through any more schooling, led to his decision, at the age of fourteen, to retire from P.S. 86 without waiting for his diploma.

* I still root for Yale. GROUCHO

16

But though he wasn't much for academic studies, he was full of ambition. He had his heart set on becoming a doctor. Fortunately for the medical profession (and also for Harpo and Chico), there were no colleges at that time that would accept a student who had not completed grade school.

So Sam and Minnie started looking around for a likely profession for their third offspring. Harpo and Chico had already embarked on careers of their own—Chico as a piano player in a neighborhood saloon, and Harpo as a delivery boy for a meat market. But what could Groucho do? He couldn't play the piano, and he had no desire to take up butchering as a substitute for surgery, "although I've since decided that there wouldn't have been much difference," he contends today.

Sam and Minnie looked to their own family for ideas for Father's career. There was Grandpa Schoenberg, Minnie's father, who had once been a traveling magician in Germany. There was Uncle Al Shean, Minnie's brother, who was already a star in show business and who later became internationally famous with his partner, Gallagher.

And there was Herman Schultz—a very distant relative. No one to this day is quite sure to which side of the family he belonged. But according to Marx legend there seems little doubt that Herman Schultz was the most colorful and enterprising of anyone on the family tree.

Herman Schultz was a chiropodist by trade, but when business was slack he was a professional firebug. He would go around setting fire to hotels so that their respective owners could collect the insurance money.

"His specialty was hotels in the Berkshires—especially in the dry season," relates Father. "Herman would disappear for months at a time, and come back with a fistful of money. We didn't know he was doubling in arson at the time. All my folks knew was that he seemed very successful, and that whatever he was doing it might be a good idea for their son Julius to learn the same trade. Then one day we got a letter from Sing Sing, and my folks began to doubt the advisability of apprenticing me out to a combination chiropodist and arsonist."

That narrowed the field right down to show business. My father was hardly any better prepared for a career in the theater than he was for one in medicine. His experience before the public had been limited to infrequent appearances as a boy soprano in a local church choir.

His first job (which he obtained by answering a newspaper ad) was with a small-time vaudeville act called the Le May Trio. This paid him four dollars a week and offered him a splendid opportunity to see the United States. After touring from New York to Colorado, without being enthusiastically received anywhere, the Le May Trio got canceled in Denver, and Le May absconded with all the salary money.

Since Le May had failed to pay him for the preceding weeks as well, my father found himself stranded in Denver without train fare home. He took the only job available—piloting a horse-drawn grocery wagon over a precipitous mountain trail between Victor and Cripple Creek, Colorado.

He'd had no experience with horses before, except to give an occasional lump of sugar to the steeds being used in those days to hold up New York's mounted police force. But somehow he managed to keep the job for two months, by which time he'd saved enough money to buy a train ticket back to Manhattan.

A number of other ill-paying and short-lived theatrical jobs followed in quick succession. The high point of these was a melodrama called *The Man of Her Choice* in which my father played the love interest. Evidently he played it too well, even though he was only seventeen, with just an academic knowledge of the facts of life, for his acting of the part soon got him in trouble.

It seemed that Elmer Harrison, who was producing the show and also doubling as the villain, was going steady with Rozella Keyes, the leading lady. One night during a performance, Harrison openly accused Father of taking onstage liberties with his girl friend.

"I might have been a little enthusiastic when I kissed her,"

18

claims Father in defense of his behavior at the time, "but other than that, I wasn't doing anything that Errol Flynn wouldn't be caught doing."

At any rate, one word led to another, Father kicked Harrison on the shins, and a barroom brawl ensued in front of the audience. This caused the curtain to be rung down prematurely, the act to be canceled, and Father to be fired.

But at least he was in New York, not in Denver.

Harpo and Chico, meanwhile, were pursuing their own careers with varying degrees of success. Harpo was working as a bellhop in the Hotel Seville (on Twenty-eighth Street, not in Spain), and Chico was song-plugging for Shapiro-Bernstein Music Publishers.

But my grandmother was not completely satisfied with the progress her "boys" were making. She decided that they should have an act of their own. Chico was not available—he was still with Shapiro-Bernstein—but Harpo, Gummo, and my father, under Minnie's prodding, were willing to take a crack at it.

The result was an act called (among other things) "The Four Nightingales." The fourth nightingale was a fairly attractive girl whose name was Janie O'Riley. The ostensible purpose of the act was to sing harmony. Gummo and my father (so I've been told) were pretty good vocalists at that time, but Harpo could only sing a few discordant bass notes, and Janie always missed the high ones.

Altogether, it was a pretty untalented crew. Nevertheless, they managed to get bookings in small theaters in towns such as Boston, Jersey City, and Harrisburg—in fact, any place where the management of the theater wasn't too particular about the kind of entertainment it gave its patrons. Of course, each booking only lasted until the manager actually heard the Four Nightingales sing. But my grandmother was a good promoter, and whenever it was beginning to look as if they'd never get another booking, she'd always manage to pull one more out of the hat.

She couldn't keep this up indefinitely, however. Averaging one performance a theater, the act soon ran out of places where it could be booked. And the time eventually came when every theater man-

19

ager east of Chicago started running when he saw Minnie Marx approaching.

Unhappy but far from discouraged, Minnie packed up the entire family, including Uncle Julius, Grandpa Schoenberg and Janie O'Riley, and settled down in the Windy City. Chico, still plugging away for Shapiro-Bernstein, remained behind in New York, and no one knew what had become of Herman Schultz.

Using Chicago as home base, the Four Nightingales embarked on an extensive tour of the South and Midwest. Harpo was still singing off key, Janie O'Riley was still missing the high notes, and the act was still getting its customary lukewarm reception everywhere it played. They were frequently being canceled by irate managers, and at least once a month they found themselves stranded without funds in some whistle-stop town.

Somewhere during all this, they stopped calling themselves "The Four Nightingales" and changed the name of the act to the "Marx Brothers & Co." Presumably this was to hide their identity, but essentially the act was the same. They were fooling no one, and by the time they pulled into a place called Nacogdoches, Texas, they were prepared for what could conceivably be a last-ditch stand.

Their first performance in Nacogdoches was at a matinee. It was a real honky-tonk kind of theater. "The audience was full of big ranchers in ten-gallon hats, and a few small ranchers in five-gallon hats," Father told me.

The first part of the performance went fairly well, but in the middle of the show the audience suddenly got up en masse and disappeared through the front exit. Investigation disclosed that the customers had gone outside to view a runaway mule.

My father and his brothers, though accustomed to insults, were enraged by this one. When the customers filed back into the theater, thirty minutes later, the Marx brothers were no longer interested in giving a good performance. All they wanted to do was get even with the audience, and the only way they knew how was to burlesque the kind of singing they had been doing so seriously.

This quickly evolved into a rough-house comedy bit, with the

20

Marxes, led by my father, flinging insults about Texas and its inhabitants to the audience as rapidly as they could think of them.

Since this happened over thirty years ago, my father is not very clear about the exact phraseology of some of these insults, but he does remember calling the Texans in the audience "damned Yankees" and throwing in a couple of lines that went something like:

> Nacogdoches
> Is full of roaches.

And:

> The Jackass
> Is the finest
> Flower of
> Tex-ass.

Perhaps it's just as well that Father can't remember any more of them. But at any rate they did serve to launch him on a successful career of ad libbing. At the time, however, they were not looking for laughs; they fully expected to be tarred and feathered and run out of town on a rail. But instead the audience loved their clowning and greeted their insults and the most tired jokes with uproarious laughter.

And so they were suddenly comedians, with their fame traveling all the way to Denison, Texas. The manager of the theater in Denison not only wanted to book them, but he offered to raise the salary for the whole act from fifty to seventy-five dollars a week if they'd throw in an additional comedy sketch. Denison was going to be entertaining a teacher's convention, and the manager expected a sellout.

My father jumped at the offer, but Harpo and Gummo considered this move pure insanity. How could they promise to deliver a sketch they didn't even have?

"There's going to be a teachers' convention there," said my father, "so we'll give them a school act."

School acts were all the rage in those days—Gus Edwards having

21

started the craze—and they had seen a number of them. "We'll make up one of our own," added my father.

Harpo and Gummo were still not convinced, but having no alternative to suggest, they put their heads together with my father and the three of them dreamed up an act called "Fun in Hi Skule." This was a hodge-podge of all the comedy bits they had seen and heard in other school acts, plus some original material that was inspired by their own school days.

Being the most literate of the group,* my father, played the schoolmaster in the act. And to look the part, he hid himself behind a black mustache and wore, for the first time, his famous frock coat (which he borrowed from Uncle Julius, who was also along on the trip).

"I tried to borrow the mustache from Uncle Julius, too, but he was very proud of his mustache and wouldn't stand still long enough for me to cut it off. So I had to paste a phony one on."

Harpo played the part of a moronic country bumpkin—a standard character in those days—and to make sure he looked moronic, he wore a wig which he improvised out of some old rope.

"The school act went over big for the teachers' convention," boasts my father, "and after that we were a pretty big hit everywhere else we played in Texas. I guess we could have stayed there indefinitely, but after we got ourselves reasonably solvent, we decided to go back to Chicago. After all, how long can anyone eat chili con carne?"

* *Faint praise.* GROUCHO

22

CHAPTER **4**

THE MARX BROTHERS in "Home Again" took Chicago and New York by storm when they finally got there. In fact, their rough-house brand of humor was so popular with the sophisticated audiences at the Palace and they were brought back for so many return engagements that they became known as the Palace Stock Company.

Of course, it took them many years to make the transition from small-time to big-time vaudeville—years that saw a number of interesting developments in the lives of my father and his brothers.

For one thing, Chico quit the song-plugging business shortly after the Texas tour, and joined forces with his brothers. Not only did he join them, but he persuaded them to abandon "Fun in Hi Skule," and do a one-hour musical show called "The Cinderella Girl." The book was written by Jo Swerling, one of the authors of *Guys and Dolls*, and the lyrics by the late Gus Kahn, who turned out to be one of this country's most distinguished lyricists.*

"The Cinderella Girl" was an immediate flop, and they did a number of other shows that weren't much more successful before they arrived at the Palace with "Home Again." But "The Cinderella Girl" was still a turning point, for it established a pattern for their later successes. For the first time in their vaudeville careers, Harpo, Chico and Father were a team, portraying essentially the same comedy characters that won them fame later on. Furthermore,

* *And also your father-in-law.* GROUCHO

23

the new show featured Chico at the piano, and offered the customers a line-up of nine lively chorus girls. Thus sex was introduced into a Marx Brothers' show for the first time (and, according to reliable sources, into their personal lives as well *).

And it was only fitting that Chico should be the one to introduce it. "Chico was a real sport and a heavy spender, with the soul of a gambler and a bankroll to match," maintains Father. "When he wasn't shooting dice or playing cards, he was usually being pursued from town to town by an irate husband, or a father with a shotgun."

Despite Chico's talent for getting himself in romantic and financial difficulties in every town along the Keith and Orpheum Circuits, the Marx Brothers couldn't have survived without him. His piano playing, though not in a class with Paderewski's, was definitely unique, and his tricks on the keyboard were a great favorite with audiences everywhere.

So much so that Harpo decided that he too would play a musical instrument in the act. He chose the harp. He'd heard his grandmother strum one, and if she could master it, so could he—if he could get one, that is. He finally persuaded my father to send away for a harp, and after it caught up with them in Decatur, Illinois, he buckled down to the business of learning how to play it.

Practicing diligently in his dressing room between performances, Harpo taught himself a few simple chords after only a week. And within two weeks he was playing duets with Chico in the act.† The harp was a big hit with audiences,‡ so it stayed in the show permanently.§

Father, meanwhile, had bought himself a secondhand guitar, and he too was practicing in his dressing room at every opportunity. He had no desire to play it in the show, however; he simply enjoyed music.

---

* You can say that again. GROUCHO, HARPO, and CHICO
† That'll give you an idea of the act. GROUCHO
‡ That'll give you an idea of the audiences. GROUCHO
§ And I stayed out when he was playing. GROUCHO

In addition to trying to master the guitar, my father soon found on his hands the responsibility of managing the act. Being the oldest, Chico had assumed the managership when he first joined the Marx Brothers. Part of his job was to collect the salary money from the theater managers and distribute it among the cast.

"But we discovered very quickly that this wasn't a very practical idea," says my father. "There were substantial deficits every week, and they became more substantial as Chico's interest in the galloping ivories increased."

When it became obvious that Chico would never make good the deficits, Father stepped in and took over the reins. Actually, this suited Harpo and Chico fine, because one of the manager's chief functions was to get down to the theater early in the morning and run through the musical numbers with the pit orchestra. Absolved of this responsibility, Chico and Harpo could sleep until noon, and usually did.

Father, for some reason or another, was always the most serious member of the group, and indulged in few of the pastimes that other actors found so engrossing. He hated staying up late, he drank very little, except for an occasional beer, and he disliked all forms of gambling. Not that he disapproved; he just didn't get any kick out of that sort of thing. While his brothers were out on the town, or looking for suckers in the local pool hall, he'd be in his hotel room, reading or practicing the guitar, or thinking up jokes for the act.

Reading was one of his favorite forms of relaxation. He devoured everything he could get his hands on, from Variety, to political magazines, to books on American history. He was a great newspaper reader, too, and read every section thoroughly, except, paradoxically, the comics. (I also suspect that during his extensive reading he must have come across at least one handbook on how to play pool, because even though he was in his hotel room every evening, he's a pretty handy fellow with a pool cue today.)

One pleasure he did approve of was cigar smoking. He was an inveterate cigar smoker by the time he was twenty. He had picked up the habit from an old vaudevillian who had tipped him off that a cigar was one of the most useful props an actor could carry with him on the stage. "If you forget a line," confesses my father, "all you have to do is stick the cigar in your mouth and puff on it until you think of what you've forgotten."

In those days he smoked nickel cigars. Only once did he loosen up enough to spend a dime for one. This was the result of an advertisement he had seen for a brand of ten-cent pure Havanas called La Preferencias. The ad fascinated him, for it promised the smoker "Thirty glorious minutes in Havana."

Figuring he'd never get to Havana any other way, he purchased one La Preferencia and brought it back to his room. Then he set his alarm clock for thirty minutes hence, lighted the cigar and stretched out on the bed to enjoy his trip.

Twenty minutes later the cigar had burned down so short that it was scorching his fingertips. Feeling that he'd been victimized, he brought the remnants of the cigar back to the man who had sold it to him and laid it down on the counter.

"The ad said thirty minutes in Havana," he complained, pointing to his watch. "It's only been twenty minutes. What are you going to do about it?"

In the face of such righteous indignation, the cigar salesman had no alternative but to give him a second stogy without charge. The second cigar survived the alarm clock test for only fifteen minutes. Again Father took it back, and again the salesman gave him a replacement.

The third and fourth cigars proved to be no better. And when my father trotted in with the fifth one burned down to a nub, hopeful of a sixth La Preferencia free of charge, the salesman was convinced that he was the victim of a skin game and booted him out onto the sidewalk.

"You couldn't believe the advertising in those days any more than you can now," points out Father, still smoldering over the outrage.

26

In addition to smoking nickel cigars, Father had other ways of conserving money. While his brothers would generally be holed up at one of the more expensive hotels, he'd be staying at some shoddy place whose rates were in keeping with his income.

Since the entire act of twenty people was only getting six hundred dollars a week, his income wasn't much. Still, he always managed to bank some of it, and constantly harped on his brothers to do the same—to no avail.

On one of their vaudeville tours through the hinterlands, my father and his brothers found themselves on the same bill with a monologist named Art Fisher, whose hobby was giving people nicknames. A few hours spent with my father convinced Fisher that he ought to be called "Groucho." The origin of "Harpo" is, of course, obvious. And "Chico" evolved from the fact that he was such a notorious lady-killer, ladies in those days being known as "chickens." Gummo was so named by Fisher because he always wore "gum-shoes," whether it was raining or not. Soon my father and his brothers found themselves using the new names in place of their real ones.

It wasn't many months after this historic event that the First World War came along. Chico, Harpo, and my father volunteered for the service but were rejected because they didn't have 20–20 vision. But war was hell for the Marx Brothers just the same. It took Gummo, their straight man, and good straight men were hard to find.

To fill the vacancy left by Gummo, my grandmother shipped Zeppo on to them. Zeppo, who was still going under the name of Herbert, was only sixteen, but he'd had his fill of school and spent most of his time ditching classes. Making him the Marx Brothers' straight man was the severest punishment Minnie could devise.

"Mom knew what she was doing," maintains Father. "Some of those one-night stands we played were a hell of a lot worse than Siberia."

A year of peaceful army life was enough to convince Gummo

that anything was better than being an actor, so when the war ended he stepped out of the act for good. As a result, Zeppo had a permanent job and also a permanent nickname. (There are many versions of the origin of the name "Zeppo," but they are all so conflicting that the reader would do just as well to make one up for himself.)

Zeppo's chief claim to fame, whenever anybody talks about the Marx Brothers, is that "he was the good-looking one." But actually he had talent as a comedian, too. Once, when my father took sick during *Animal Crackers*, Zeppo understudied for him. After he recovered sufficiently, my father went down to the theater to watch him perform.

"He was so good the audience couldn't even tell the difference," claims Father. "I could have stayed out front every night, and no one would have missed me at all. And I would have, too—if I could have smoked in the audience."

But four comedians would have been too much for one vaudeville act, so Zeppo took over the juvenile chores. By the time they scored their first big success in "Home Again" at the Palace in 1919, Zeppo was not only a first-class straight man, but also an accomplished adagio dancer.

"Home Again" landed them in the big time for good. Oddly enough, it was written by their uncle, Al Shean, who was already an important star in vaudeville. Uncle Al didn't know whether or not his nephews had any talent, but he felt sorry for them after watching them flop in show after show. So when Minnie had begged him to help her boys, he sat down in her kitchen and started writing "Home Again" on a piece of scratch paper.

Al Shean wasn't actually a writer, but he knew enough about the theater to outline a good basic premise. With that to start from, Father and his brothers added some of their own wild jokes and comedy bits and tried the show out in the small-time vaudeville houses around Chicago. "Home Again" caught on almost immediately, and was soon booked into the big-time—the Majestic Theater, in Chicago. Two rave reviews—by Percy Hammond and Ashton Stevens—assured their success and led to their being booked at the Palace in New York several months later.

"Home Again" played the Keith Circuit in New York City for a solid year. By that time, the Marxes were getting fifteen hundred dollars a week for the act and eating well.

One evening, when they were playing the Fifth Avenue Theater at Twenty-ninth Street, Father and his brothers went across the street between performances to have their dinner. They lingered too long over their coffee and didn't get back to the theater until the curtain was going up. Having no time to paste on his phony mustache, Father grabbed some black makeup, smeared some under his nose, and ran out onto the stage.

The laughs were just as loud with the makeshift mustache, so Father decided he'd stick to a painted one permanently. "It was a lot easier to put on, and besides it didn't smell of ether like the glue on the phony one did."

But the manager of the theater was furious about the switch. "Hereafter," he said, "I want the same mustache you gave 'em at the Palace!"

"You can have it," said my father, picking the mustache up off the dressing table and handing it to him.

During the Marx Brothers' long stand in New York, the girl who had been dancing with Zeppo quit the act.

My mother, whose name was Ruth Johnson at the time, applied for the job and got it—probably on account of her looks more than her dancing ability. She was eighteen and strikingly pretty, and Zeppo envisioned a chance to combine business with pleasure.

He took her to dinner at Luchow's the night he hired her, and in the restaurant they ran into my father, who was dining with Gracie Allen. Gracie Allen, of course, hadn't married George Burns yet, and my father took her out quite often.

Zeppo introduced my father to the new dancer, my father complimented him on his good taste, and then said to her, "I wish I could say the same for you."

The next day Zeppo escorted Mother to the theater for rehearsal. Backstage they bumped into Father once again. He was carrying his guitar in its leather case, and he was on his way up the circular stairway leading to the dressing rooms.

Noticing Mother, he leaned over the iron railing, wiggled his eyebrows at her suggestively, and said, "I ought to get married, so I'd have someone to carry my guitar!"

CHAPTER 5

I WAS only a year old when my parents took me to London. They made the trip because the Marx Brothers were to appear there in a new act called "On the Mezzanine." It was the follow-up to "Home Again," a little more sophisticated perhaps, and it had been so successful in America that London booking agents were anxious to treat English audiences to the same.

But the first night audience in London didn't appreciate or understand the Marx Brothers' wild brand of comedy. Jokes that slayed New York audiences went completely over the Londoners' heads. "It was so silent in the theater that you'd have thought we were playing *Hamlet,*" recalls my father. Near the finish of the show the audience started to hoot and jeer and hurl pennies on the stage. Penny-throwing was an old British custom, the epitome of adverse criticism in the music halls. When a performer, especially an American, received that kind of treatment, the wisest thing to do was to hop the next ship out of Liverpool.

But my father never accepts defeat without putting up a stiff fight. Besides, he's extremely susceptible to seasickness, and the mere thought of boarding a ship again after he had just got off one was enough to make him turn green. So instead of retreating to the wings, he stepped bravely to the footlights, lugubriously surveyed the customers for a moment, and then said, straight-faced, "We don't mind being insulted, but if you must throw coins, how about throwing something that'll do us some good—like shillings or guineas?"

31

That brought down the house, and although it didn't prevent the manager from canceling the act immediately after the performance, it changed what had promised to be a complete rout into a minor victory. My father's wisecrack on the brink of defeat not only won him the sympathy of the audience, but the line became famous throughout London and resulted in the act's being booked by a rival theater circuit.

For their second attempt at what my father calls "licking the Redcoats," the Marx Brothers reverted back to "Home Again." Its humor was a little dated, but they felt that it might be more in the tradition of what English music-hall audiences expected. They were right. "Home Again" was a huge success in London, and afterwards it toured the provinces for months before the Marx Brothers finally returned to the United States.

Although it's difficult for me to differentiate between what I actually remember about my father in those days and what I've been told, I seem to recall seeing a man of his description hanging around when I was still in a crib. He was about thirty at the time, gaunt, bushy-haired and bespectacled, and my mother always called him "Grouch."

There was no such thing as a nurse or housekeeper to look after me. For a while there wasn't even a house. Just hotel rooms. It seemed to me we were always traveling—for what purpose I didn't know.

The three of us usually shared one room in a hotel, and not a very good hotel at that. The Marx Brothers were working steadily, but fifteen hundred dollars a week for the whole act was not really very much. Their individual salaries amounted to about two hundred dollars a week, and out of that they had to pay their own traveling expenses and hotel bills. And since my father now had a family, he was more determined than ever to save what money he could.

While he was not at the theater, my father seemed to spend much of his time in the bathroom. My mother had discovered soon after I was born that my father enjoyed taking care of me.

He didn't even seem to mind washing diapers, so whenever possible she turned this chore over to him. When he wasn't washing diapers, he was forced to spend most of his leisure hours in the bathroom because it was the only place he could read and play the guitar without waking me up.

In addition to the inconvenience of three in a hotel room, there was the problem of what to do with me during the show, since my mother was still dancing in the act. Baby sitters were unheard of in those days, and they couldn't leave me at the theater during the performance because most vaudeville houses didn't have individual dressing rooms.

My father finally had to prevail upon a troupe of acrobats on the same bill to stay with me in the hotel room while the Marx Brothers were on the stage. The acrobats opened the show, and after their performance just had time to rush back to the hotel before my mother and father had to leave for the theater.

This arrangement worked out for a while, but finally my father had to let the acrobats go. They were conscientious baby sitters, but they couldn't refrain from practicing their acrobatics in our hotel room. Aside from what this was doing to the furniture, the guests in the room below were constantly complaining to the manager about the disturbance overhead. The manager quite often thought it was my father beating up my mother and wanted to throw us out.

The baby-sitting problem came to an end as a result of a small feud Zeppo had been carrying on with my mother ever since she had thrown him over in favor of my father. For the climax of their adagio dance, my mother was supposed to do a very fancy back bend, with Zeppo helping her up again at the finish. At their best, I understand, they wouldn't have given Fred Astaire and Ginger Rogers anything to worry about, but they served a definite purpose: they gave my father and Harpo and Chico an opportunity to be off the stage for a few minutes.

After they had been dancing together for some months, Zeppo discovered that my mother couldn't extricate herself from the

33

back-bend position very gracefully under her own power. To torment her, he'd frequently let her struggle with the problem for what, on the stage, seemed like an interminable length of time before he'd condescendingly help her up. This made my mother look pretty ridiculous, and at the conclusion of their act there would always be an unpleasant scene in the wings.

But my mother liked being a part of the show, and she put up with Zeppo's unchivalrous behavior until "On the Mezzanine" was playing the Biltmore Theater in Los Angeles several years later. The incident that brought things to a head occurred one night during the performance. Zeppo, while swinging my mother around by her hands, somehow let her slip through his grasp and she sailed into the orchestra pit, landing in the percussion section.

"The manager," relates my father, "rushed backstage after the show and said he thought it was the greatest finish to a dance routine he'd ever seen."

My mother, however, was not so pleased. She was pretty shaken up by the experience and accused Zeppo of doing it deliberately. She felt he was trying to get even with her for what she had told him a few days before. She had told him that his hands were as rough as alligator skin and that he ought to do something about them.

Zeppo's excuse for the slip during the number was that he *had* done something about them. For several days he had been using almond-cream lotion to soften his hands. He had put some on before this performance, and it had made his hands slippery.

My father hates family warfare of any kind, and when the problem was brought to him for arbitration, he voiced the opinion that there was justification for complaint on each side, and that the two of them ought to make more of an effort to get along, at least professionally.

But when my mother and father returned to our hotel room around midnight, I overheard her telling him tearfully that the Marx Brothers would have to choose between her and Zeppo. Evidently she felt that out of loyalty to his own wife he would decide in her favor. She was young and innocent and hadn't been married to him long enough to realize that, although he'll go out of his way to be fair, he doesn't like ultimatums. Besides which, he'd been thinking for a good many months that a wife's place is in the kitchen, not in the percussion section.

"Ruth," he said, "we've been known as the Four Marx Brothers for a number of years now. I'm not going to change it just because you can't get along with Zep."

"It's impossible to get along with that man," replied Mother. "He's much too fresh!"

"All right," said Father. "Then turn in your uniform. And tell the coach you won't be out for spring practice."

This didn't get the laugh he'd been expecting, and when he saw the tears well up in my mother's eyes, he temporarily softened. "Come now, Ruth. It isn't as bad as all that. Taking care of your son is a more important job than doing that bad imitation of Irene Castle."

"It isn't that," sniffled my mother. "I just don't want Betty taking my place!" (Betty, Chico's wife, was also in the act, and there was some jealousy between them in those days.)

"She's turning in her uniform, too," said my father. "I've already spoken to Harpo and Chico about that. No more wives in the act. Wives are a nuisance. There's only one place for a wife, and I won't go into that with a child present."

With my mother assuming most of the baby-tending chores, my father volunteered for the early morning duty, which consisted of taking me to breakfast and for a walk afterwards. Even though the show kept him up late, my father liked to rise early and read all the papers at the breakfast table. That way he'd be through with them by the time the noon editions came out.

I remember one walk in particular. We were in Boston for the out-of-town try-outs of *I'll Say She Is*, the Marx Brothers' first legitimate show. It was a wintry morning, and my father had dressed me in a white sailor suit. Why, I don't know. I guess he didn't realize that I'd be out of uniform in a white sailor suit in the winter.

Going through the park, I ignored my father's advice not to stray onto a large mud puddle that had frozen over, and he didn't notice that I had, because he was strolling along with his head buried in the newspaper. Suddenly the thin ice cracked, and I fell through into the shallow but muddy water. My sailor suit and face were the color of chocolate when I sheepishly presented myself to my father on the sidewalk. I expected him to be angry, but instead he doubled over, laughing. When his laughter subsided, all he said was, "I never thought the day would come when a son of mine would be imitating Jolson."

At dinner time, the three of us would generally go out to a restaurant together. In those days, we never went to a very fancy eating place—it was usually Child's or some cafeteria.

One evening—I think it was at Child's in Boston—we were seated near a prim-looking dowager at a table by herself. She was obviously quite distressed at finding herself so close to a couple with an obstreperous child in a high chair, but she was doing her best to ignore us.

I finished dinner first and was given permission to get out of the high chair. I entertained myself by mopping up the dirty floor with a piece of toast. When I tired of pushing the toast around, I casually tossed it over my shoulder and it landed on the dowager's plate of ham and eggs.

My mother was horrified. "Grouch," she whispered, "please go over and apologize to that woman."

Rising obediently, my father approached the dowager. She was glaring at him, but he maintained his composure admirably.

"Madame," he said with a deep bow, and the proper amount of contrition in his voice, "I'm sorry my son threw that toast in your plate. And if he ever does it again, I'll have him throw the jam in with it."

As I grew older I realized that my father could never quite decide whether to be a strict disciplinarian or a pretty soft touch. I think he felt that, for our own good, a little discipline was necessary. And our own good was always uppermost in his mind. But whenever he was at the point of meting out punishment, his sense of humor would get the best of him.

36

He didn't believe in spankings, and if Mother dared lay a hand on us, no matter how justified she was, he'd become furious. He used to say that grownups didn't have the right to "slug" children who were too small to defend themselves. And besides, he felt, it wasn't safe. When the children grew up and were large enough, they might hit him. He always took the long range view.

If my sister or I did something really bad—like lying or breaking a piece of furniture—he'd put us to bed and threaten to make us go without dinner. He maintained this was more effective than spankings. I don't know how effective it was, but it was certainly more pleasant, especially since, in all the years I was growing up, he never once carried out the threat about no dinner.

After I'd been incarcerated in the bedroom for a while, he'd open the door and say, in a grim tone, "Do you think you can behave yourself from now on?"

I'd, of course, answer "Yes," and he'd reply, "All right, put your clothes on and come down to dinner. I don't know why I should have to eat that dinner, and not you."

He punched hard to cover up his soft spots. He didn't have the heart to make anyone go hungry. Besides, he liked having his children around him at the table, and if it came to a choice, he preferred children's company to that of the grownups. This was always a source of contention whenever he and my mother were having ten or twelve people in to dinner. Mother believed that we should eat early on those occasions and be packed off to our rooms before the company arrived.

But father would have none of that. "I don't get to see the kids all day. When am I going to see them if I can't eat with them?" he'd ask, even if he'd been around the house steadily for the past two weeks.

At the dinner table, he was always very conscious of whether we were eating or not. Frequently he'd interrupt his stories to bark out, "If you don't drink all that milk, you're not going to get any dessert." If that didn't work, he'd try another tack. "Don't you know that milk is good for you? It builds bones. It's good for your teeth. I always drank my milk when I was a boy, and look at my teeth—filled with cavities."

Often his exhortations at the dinner table varied in accordance with what the medical writers were currently saying. One night he might admonish you for concealing your helping of spinach beneath an empty baked potato skin, and a couple of meals later he'd say to my mother, "Don't force them to eat if they don't want to, Ruth. I read a long article in *Harper's* today by a doctor who thinks spinach is absolutely worthless—maybe even injurious. Leave them alone. Children are like animals—they'll eat when they're hungry."

A couple of months after he first told me spinach was worthless, I tried leaving the spinach on my plate untouched. Glancing at my plate as the housekeeper took it away, he shook his head ominously and said, "No spinach, no dessert."

I reminded him that he had told me spinach was worthless.

"That'll teach you not to believe everything your father tells you," he replied, handing me the cake platter.

It was a pretty confusing atmosphere in which to grow up. You never knew from one day to the next just what his views were on spinach. Or on anything else, for that matter.

He went through a long period once when his sole purpose in life, it seemed, was to keep me from putting too much sugar on my breakfast cereal. This phase reached a climax when we were still on the road with *I'll Say She Is*.

It was in Philadelphia, about a month before the show was to open on Broadway. They had been touring with *I'll Say She Is* for about a year, and it had met with considerable success everywhere on the road, but they had hesitated about bringing it to New York's legitimate theater because of its slapstick overtones. After a year of touring, however, they had no choice but to tackle New York; there was no place else to go.

But it was imperative that their first legitimate show be as good as possible when it reached New York. If they flopped there, they'd be through in show business. The Marx Brothers had had a fight with B. F. Albee, who controlled the two biggest vaudeville cir-

38

cuits, because they disagreed with his dictatorial booking methods. As a result, they couldn't get booked in any major vaudeville theater in the United States.

Because of the importance of the impending event, Father and his brothers frequently stayed at the theater after their nightly stint, smoothing out the rough spots in the show and devising new routines. It was usually late when my father returned to the hotel, and he wouldn't feel like taking me to breakfast in the mornings. To spare my mother the pleasure, Father bribed Ed Metcalf, one of the bit players in the show, to get me up every morning and take me to breakfast. Metcalf was a burly, red-faced Irishman who played the part of the detective in Harpo's renowned knife-stealing scene.

My father had warned Metcalf not to let me pour the whole bowl of sugar over my oatmeal, but Metcalf construed it to mean no sugar at all. Every morning, for four successive days, he foiled my attempts to get the sugar bowl. By the fifth day, I was getting pretty sick of him, and when he still refused to allow me even one small spoonful, I blew my three-year-old top, and said, "Pass the sugar, you son of a bitch!"

Metcalf wasn't familiar with the works of Dr. Spock, and didn't quite know how to handle the situation. His first impulse, of course, was to wallop me, but not knowing how my father might feel about it, he refrained from brute force and escorted me back to the hotel, remarking along the way that my father would undoubtedly give me a sound thrashing.

After Metcalf had departed, my father sat me down and shook his head in silent disapproval. After what seemed like hours, he finally said, "Arthur, I'm surprised at you, treating Mr. Metcalf that way."

"Well, he wouldn't let me have any sugar," I complained.

"That's no way to get it," said Father patiently. "If you expect him to be nice to you, you should say, 'Please pass the sugar—you son of a bitch.'"

CHAPTER 6

I'll Say She Is sneaked into New York and opened at the Casino Theater on May 19, 1924. Its opening was completely unheralded. Most of the first-string critics didn't even want to waste an evening reviewing it and wouldn't have if there had been anything else doing in town that night.

Alexander Woollcott wasn't planning to attend under any circumstances. He was going to play poker that evening. But he had forgotten to notify his assistant to cover the event, and at the last moment he got stuck with the job and dragged one of his friends, Franklin P. Adams of the *World*, along with him.

It was a lucky thing for the Marx Brothers that it turned out this way, for Woollcott was one of the most influential critics in New York at the time, and he was ecstatic in his praise of *I'll Say She Is* the next morning. He wound up his review by writing, "If, thus badly recounted, it does not sound amusing, will you take the word of one who, at its conclusion, had to be picked up out of the aisle and placed gently back in his seat, that it is all of that?"

The other critics—Percy Hammond, Heywood Broun, George Kaufman, and George Jean Nathan—were equally enthusiastic, and *I'll Say She Is* settled down in New York for a two-year run. The Marx Brothers were suddenly the darlings of Broadway.

I'm not sure what *I'll Say She Is* was about, and neither are my father or his brothers. They tell me that the man responsible for it was a shoestring producer named Joseph M. Gaites. Gaites had had a load of scenery on his hands left over from two previous flops; and in an attempt to recoup some part of his investment, he had hired Will Johnstone, cartoonist for the New York *Evening World*, to write a musical around the scenery. Johnstone combined a few new ideas of his own with a number of sure-fire sketches the Marxes had been using on the road for years and pieced the whole thing together with some song and dance routines supplied by his brother, Tom. The result added up to one of the biggest hits New York had seen in many years.

Father took me backstage several times and let me view the matinee performances from the wings. I regret that I was too young to appreciate the comedy (and also the scantily-clad chorus girls who were milling around me in the wings), but I vividly recall two of the most celebrated routines in the show.

One was the sketch where the detective (Ed Metcalf) was congratulating Harpo on his honesty. As Metcalf shook Harpo's hand vigorously, silverware began to fall clatteringly to the floor from Harpo's sleeve. The detective couldn't believe that he'd been deceived so completely, and shook hands with him again. More silverware rained on the floor. They kept this up for a good fifteen minutes, by which time the audience was paralyzed.

The other scene I remember was the one in which my father, as Napoleon, was bidding farewell to Josephine before he departed for the battlefield. He made love to her passionately and whispered sweet words in her ear such as, "Your eyes shine like the pants of a blue serge suit." And after he had caught her with another man, "Jo, you're as true as a three-dollar cornet."

It was a little disturbing seeing my father make such ardent love to a woman who was not my mother, but after I'd seen the show a few times I grew accustomed to it and accepted his explanation that it was all part of a day's work.*

With the success of *I'll Say She Is*, our nomad existence came to an end. We settled down in a spacious but not very luxurious apartment on Riverside Drive.

* *Why do you think I went into that sort of work to begin with?* GROUCHO

41

Not long after the opening, my father made his first extravagant purchase. He bought a seven-passenger Lincoln sedan for six thousand dollars. The car seemed as tall as it was long; it had a window separating the driver's compartment from the back seat, and it was loaded down with all kinds of nickel-plated trimmings.

The Lincoln was delivered to my father at the stage door of the Casino Theater one Wednesday afternoon during the matinee. He was pretty excited about it. At one stage of his vaudeville career he and his brothers had all owned motorcycles and had traveled from town to town on them, sometimes transporting chorus girls on the handlebars.* But this was his first full-sized motor vehicle.

Chico was on the stage doing his piano solo when the Lincoln arrived, and the Napoleon sketch was to follow. Father couldn't wait for the show to be over before trying out his new car. Figuring Chico would be on for another ten minutes, he hopped in the Lincoln, dressed as Napoleon, and went for a spin around the block.

The Lincoln performed smoothly, but my father had not counted upon the crosstown traffic's being so heavy, nor had he taken the one-way street into consideration. About the time the Napoleon sketch was to start, he was wedged in between two trucks three blocks from the theater, still trying to find a street where he could make a left turn.

"Chico had to play fourteen encores," contends my father. "And this was pretty difficult since he only knew ten numbers."

In his desperation to get back to the theater, he made an illegal left turn, and a policeman stopped him. One look at my father dressed as Napoleon was enough to convince the gendarme that he was a refugee from Bellevue's psychiatric ward.

"But I tell you I'm one of the Marx Brothers," insisted my father, "and I'm due on the stage right this minute."

"If you're one of the Marx Brothers," said the skeptical cop, "let's hear you say something funny."

"If you're a policeman, let's see you arrest somebody!" retorted my father.

* *Sometimes? Always!* GROUCHO

42

There was no reason why that line shouldn't have landed my father in the nearest jail, but evidently the policeman felt that only a Marx Brother would have the nerve to say such a thing, and not only let him go, but escorted him back to the theater.

The following Sunday my father, sportingly dressed in a pair of long knickers, said, "Ruth, let's go for a spin in our new car." It was a beautiful spring day, and my mother and I were looking forward to an outing in the country as we climbed into the front seat beside my father.

But we got no farther than Central Park. There my father parked the Lincoln under a tree and alighted.

"Why are we parking here?" asked my mother. "I thought we were going for a ride."

"Riding on Sunday is for yokels," answered my father.

He forthwith produced a duster, a jar of auto wax and some rags. "I have to polish the car. You and Arthur can sit on the grass and play."

Stripping down to his undershirt, he labored over the car for the next three hours and even polished the nickel plating. After the car was as shiny as Father could make it, we piled in and drove back to the apartment. That was how we spent every Sunday for the first year we owned the car.

Though you wouldn't suspect it from the way he spent his Sundays, Father was the toast of New York in those days. All the famous wits of that era—Dorothy Parker, Bob Benchley, George Kaufman, Heywood Broun, F. P. Adams, Harold Ross, George Jean Nathan and Alexander Woollcott—took the Marx Brothers to their bosoms and were fighting for their company. They were being quoted in all the columns, and wined and dined by the Long Island social set.

Suddenly finding himself accepted by Manhattan's brightest intellectuals was an enjoyable novelty for my father, but he never reveled in it the way his brothers did.

My father has never been a very gregarious fellow. Beneath his confident and caustic exterior lurks an enormous inferiority complex, largely born of his limited formal education. He has many close friends, most of whom are writers, but he prefers to see them individually or in small groups. And sometimes he prefers not to see them at all, or even his family.

"I'm a born hermit," he once told me. "My idea of a good time is to lock myself in my room with a big Havana and read the *New Yorker.*"

Harpo, Chico and Zeppo, however, were born mixers, the life of any party. They were expert bridge and croquet players, they could do card tricks and they could entertain musically. Father might sing a song or two if he were in an exceptionally amiable mood, but generally he had to rely on conversation to make himself noticed. And for this he felt hopelessly inadequate alongside Kaufman, Benchley, Woollcott, Parker and the rest of the crowd.

Frequently he wasn't quite sure what they were talking about, but feeling that he might not get another invitation if he remained too quiet, he took to breaking into the conversation by twisting their pontifical statements around into jokes, or making outrageous puns on their big words. Today he considers pun-making on a par with wearing lamp shades as women's hats, but in the Roaring Twenties it was not only an acceptable form of humor, but more important, it enabled him to enter into the most intellectual discussion without running the risk of revealing his ignorance.

"They never caught on to me," confesses Father proudly. "They thought I was a great wit."

But he knew when to listen, and he learned a great deal from his new friends. He read the books he heard them discuss, saw the plays they recommended, and even started doing some writing of his own. Before long he was a frequent contributor to F. P. A.'s "Conning Tower," and he was also beginning to get his humorous articles published in all the national magazines.

Today he's one of the few entertainers I know of who doesn't have to have his articles "ghosted," but because he's in such a high income-tax bracket, it's almost impossible to get him to write any-

44

thing. Over the years, however, he has published two books, *Beds* and *Many Happy Returns*, and they are still very funny. But as far as he's concerned, the high point of his literary career came when H. L. Mencken printed an excerpt from one of his articles in *The American Language*.

His self-education was pretty rapid because he admired writers and liked to be around them. Of course, he was also quite friendly with the old vaudeville crowd—Al Jolson, Jack Benny, George Jessel, Fred Allen, George Burns, Will Rogers, Ben Bernie and Eddie Cantor—and continued to see them occasionally at the Lambs or the Friars.

Jessel has always been able to make Father laugh, and as a favor to him, he joined the Hollywood chapter of the Friars Club a couple of years ago. But Father doesn't like club life, and, after a few months, he dropped out. The Friars were disappointed over losing him, and wanted to know why he was resigning. They weren't satisfied with his original explanation—that he just didn't have time to participate in the club's activities. He must have another, more valid reason, they felt.

"I do have another reason," he wrote back promptly. "I didn't want to tell you, but since you've forced the issue, I just don't want to belong to any club that would have me as a member."

Father might have been the toast of New York when we were living on Riverside Drive, but I wasn't aware of it. All I knew was that the other children on the block had fathers who went to work every morning and came home at six o'clock. Mine hung around the apartment all day, like a bum, and read or played the guitar, or took me for long walks in the park. Finally I went to him and told him that my playmates wanted to know why he didn't go to work in the daytime, like the rest of the fathers.

"You go back and ask them what their fathers do at night while I'm at the theater," he advised me. "On second thought, maybe you'd better not. It's an unfair question."

Actually, there were a great many advantages, I discovered, to

45

having a father who was available during the day. And I think the other children in the neighborhood appreciated having him around, too.

My father loved children—he still does—and was never so busy that he couldn't take time out to entertain them. He'd sing and play the guitar for us, he'd participate in our games, he'd treat the neighborhood to ice cream cones, and he loved to engage in long conversations with my friends.

Father was sort of the Hans Christian Andersen of Riverside Drive and One Hundred Sixty-first Street. One of his favorite pastimes was story-telling. If other children were around they could get in on it, too. But always, before leaving for the theater in the evenings, he made it a point to sit down in the massive chair in front of the fake fireplace, light up a cigar, and tell me a special bedtime story.

Generally he'd stick to the tried-and-true classics, but they weren't very true when he got through with them. He'd keep the story structure of the original, but you'd hardly recognize it. It would be part Robert Benchley, part Ring Lardner, and part (a big part) Groucho Marx.

I can still remember his version of Little Red Riding Hood:

Once upon a time there was a little girl named Red Riding Hood. They called her that because her father was a Rhode Island Red, and her mother was a great admirer of Lenin and Trotsky.

She lived with her mother and father in a nice house on the edge of a dense woods, or the rough, as it's known in golfing circles, and I ought to know because I've been in plenty of it.

One day Little Red Riding Hood's mother went to Red Riding Hood and said, "Red, your grandmother is very sick. She had a little too much firewater last night at the speakeasy, and she's nursing a hangover. So I want you to take this basket of food over to her dump. It's filled with all kinds of goodies: sturgeon sandwiches, knackwurst and sauerkraut, baked beans, chopped chicken liver, antipasto, chow mein, and a bottle of vino right off the boat. It'll

46

give her the strength she needs to get to the speakeasy by the time it opens tonight. So hurry over to Granny's with this garbage and no dallying along the way. Don't stop to speak with anyone—not even Lee Shubert. And keep your hands off that bottle of vino—it's poisonous."

So Little Red Riding Hood put on her cape and started down the path through the woods. It was a nice day, and she was enjoying the walk, and wondering if she could open the bottle without a bottle opener, when she bumped right into a wolf, whom she mistook for the iceman.

"Oh, hello, Mr. Iceman," she said. "Mother's waiting for you."

"You don't see very well," said the wolf. "I'm not the iceman. I'm a wolf, and I'm hungry. Where are you going with that basket of knackwurst?"

"I'm taking it to my Granny's," said Red. "She's been hitting the bottle too much lately, and her tummy's all upset."

"That bootlegged stuff is all alike," said the wolf. "Why doesn't she make her own?"

"She's very old," said Red, "and she doesn't have much time to live. She doesn't want to waste her declining years fooling around with a home-made still."

"Where does your grandmother live?" asked the wolf. "Maybe I'll drop in on her sometime, and sell her a few cases. I'm on the wagon, and have no use for the stuff myself."

"She lives in that cute little house on the edge of the fifth fairway—you know, the water hole."

"That'll be very convenient since I'm on the water wagon," said the wolf. This wolf was nobody's fool when it came to pulling off a few nifties, and they both split their sides laughing, following which the wolf tipped his hat good-day and trotted off down the path in the direction of Red Riding Hood's grandmother's.

At Granny's house, the wolf knocked on the door, and when Granny said, "Who's there?" the wolf replied in a high pitched voice, "It's me—Little Red Riding Hood—and I've come to bring you some knackwurst from Barney Greengrass."

47

"I don't like knackwurst. Have you any sturgeon?"

"Don't look a gift knackwurst in the mouth," said the wolf.

"All right," said Granny. "Come in."

The wolf rushed into the room, and before Granny knew what was happening, the wolf ate her up, hangover and all. Then he put on her nightshirt and cap, jumped into the bed and pretended to be Granny.

A little while later, Red Riding Hood knocked on the door, and the wolf said in a bass voice, "COME IN, LITTLE RED RIDING HOOD."

Red was a little mystified by the bass voice, but figuring that perhaps Granny had a cold, she opened the door and went in anyway.

The wolf was lying in bed, trying to look like a grandmother. He wasn't succeeding much, but Red was pretty nearsighted and besides she was easily fooled. She was smart enough, however, to notice that her Granny wasn't quite the same.

"Why, Granny, what big hairy arms you have," exclaimed Red. "You look exactly like Jess Willard."

"Jess Willard should look so good," replied the wolf.

"Why, Granny, what big legs you have! You look exactly like a ballet dancer my daddy used to go around with."

"Your daddy should live so long," replied the wolf.

"Why, Granny, what big eyes you have. They're as big as saucers."

"I can see a lot better than you can," replied the wolf.

Red was pretty frightened by that time, but even so, she should have known better than to give the wolf a feed-line like she gave him next.

"Why, Granny, what big teeth you have!" she exclaimed.

"ALL THE BETTER TO EAT YOU UP WITH," said the wolf.

And with that he tried to jump out of bed and eat Little Red Riding Hood. But he was so slowed up from eating Red's grand-

48

mother that he could hardly move, which gave Red a splendid opportunity to yell for help.

"Keep quiet," said the wolf. "This story's supposed to end with me eating you up. And if it doesn't turn out that way, I have to give my advance back to the publisher."

"That's your hard luck," said Red, and then she cried out, "HELP, HELP!"

And just as she did a golfer who had heard her scream clear over on the fifth green, rushed into the cottage and hit Little Red Riding Hood over the head with his putter.

"That'll teach you to scream when a man's putting," said the outraged golfer. "On account of you I lost a ten-dollar Nassau."

And then he pulled out a gun and shot the wolf, and himself, and they all lived happily ever after.

I was pretty young to appreciate the humor in his stories, but what difference did that make? He told them well, and he could always manage to stretch a ten-minute story into an hour. And when bedtime is fast approaching, a story's length is more important than its meaning.

The other children who heard his stories were a little mystified by them, too, but they seemed to enjoy them just the same. They liked being with him. And it wasn't because he was a celebrity, because I don't believe many of the children (or even the grownups) in the neighborhood realized he was a star. (I know I didn't.) Riverside Drive and One Hundred Sixty-first Street wasn't a very theater-conscious community, and besides, my father wasn't easily recognizable in those days. He didn't wear a mustache in private life, and only his close friends and people in theatrical circles knew him as Groucho Marx.

Outside of the theater, he still clung to the name of Julius H. Marx (he didn't change it officially to Groucho until years later), and from appearances he could have been an ordinary young businessman. His glasses and habitually intense expression gave him a

studious look; he lived modestly, displayed no theatrical manner-
isms and stayed in the background as much as possible. He wears
a real mustache full-time now, and his television program has made
him so nationally known that it's almost impossible for him to
play an anonymous role. There are occasional opportunities,
though, when he comes across some poor soul who doesn't have
access to a television receiver.

I was with him the last time he met such a person. It was in
Phoenix, Arizona, where he had gone to watch the Giants in
spring training.

One morning, dressed in blue jeans and a rumpled polo shirt,
my father strayed over to a combination curio shop and fruit stand
that was across the street from the resort where we were staying.

"I'd like some fruit," Father said to the proprietor, a timid-look-
ing woman, who obviously didn't recognize him, but was terribly
anxious to please.

"Certainly," she said. "What kind of fruit?"

"Do you have any wax fruit?" he asked.

She shook her head.

"I'm sorry to hear that," he said, feigning disappointment.

"Why do you want wax fruit?" she asked, puzzled.

"I'd like to put some in my room," he explained.

"What for?"

"Well, supposing some company drops in. I should have some
fruit around, if I'm any kind of a host."

"Why don't you get some real fruit?" she asked. "We have lots
of real fruit, and it's pretty cheap this time of year."

"No, I don't want real fruit," he said, shaking his head solemnly.
"It rots, and the first thing you know you're stuck with it. But wax
fruit will last you a lifetime. You don't have to run out every time
company's coming, and buy more."

"But what good is wax fruit?" asked the woman.

"I'll tell you what's good about it," explained my father. "Wax
fruit looks better than real fruit."

"But you can't eat it."

"No, but it looks nice. And besides, I don't want my company coming over and eating my fruit. If they want to eat fruit, let them eat fruit at their own house."

"I'm afraid I can't help you," she said.

"For your own good you ought to put in a line of it," my father advised her. "I'll bet you'd clean up with a good line of wax fruit here."

She looked doubtful; there wasn't another customer in the store.

"How's business?" asked my father.

"Terrible!"

"How come?"

"Well, the curio shop down the street gets all the business."

"Do they have wax fruit?"

"No. They have a wooden Indian out front, and people stop to have their pictures taken with it, and then they drift into the store."

"Why don't you get a wooden Indian?"

"Can't afford it."

"What about a real Indian?"

"Can't afford that either. A real Indian would cost me about eight dollars a day."

"How much can you afford?"

She thought it over for a moment. "Well, no more than a dollar a day."

"I couldn't work for that," said my father.

"Are you an Indian?"

"No, but I used to watch Jim Thorpe play football, and I once passed through the depot at Albuquerque. I know how they act. But I couldn't do it for a dollar a day. Ten years ago, perhaps, but not with the inflated dollar today. It would hardly pay for my gas back and forth to Los Angeles."

"You couldn't commute from Los Angeles," she said.

"Why not? It's only four hundred miles. I really hit it up when I'm on the road."

"You just couldn't," she said. "You'd have to live here."

51

"That's out of the question. My brothers wouldn't stand for it."

"Your brothers?"

"Yes. Jimmy and Al Ritz. That's Jimmy over there"—he pointed to me—"and I'm Harry Ritz. We're a nightclub act, but we don't work much. I thought maybe I could fill in as an Indian when we're not working. But I guess I'll have to forget it."

Before we left Father bought a bag of real apples. Just as we were leaving the store, he took an apple from the bag and bit into it crunchingly. "Say, this is quite good!" he exclaimed to the bewildered proprietor. "Are you sure it isn't wax?"

The lady was still shaking her head as we crossed the street.

CHAPTER 7

MY MOTHER never quite understood my father's sense of humor. And since his sense of humor motivates a good deal of what he says and does, it naturally follows that she never quite understood him, either.

She realized, of course, that she was married to an extremely funny individual. And at times he could make her laugh as heartily as anyone else. But she was a shy and retiring person and could never get used to the way he would openly defy convention simply, it seemed, to see how many people he could shock.

By "shock" I don't mean that he was vulgar, for I know of very few men who shy away from dirty stories and ribald speech more assiduously than he does. He considers smut the easy laugh department. He never used it on the stage, and he rarely uses it in private life.

Actually it was not so much *what* Father said that annoyed Mother. Her chief complaint was that he didn't know when to be funny, and when to act like a normal human being. He knew, of course, but he's an individualist, and sometimes he just can't resist his impulse to do something that'll get a laugh. And the more solemn the occasion, the lower his resistance.

Mother's first warning of things to come occurred at their wedding, in 1919. The ceremony was to take place in her mother's apartment in Chicago. Her mother had never met my father, but she was a little wary of him because he was in show business. So were the ministers they tried to get to marry them. They were turned down by five different clergymen before Jo Swerling, who was their best man, could convince a minister that it would really not damage his reputation to marry a show-business couple.

Father showed his gratitude to the minister for appearing by heckling him unmercifully all through the ceremony. (Harpo can attest to this, because he was hiding behind a potted plant at the time and was moving the plant around the room, to make it appear that the plant was walking.)

When the minister intoned, "We are gathered here to join this couple in holy matrimony," Father interrupted him with, "It may be holy to you, Reverend, but we have other ideas."

Coming down the home stretch—and pretty relieved that the ordeal was almost over—the minister asked, "Do you, Julius, take this woman to be your lawful wedded wife?"

"Well, we've gone this far," replied Father. "We might as well go through with it."

Very few women would stand for that sort of thing, much less think it funny. Mother put up with it for twenty-two years—a record, I'm sure, that will last forever—but it never ceased to disconcert her.

What was even more disconcerting to Mother was that on an occasion when an air of jocularity was indicated, he might sit in the corner all evening, gloomily discussing the world situation. And if she made an attempt to prod him into livening things up, he'd retreat even farther into his shell, start yawning at eleven o'clock, and shoo all the guests out of the house by eleven-thirty. Or if it were at someone else's house, he'd announce that he was coming down with a cold and that he had to get home and take a sleeping pill. He never actually does catch a cold, but gets what he now refers to as a "grippy feeling," the symptoms of which are cold feet and the fact that his pipe or cigar doesn't taste good. This usually comes on about a week before he has to submit to an ordeal he isn't particularly looking forward to—like a big party, or the starting date of a picture, or a benefit where he has to make a speech, or sometimes it's even noticeable the night before his television program is filmed. As soon as the ordeal is over, however, he's in perfect shape. But since he's pretty much in demand these days, both professionally and socially, he goes through one "grippy feeling" after another.

But he never had a grippy feeling when he took the family out to dinner at a restaurant. On these occasions, Mother could always count on him for big jokes, especially if the restaurant was crowded, and he hadn't made a reservation, and the headwaiter didn't recognize him.

"Name, sir? There'll be a short wait."

"Jackson," Father would usually reply. "Sam Jackson. And this is Mrs. Jackson, and these are all the little Jacksons."

Jackson was his favorite nom de plume, and Mother would always do a slow burn whenever he used it at a time like this. She knew that if he'd give the headwaiter his real name we'd probably get a table immediately.

"Grouch!" Mother would whisper. "Tell them who you are."

"Why should I?" he'd reply. "If I can't get in under the name of Jackson, then I don't want to eat here. I don't like restaurants where you have to be a celebrity in order to get in."

"Then you should have made a reservation," she'd say. "You just can't walk into a restaurant on a Thursday night without a reservation and expect to get seated right away if you don't tell them who you are."

At this point we'd either leave for another restaurant or else he'd appear to give in to her request and tap the headwaiter on the arm. "My wife wants me to tell you who I am," he'd say. "My name's not really Jackson. It's Abe Schwartz, and I'm in the wholesale plumbing supply business. And this is Mrs. Schwartz, and all the little Schwartzes."

If the headwaiter thought he was peculiar, the waitress, when we'd finally be seated, considered him completely mad.

"Miss," he might begin, glancing up from the menu, "do you have frog's legs?"

"I'll ask the chef," she'd reply.

"No, you're not supposed to say that," Father would explain in a patient tone. "When I say, 'Do you have frog's legs?' you're supposed to answer, 'No, rheumatism makes me walk this way.' "

She'd nod, bewildered, and he'd say, "Okay, now let's try it again. Miss, do you have frog's legs?"

Her face would go blank. "It isn't on the menu. I'll have to ask the chef."

He'd shake his head. "Now you've spoiled it. We'll have to start all over aga——"

"Grouch," Mother would interrupt. "This girl is busy. Why do you waste her time with such foolishness?"

"It's not foolishness. It might come in very handy to her someday. Supposing vaudeville comes back, and she wants to get up an act. Look at the shape she'd be in with this sure-fire material. She wouldn't have to run around trying to find someone to write some stuff for her at the last minute. She'd have it right on the tip of her tongue."

He had many variations of this routine, all stemming from old and tired vaudeville jokes, and none of them ever failed to infuriate Mother. She used to say that if he wanted to make himself look ridiculous that was his business, but she wished he wouldn't do it when he was with her.

This was like asking Ben Hogan to stop playing golf. He couldn't—he got too much fun out of it, especially if he thought it amused me or a close friend of his who happened to be along. Besides, and at the risk of sounding traitorous, I suspect that it was really a way of drawing attention to himself without actually revealing his true identity. For a number of years he had a fixation about not wanting to get any special privileges just because he was a celebrity. He couldn't bring himself to walk into a restaurant and say, "I'm Groucho Marx." But at the same time he couldn't completely reconcile himself to being unrecognized. So he took the reverse tack, making himself conspicuous by other methods.*

He was never at a loss for other methods. Just when Mother

* *Take it easy with that probing. If I want to be analyzed, I'll go to a psychiatrist.* GROUCHO

56

would think he was going to behave himself for a change, he'd come up with some fiendish new scheme.

Father hates sight-seeing, for instance, but once when we were on a trip to Salt Lake City with him, Mother talked him into going on a guided tour through the Mormon Tabernacle. Father's deportment was admirable through most of the proceedings, and he even seemed to be interested when the guide stopped the group in the main auditorium and started to lecture us about the fine acoustics in the building. This is the high point of the tour, and the guide always finishes his talk by announcing that the acoustics are so amazing that you can "actually hear a pin drop. To prove it, ladies and gentlemen, I'm going to drop a pin, and I want you to be very quiet and listen to it drop."

A rapt silence settled over the group as the guide took a pin from his coat pocket, held it in the air dramatically for a moment, and then let it fall to the floor. You couldn't hear the pin drop, but the people, obviously mesmerized by the ritual, imagined that they did, and nodded their approval.

"I see you all heard it," said the pleased guide, ready to move on to another point of interest.

"I couldn't hear a thing," answered Father in a loud tone from the rear of the group. "Would you mind dropping it again? And use a bigger pin this time—a bowling pin. I'm a little hard of hearing!"

A burly guide approached him from the rear and tapped him on the shoulder. "We don't want any wise guys around here, Mister. We'd like you to leave now, without giving us any trouble."

"I'm not a wise guy. But I paid my money, and I think I'm entitled to hear a pin drop."

"Would you like us to call the police?"

"You can't arrest me. Do you know who I am?"

Father was aroused, and Mother, though annoyed, was at least pleased that he was going to abandon his mantle of anonymity to save us from complete disgrace.

"No, who are you?" asked the guide.

"My name's Jackson," said Father. "Sam Jackson. And this is Mrs. Jackson, of the Stonewall Jacksons."

The Jacksons were promptly expelled from the Mormon Tabernacle, and Mother and Father didn't speak for the remainder of the trip.

Their marriage was liberally sprinkled with a number of other instances of Father's unruliness, but I doubt if anything made more of an impression on Mother than an incident that took place in Chicago in 1927.

Father and his brothers were appearing there in *Cocoanuts*, a satire on the Florida land boom written by George Kaufman, Morrie Ryskind and Irving Berlin. It was their second legitimate show, and it, too, had been a resounding hit on Broadway before they started touring with it.

Chicago was their first stop, and a long one. *Cocoanuts* played Chicago for about six months. During that time the Marx Brothers were much sought after socially. Being on the stage every night except Sundays, my father, of course, didn't have much time for socializing, but my mother was pretty free to do as she pleased, and since it was all right with my father, she'd frequently accept invitations without him and meet him after the show for a late supper.

In those days around Chicago, spiritualism was having a resurgence, especially among some of the ladies of the social set with whom my mother had become friendly. Their idol was a middle-aged, African Negro woman who called herself the Great Narobi, and whose work in communing with the world of spirits had already won her considerable fame. Every evening, including Sunday, she held a séance in her headquarters, a dignified-looking brownstone mansion on Grand Boulevard, and the cream of Chicago society swarmed there to witness her phenomenal spiritualistic feats.

After a few weeks of fraternizing with a group of women who took spiritualism seriously, my mother was soon converted and attended several of Narobi's séances herself. The séances impressed her greatly, and she'd come home and tell my father how Narobi had been in touch with George Washington that evening, or perhaps one of Mother's dead ancestors.

My father believed not a word of this. He labeled Narobi a fake and anyone who believed in her hopelessly gullible.

"You may not believe it," said my mother, "but an awful lot of very well-educated, bright people think there's a lot to it."

"If Narobi's so smart," scoffed my father, "why doesn't she get one of the spirits to tell her who's going to win the fifth race at Belmont tomorrow? If she could do that, she wouldn't have to earn a living holding séances in a broken-down mausoleum."

"If you'd go see her just once," promised my mother, "you wouldn't be so cynical."

She finally persuaded him to attend a séance with her, and on the following Sunday evening he found himself sitting amongst the audience in Narobi's dimly lit mansion. It was a distinguished-looking group that had gathered there. The women were dressed in evening gowns and the men in tuxedos. Mother had not been able to persuade Father to wear a tuxedo,* but she was pleased at having him there, anyway.

After a short wait in the incense-filled room, the curtains parted and Narobi, flanked by two husky Negroes, stepped out and made a short obeisance to her followers. At this point, according to my father, Narobi stretched out on a couch, and one of her assistants announced that she was going into a trance.

It took Narobi only about ten minutes on the couch with her eyes closed to make the transition from Grand Boulevard to the spiritual world. Then she sat up very slowly and stared out into space.

"Narobi is now ready to commune with the world of spirits," announced one of the assistants. "If any of you have any questions you'd like answered, please raise your hands."

My father's hand shot up first.

"Very good, sir," the man said to him. "Please rise and direct your question to the Great Narobi."

* I compromised by wearing a beret. GROUCHO

59

My father stood up, waited for complete silence, and then said, "Narobi—what's the capital of North Dakota?"

It got a big laugh, even from the spiritualistically minded audience, but my father was escorted to the door by the two robust Negroes and told never to return again.

CHAPTER **8**

FATHER NEVER WANTED to play Hamlet.* But during the First World War he had dreams of becoming a farmer.

So compelling was this idea that he talked his brothers into pooling their financial resources with his and purchasing a five-acre farm in La Grange, Illinois. They were going to raise chickens and grow vegetables for the war effort.

Since La Grange was within easy commuting distance of Chicago, they figured they'd be able to attend to the farm chores in the forenoon before leaving for any vaudeville engagements they might be fortunate enough to have.

It seemed like a practical arrangement, and anyone but the Marx Brothers probably could have made it work. Unfortunately, the Marx Brothers didn't know anything about chickens, and the chickens didn't know anything about the Marx Brothers. Like good farmers, Father and his brothers rose at five o'clock the first morning and attended to the chores.

"By the second morning we weren't so enthusiastic," recalls Father. "We didn't get up until six. By the third morning we were getting up at seven. And by the end of the week we were getting up just in time to have a leisurely breakfast around eleven o'clock, and then, if we were lucky, we had to leave for the city to go to work."

---

* *I don't even want to see it.* GROUCHO

61

Even when they weren't working, Father and his brothers refused to hang around the farm. They'd find other reasons to go to the city. Chico would have a date at a pool parlor. Father would be off to see the Cubs or the White Sox play baseball. And Harpo and Zeppo would be out looking for card games.

While they were pursuing their various interests, the farm would be left in Sam and Minnie's care. Sam knew even less about chickens than he did about tailoring. As a result the chickens were dying off rapidly, and the five acres were going to seed.

The Marx Brothers didn't care. They were embittered on the subject of chickens by the time they had owned the farm for a couple of months. The chickens weren't laying. Not only weren't the Marxes getting fresh eggs, but it embarrassed them to have to admit in front of visiting friends that there were none for them to take back to the city.

But my father and his brothers were an ingenious, never-say-die lot. They overcame this problem by buying eggs at the grocery store and planting them under the hens whenever they got word ahead of time that friends were coming out to the farm to inspect the place.

"We fooled quite a few people," admits Father. "Even the hens got to like us. As a matter of fact, one Rhode Island Red told me that she had never had a softer job. She hoped it would keep up."

It didn't keep up for long, however. It couldn't—not when things reached the stage where even Sam wasn't willing to remain behind on the farm and take care of the fowls.

"I knew we were licked when I caught him sneaking out to a pinochle game one Monday morning around nine o'clock," relates Father. "We put the farm up for sale that same afternoon."

After this experience, Father realized that he wasn't cut out to be a farmer. But like most boys born and brought up in the city, he still had dreams of owing a house in the country. Being the cautious type, Father didn't buy his first house until after *Cocoanuts* was firmly established as a Broadway hit in 1926.

He could have afforded a house before that, if he had been willing to buy it through the time-honored mortgage plan. Apparently all the melodramas he had seen in the past, in which leering villains foreclosed mercilessly on destitute heroes and heroines, had left their mark on him. He refused to let himself be put into such a vulnerable position and wouldn't buy a home until he could pay cash for it.

Our first house was in Great Neck, Long Island, and my parents found it on one of the few Sundays Father spent driving our Lincoln instead of polishing it. It cost $15,000, and was on a wooded corner lot that covered a whole acre. It was made of brown stucco, and it had three stories, ten rooms, a steep-pitched slate roof, and an even steeper bluestone gravel driveway that washed down to the street corner in every rainstorm. After each rainstorm, Father rushed down to the corner with shovel and wheelbarrow and hauled the expensive bluestone back to our driveway.

Great Neck was just rural enough for Father's tastes. It was forty-five minutes from Broadway via the Long Island Railroad, and the closest chicken was in the poultry market in what was then a very tiny suburban village. In those days, before it became over-populated, Great Neck was more or less a show-business colony. Some of our neighbors whom I can remember were Al Jolson, Ruby Keeler, Eddie Cantor, Jane Cowl, Sam Harris, Larry Schwab, Rube Goldberg, Ed Wynn, Nunnally Johnson, Sam Hellman, and Ring Lardner. In addition to the fact that he was friendly with most of this crowd, Father liked Great Neck because it enabled him to live the life of a country gentleman.

He worked nights, and, except for two matinees a week, his days were free. He could sleep as late as he pleased without having it on his conscience.

Once he was awake, however, he was a very enthusiastic and conscientious young home-owner. If anything, he was a little too conscientious to suit my mother. She felt, and often said so, that it was a woman's job to run the house, and a man's job to earn a

63

living. He agreed with her in principle, but since his job enabled him to do both, he frequently did, whether she fully appreciated his interference or not.

He couldn't help it. He'd been living in hotels, apartments and boarding houses all his life, and when he finally became a home-owner, nothing—not even an indignant wife who wanted to assume the responsibility herself—could allay his enthusiasm for getting deeply involved in its management.

At first he was mainly concerned with the care of the grounds and the planting of a fruit orchard. His idea of a perfect dessert is a bowl of fruit, and he had wild dreams of stepping out of the back door someday and being able to pick apples, pears, peaches, cherries and plums right off his own trees. It never happened this way, because we had to move away before the trees reached a fruit-bearing age.

"The story of my life," insists Father. "I've spent a fortune buying fruit trees and raising them. And every time they reach the stage where they're about to bear fruit I move to another house."

At the time, however, Father had no idea that this would be their fate—or rather his fate. He treated them with tender care and spent many an hour at the nursery in the village of Great Neck, trying to find out why they weren't already bearing.

"What's the matter with those crooked fruit trees you sold me?" he'd ask the man at the nursery. "They're not doing anything."

"But Mr. Marx—they're baby trees. Give them time."

"I don't want to give them time. I'm not getting any younger, you know. Pretty soon I'll be too old to eat. And in the meantime, I'm spending a small fortune for fruit at the market."

To appease him, the nurseryman would stick Father with thirty or forty dollars' worth of the latest gardening equipment and send him home believing that he was a natural-born horticulturist.

This he wasn't. He was fair when it came to pulling out weeds, he could mow a lawn adequately, he could clip a privet hedge very unevenly, and he could tell the difference between roses and lilacs. But Luther Burbank had nothing to fear from him. Eventually,

Father realized this, and hired a gardener. But his interest in his fruit trees never waned.

He watched their progress closely from day to day; and if one of them became diseased and looked as if it were going to die, he'd feel as depressed over this as he would over the illness of a good friend. Back he'd go to the nursery, sometimes accompanied by the gardener, but more often with me, and there would be a long conference with the nurseryman about insect sprays, plant food and fertilizers.

When he wasn't trying to prod his fruit trees into growing faster, he'd be chopping down other trees. Father likes a lot of light in his houses, and we had a number of stately shade trees on the premises that kept our rooms continually dark during the day.

So he bought a two-handled lumberjack's saw, and, with me assisting, started hacking away at the tall timber and cutting the trees up into logs for the fireplace.

We soon had plenty of daylight in the house—just as we had an abundance of lamplight at night. Father wouldn't stand for any lamps or wall brackets that weren't practical enough to take hundred-watt bulbs. If Mother brought home a lamp purely for decorative purposes, Father would make her take it right back. He's still that way. When he goes on a trip, he carries a couple of hundred-watt bulbs in his suitcase, just as a precaution.

"I've spent too many nights groping my way around hotel rooms and going blind reading by those dim yellow lights they give you," says Father.

In Great Neck, Father was not concerned just with growing fruit and keeping the house light. As time went on, he became interested in all phases of running the house—even the marketing. Mother was a good shopper, but Father didn't trust her judgment entirely. He had to go along.

First of all, it gave him the opportunity to wander through the grocery store, gossiping with the clerks and some of the customers. And secondly—and more important—there was then no chance of the wrong kind of rye bread or pumpernickel being smuggled into our house. Father's very fussy when it comes to rye bread and pumpernickel. He'll have no truck with any sliced-at-the-factory packaged brands that are rye bread and pumpernickel in name only.

If Mother were busy at home, Father would frequently offer to do the shopping for her. And just as frequently she would take him up on this.

Even though she didn't particularly like his interfering with the running of the house, there were certain advantages to his doing the marketing. He'd usually go to the most expensive food specialty shop in town—the one he had warned her not to patronize—and he'd come home loaded down with all kinds of imported delicacies and out-of-season fruits and vegetables.

"Why don't you buy this kind of cheese when you go shopping?" he'd say smugly. "That cheese you bring home tastes like it was made in a soap factory!"

"Because they only have processed packaged cheese in the regular markets. And you told me not to go to the one you just went to. You said they were highway robbers."

"They are. But they have good stuff. Even their meats and vegetables are better, if you want to know the truth."

But as soon as Mother would start patronizing an "extra fancy" market on her own and the bills rolled in, Father would become furious.

"I don't know why it costs us so much for meat this month," he'd say, riffling through the bills. "Why, the average family could live all year on what it cost us for meat this month."

"The average family doesn't buy their meat at Kleinhardt's."

"Then why are we buying our meat there? I'm sure the stuff is just as good at the A & P."

"You told me to go there."

"Well, you're the woman of the house. You should know better."

Father would rather do anything than admit he's wrong—even if it means risking his life. I know of no better example than the time back in 1927 when his stubbornness was nearly responsible

66

for wiping out the entire Marx family and a Swedish nurse named Sadie.

It was on the day we were bringing Mother, Miriam, and the nurse home from the hospital in New York City, where Miriam was born.

Father, in his anxiety to get Miriam home safely, was driving very slowly and cautiously, even for him. And when we approached the railroad crossing in Great Neck, he slowed the Lincoln to such a snail's pace that it stalled—right on the tracks.

Father stepped on the starter several times, but the engine wouldn't respond. At that moment we heard the familiar tooting of a Long Island Railroad train approaching around the bend.

"The 3:02 is right on time," remarked Father, glancing calmly at his wrist watch.

"My baby!" screamed Mother. "Let's get out!"

"And leave a six-thousand-dollar car on the tracks?" replied Father. "Not I. These cars don't grow on trees, you know."

"I don't give a damn about the car," said Mother hysterically, as Father tried in vain to get the engine started.

"Well, I do," replied Father. "She's got a lot of miles in her yet. She just flooded, but I'll get her started. Just be calm, everybody— be calm!"

But nobody was calm, and he couldn't get the engine started. The train came in view, Mother grabbed Miriam from the arms of the nurse, alighted from the car and urged the rest of us to run for our lives. But Father remained at his post, refusing to be swayed by female hysterics.

As the train drew closer, Father suddenly shouted out the window, "Hey, Ruth—in case I get killed, the key to the vault is behind *The Works of Shakespeare* in my study!"

Mother shuddered and refused to look. Father was quite pale himself. He sat there, grimly trying the starter, and, out of the corner of his eye, watching the train come closer and closer.

I often wonder what would have happened if the train hadn't turned out to be a local that had already started to slow down for the Great Neck station before it ever rounded the bend. Fortunately, it was, and it came to a grinding halt just ten feet short of the Lincoln.

"Damn!" said Father, as we all piled back in the car. "Now I have to find a new hiding place for the vault key!"

Mother was furious with Father during the rest of the ride home. In fact, she's never quite forgiven him for subjecting her to such a harrowing experience—but he insisted that he had done the only thing possible under the circumstances.

"After all," he said righteously, "would a captain desert his sinking ship? Would Lord Nelson quit Trafalgar?"

CHAPTER 9

I DON'T KNOW whether or not the incident at the railroad crossing had anything to do with it, but soon after that Father hired a chauffeur named Otto.

Having a chauffeur to drive him to and from the theater, while he sat in the back seat puffing importantly on a large cigar, was the fulfillment of a boyhood dream. But Otto was not with us for long. He cracked up the Lincoln one day while he was out driving by himself, and we soon had a new chauffeur—in fact a succession of new chauffeurs.

Father never had much luck with chauffeurs. Either they talked too much while he was in the back seat trying to think up new ad libs for the show, or else he just didn't approve of their driving. It was usually the latter.

Father's one of those people who hates to drive, but who trusts very few others behind the wheel of an automobile—especially his automobile. He'd deny that he's a back-seat driver—and I'd be the last person in the world to accuse him of it—but God help you if you don't keep your eye on the road every second, obey all the traffic laws, and follow his directions on how to get some place, which will usually land you eight or ten miles from your destination. . . .*

* *That mule in Chapter III never complained about my directions.*
GROUCHO

I once took a trip through Texas with him. I was the driver, and he was the map reader. We were trying to make Dallas by dinner time. Dallas was three hundred miles from our starting point. By dinner time, we were six hundred miles from Dallas.

There was another reason why Father eventually abandoned the idea of having a driver. Chauffeurs always doubled in butlering—at least the ones who worked for us did—and Father didn't approve of fancy service at the dinner table. All he asked for was good, simple cooking. It angered him to have to wait for the meat, the potatoes, and the vegetables to be brought in one at a time on separate platters and passed slowly around the table by the butler.

"What became of the potatoes?" he'd bellow impatiently, after he'd helped himself to the meat, and the butler had disappeared inside the kitchen for a moment. "Did that guy get lost or something?"

"Give him time, Grouch. He probably had to wait for Hazel to dish them out."

Father would give him another ten seconds, during which time he'd be glowering at the meat on his plate. If the butler hadn't returned by then, there would be another explosion.

"This is a hell of a way to have to eat," he'd say in a loud tone. "By the time I get the potatoes and vegetables, my meat'll be ice cold. Why can't we just put all the food on the table at once, and help ourselves? That's the way we did it when we were kids."

"No one does it that way any more."

"Why not?"

"It just isn't done."

"Well, what about the families where they don't have anyone else to pass the food? I'll bet *they* get the meat and the vegetables at the same time."

"That's different. But if you're going to have someone to do the serving, you might as well do it right."

"Who cares what's right? I'd rather be poor if I have to go through life getting my vegetables fifteen minutes after my meat. Who are we trying to impress, anyway?"

Father couldn't understand Mother's concern about what other people might think, and the battles over this were endless. And the situation didn't improve after Father fired our last butler, for then the cook had to do the serving—and she did it more slowly than ever.

Mother and Father finally reached a compromise when they discovered that they could buy a silver serving platter that was divided into three compartments: one for potatoes, one for vegetables, and one for meat. Even with the new dish, Father would have preferred having all the food on the table at once, but in those days he was still pliable enough to make certain concessions to the female sex which he wouldn't dream of making today.

One concession he wouldn't make was eating by candlelight. Mother, like many women, felt that candles added a soothing, romantic atmosphere to the dining room. Father felt they were something out of the Dark Ages.

It was quite a shock to Mother to see Father's reaction the first time she tried lighting our dining room in Great Neck with candles only.

"What's this—a coal mine?" he said, walking straight to the electric light switch and flipping it on. "I have to see what I eat. Candles are for tea rooms and gigolos."

If they had company, he'd allow my mother to have the candelabras lit until the guests entered the dining room and were seated. Then he'd announce, "If you've all seen the candles, we'll dispense with them immediately. We just want you to know we have them."

Chances are, he wouldn't even leave the candelabras on the table. He'd put them on the sideboard. He hated to have anything obstructing his view of the person across the table from him. Table floral displays were also anathema to him, particularly if they were tall. "Who's buried under there?" he'd remark and soon the flowers would be on the sideboard alongside the candlesticks.

In addition to the fact that he insisted on the dining room being as brightly lighted as a movie set, he had—and still has—some pretty eccentric eating habits. In the thirty-three years I've known him, I don't believe he's ever sat through an entire meal without complaining about the food, the service or both.*

And he'll complain no matter where he happens to be eating— at your house, his house, or in his favorite restaurant. He's not at all biased that way.

If he's in a restaurant, he'll undoubtedly remark that the finest restaurant food in the world isn't as good as the worst home cooking.

But if he's home, and the meal isn't exactly the way he likes it, he'll say indignantly, "What can you expect? Amateur cooks! There isn't anyone I know, outside of professional chefs, who can prepare two good meals in a row."

His eating habits are impossible to figure out, but there are certain "musts" if you expect him to do a minimum of complaining. For instance, he considers no meal a meal without potatoes, even if the main course is shrimp curry with rice.

He wants a separate "side" dish for his vegetables. If he has to struggle through a meal with his string beans on the same plate with his meat and potatoes, he'll be unhappy for the rest of the evening and probably won't accept another invitation to your house.

He expects "natural" pan gravy—even if the dish is something like stuffed bell peppers.†

He refuses to eat what he calls "trick" vegetables: eggplant, squash, rutabagas, or other "trick" dishes: meat loaf, persimmon pudding, chicken à la king, creamed chipped beef, codfish cakes, tuna salad, and bouillabaisse.‡

Above all, he won't stand for music while he's eating. He isn't likely to get it, of course, in someone's home, but he won't patronize a restaurant for very long that gives its customers music, canned or otherwise.

---

* Or the company. GROUCHO
† If that's what you're serving, I don't expect to be there at all. GROUCHO
‡ And stuffed bell peppers. GROUCHO

72

There used to be an Italian restaurant in Los Angeles called Romeo's Chianti. It served the best Italian food in the city, and Father loves Italian food, but Romeo insisted on lavishing recorded Italian opera on all his patrons.

"Hey, Romeo," Father would say, "can't you turn off that lousy screaming?"

"But, Mr. Marx—all my other customers—they come here to hear music with their spaghetti."

"You call that music—all those Italians hollering at the top of their lungs? It sounds awful."

"But Mr. Marx—that's Puccini."

"Puccini was a bum. He wasn't even in ASCAP."

"Mr. Marx, you make jokes with me."

"I wouldn't kid you. I have a brother who's an Italian, and he swears it's true. So how about turning that noise off?"

After a while, Romeo took to turning off the phonograph whenever he saw Father arriving. But once we were seated he'd always sneak over to the phonograph and turn the music back on again.

"Romeo, you can't be trusted," Father finally told him. "I'm switching to Chinese food after this." And he never returned to Romeo's again.

Another thing Father always insisted on at home was eating at a "reasonable" hour. Nothing upsets him like having to wait until eight-thirty or nine for his dinner (even if he isn't hungry before then).

When he and my mother were giving a dinner party, he'd wait until the guests had had time for one drink and then he'd start asking, "Hey, Ruth—when are we going to eat?"

If she told him that dinner wouldn't be ready for perhaps another twenty minutes, and that he could help himself to some hors d'oeuvres if he were hungry, he'd say, "I don't want to get filled up on all that garbage. Why isn't dinner ready?"

"You know how it is when you have roast beef, Groucho. It's better to let the people wait than have the roast overdone."

"That's the cook's look-out. What's she been doing in that

73

kitchen all day that she can't have dinner ready on time? I'll have to give her a talking to."

Before the next dinner, he'd instruct the cook to have dinner ready at seven-thirty, and no later. That was certain to be the night that Max Gordon (who was usually an hour early), or some other of his friends, would show up late, and the roast would be overdone.

"I don't know why it's so hard to get the roast beef the way I like it," he'd say to my mother the following morning.

When she'd point out to him that well-done roast beef was the usual result of putting the roast in the oven too early, he'd shake his head sadly and mutter, "Amateur cooks—the world is full of amateur cooks!".

If he discovered, after several dinners at someone else's house, that his hosts were habitual late eaters, he'd make a mental note of it. The next time he was invited there he'd have his dinner at home first, despite my mother's protests that it was impolite and that he wouldn't like anyone to do that to him.

"No one has the right," he'd tell her, "to invite you to dinner at seven o'clock and make you wait until ten before giving you something to eat."

If he found that a couple he knew were habitual late arrivers, he had his own way of curing them of the habit. He'd start dinner without them the next time it happened.

Mother thought this, too, was impolite but Father said, "When I tell people seven o'clock, I don't see how they can misunderstand me to mean a quarter to eight. My diction isn't that bad. I can be heard in the last row of the balcony."

Father also expects his guests to leave at a reasonable hour. He doesn't like to have them hanging around until three or four in the morning. He wants to go to bed. He'll never tell anyone to leave, however. If his guests persist in ignoring his yawns, he'll stand up and make the announcement that he's tired and going to bed. "You people stay as late as you like. You know where the liquor is—enjoy yourselves!"

74

"You'd be surprised," he once told me, "how many people stay and have a hell of a time after I go to bed. One of these days I'm going to throw a party and never come out of my room at all. I think it'll be a smashing success."

This isn't a new practice with him. He was doing it when we were still living in Great Neck. I think he learned it from an experience he had with Ring Lardner, who was a frequent visitor in those days. Lardner was one of his best friends and favorite authors, and he loved to come to our house and discuss show business with Father, over a glass of brandy. Father enjoyed his company immensely, except for one thing—Lardner would never go home.

After staying up until four in the morning with him on several occasions, Father decided that he was getting too old for keeping such late hours. (He was thirty-six at the time.) So the next time Lardner visited us and showed no indication of leaving by midnight, Father stood up and said, "I don't know what your plans are, Ring, but I'm going to bed."

Lardner told him to go right ahead, and when Father came down to breakfast at nine o'clock the following morning, his guest was still sitting in the same chair, staring into space.

"I thought you were going to bed," said Lardner. "Don't let me keep you."

As much as he likes to sound inhospitable, Father has always been a very soft-hearted host. He could never say "no" to anyone who called up at the last minute and wanted to bring along an extra friend or two. And if none of his guests imposed upon his hospitality in this way, he'd usually think of someone *he* wanted to invite at the last minute.

After many years, my mother became hardened to this sort of thing, but when they first set up housekeeping, she was a very nervous and inexperienced hostess, and the slightest change in plans would upset her terribly and was almost certain to precipitate an argument.

It started with the very first dinner party they gave in the new house in Great Neck. They were having ten people in to a sit-down dinner: the George Kaufmans, the Max Gordons, the Sam Harrises, the Bobby Norths, and the Bill Parkses.

Mother was extremely apprehensive. Not only because they had never attempted to entertain ten guests before, but also because the Parkses were coming. Parks was not part of the show-business crowd. He was a wealthy manufacturer who lived across the street in a house that made ours look like a squatter's shanty. But he had become friendly with my mother and father because they were neighbors, and he had invited them to dinner a couple of weeks before. They had come home awed by the fact that the Parkses had had five servants to serve four people in the dining room.

They couldn't hope to compete with that kind of class, but nevertheless my mother was pretty jittery about returning the invitation, and she went to great pains to make her dinner as nice as possible.

We had a couple working for us, but Mother hired an extra serving girl. And Mother must have spent at least a week arranging and rearranging the table settings. This was the most difficult part of all, for our dining room was not especially large, and when the table was extended with extra leaves, there was barely room to walk around it. And even with the extra leaves it was going to be a tight squeeze to get ten place settings at the table.

But somehow she managed, and by the time the party was only an hour away, our dining room looked like a picture layout in *House Beautiful*, and Mother, in a new hostess gown, was beginning to feel confident that she had nothing to fear.

Then the phone rang, and my father answered it. "Sure, George, bring him along. This is Liberty Hall. Always room for one more."

Hanging up, he turned to my mother and said quite casually, "Put on another plate, Ruth. That was Kaufman, and he's bringing Morrie Ryskind along. Ryskind's his new collaborator. He's a lot of fun."

My mother turned white, as though she'd been mortally wounded. "How could you do such a thing to me?"

76

"What's wrong?" asked Father calmly. "We have plenty to eat, haven't we?"

"Of course we have. It isn't that. There isn't any more room at the table."

"Don't be ridiculous. We can always make room for one extra person."

"But we can't. There's barely enough room at the table for ten."

Father look unconcerned. "Then we'll set up a card table."

"Isn't it going to look awfully strange having one person at a card table?"

"Then let Arthur sit at the table with him. He wanted to stay up with the company, anyway. Now there'll be room for him."

"But, Groucho—grownups don't want children around."

"Oh, stop making such a big *magilla* out of one extra person. My mother used to cook for eleven people every night, and you never heard a squawk out of her. And if she could do it alone, I don't see why we can't—with three servants to help!"

That settled it. A card table for four was set up in a corner of the dining room. It was to accommodate not only Morrie Ryskind and me, but two others whom my mother had decided to move over from the main table. She had made this strategic maneuver at the last minute, figuring that as long as the card table had to be in the way of everything anyway, she might as well load it to capacity. With fewer people at the main table, she could make it smaller and there would be more space for the servants to move around.

Everything probably would have proceeded smoothly and according to plan if Morrie Ryskind hadn't shown up with *his* two guests.

"Mr. and Mrs. Harry Ruby," he said, introducing the song writer and his wife. "I hope you don't mind, but the Rubys didn't have anything else to do tonight either, and I thought you might need someone to play the piano."

"Don't give it a thought," said my father in a hearty voice. "This is Liberty Hall. No trouble at all."

Mother would have been glad to argue this point with him, if she hadn't been so busy helping the maid put the leaf back in the dining table again, and replacing the two place settings that had been removed. By the time this was done, the domestics were in a state of complete bewilderment from which they didn't emerge for the remainder of the evening.

It turned out to be a real Alice Adams party, with everything going wrong.

The first thing that happened was that the serving girl showed up drunk. In her first and last appearance of the evening, she came swaying through the living room with a plate of hot hors d'oeuvres and dropped them in Mrs. Parks' lap.

"She couldn't have dropped them on Ryskind," commented my father. "She had to drop them on one of the invited guests."

When the roast beef came in for the first time it was practically raw, and Father had to send it back to the oven for another thirty minutes. During the interval, the guests adjourned to the living room for another round of cocktails made of bootlegged gin and orange juice.*

Promptly upon our return to the dining room, Father removed the candles and the flowers from the table and put them on the sideboard.

"Isn't that better?" he said. "At least we can all see each other. At least, I hope we can all see each other. If we can't, I'm going to get another bootlegger."

The roast beef was finally pronounced fit by a board of experts consisting of Harry Ruby, George Kaufman and my father. But when it took the butler five minutes to serve three people, I could see that Father was getting annoyed.

"Can't he leave the meat, and we'll pass it?" he asked Mother. "So he can go get the potatoes and the vegetables?"

Mother gave him a silencing stare and resumed talking with Millie Gordon. Father went back to glaring balefully at the lonely

* *Quiet! Do you want to get me in trouble with the Coast Guard?* GROUCHO

slice of beef on his plate, then got to his feet and stormed into the kitchen. He returned a moment later with the mashed potatoes and a gravy boat and ladle and handed them to the dignified-looking Mrs. Parks.

"Here, girlie," he said, "help yourself and pass them around!"

Mother was horrified as Mrs. Parks smiled without conviction and helped herself to the mashed potatoes. But Mr. Parks laughed heartily and said to Mrs. Parks, "Groucho's got the right idea, Emily. Why can't we do the same when we have company?"

That was all the encouragement Father needed. Jumping up, he rushed back into the kitchen, came out in a moment with the peas and carrots, and started them around the table, family style.

"Now will you please sit down and eat your dinner?" demanded my mother. "Clarence can do the rest."

"Clarence is a schlemiel," said Father.

Clarence was in the kitchen out of earshot by then, and my father was happy at last. He had his meat, potatoes and vegetables all at the same time.

"Marx," said Max Gordon, "you really know how to live! If I tried that at home, Millie would bash my head in."

"Give me time," said Father. "The evening's not over yet."

And it wasn't. The worst was yet to come.

The dinner itself was considered a success. The food, for some odd reason, was good, and everyone had two and three helpings.

It was after the table had been cleared and the coffee was about to be served that it happened.

When Clarence came in with the first cup of coffee and set it down at my mother's place, Father said, "You mean to say you're going to have to make thirteen trips back and forth to the kitchen just to serve coffee?"

Clarence nodded.

"Put it all on a big tray," suggested Father. "It'll save you some work, and we'll be able to have the coffee *with* our dessert."

Clarence disappeared and returned five minutes later with thirteen cups of coffee on a huge tray.

79

"That's more like it," said Father, getting up. "And I'll go get the cream and sugar!"

Father was crazed with success. He was confident, as he dashed into the kitchen, that he had found the perfect formula for good service at home. He was not so confident as he dashed out again with the cream and sugar and collided with Clarence, who at that moment was passing in front of the swinging door with the tray of coffee cups.

All hell broke loose as the two of them crumpled to the floor amidst the clattering of falling china and silverware.

In an instant my mother was in the kitchen and out again with an armful of dish towels, and the cook was right behind her flailing a mop.

Father still hadn't had time to pick himself up. He was lying on the carpet in a puddle of lukewarm coffee, with broken cups all around him. But there was one cup that hadn't broken. It was standing right side up, with a few drops of coffee still in it. Raising himself up on one elbow, Father lifted the cup and drank.

"Are you all right?" asked the cook, bending over him.

"Of course I'm all right," said Father amiably. "It was a splendid dinner all around. There's just one thing I want to know. Why isn't the orchestra playing?"

CHAPTER 10

ACTUALLY, our life in Great Neck, in the late 1920's, wasn't very social. It couldn't be—not with Father playing in a show six nights a week and doing matinees on Wednesdays and Saturdays.

Sunday was his only night off, and that was usually when he and Mother would have company, or else go to dinner at the homes of friends. Occasionally they'd make dates for other nights of the week, but it would have to be with the proviso that their friends would be willing to go their own way after dinner, or else accompany Father to the theater and see the show.

This wasn't a very practical arrangement, since a good many of their friends lived and worked in the city and couldn't always get to a dinner in Great Neck as early as Father had to eat in order to make an eight-thirty curtain. He could have met them in the city, of course, and sometimes he did, but he preferred to dine at home because he had had his fill of eating out when he was in vaudeville.

Sunday night was also the only night of the week when Father could see a show other than his own. Because it was such a rare treat for him to be in the audience instead of on the stage, he was usually in a very good mood when he went to see someone else perform.

One Sunday evening he took Mother to the Winter Garden, where the great Houdini was appearing. During his act, Houdini announced that he was going to do his famous needle-threading trick. He would put some thread and a dozen sewing needles in his mouth, and the needles would come out on the thread. And to prove to the audience that he didn't have some needles already threaded concealed beneath his tongue, Houdini asked for someone from the audience to come up on the stage and examine his mouth.

Father volunteered and took his place on the stage beside Houdini.

"Very well, sir," said Houdini, "now, before I do this trick, I want you to examine my mouth very carefully and tell the audience whether or not you see anything in there."

Houdini opened his mouth wide, and Father peered in.

"I see something," said Father.

"You do?" said the surprised Houdini. "What do you see?"

"Pyorrhea!" answered Father, and he returned to his seat.

Most nights, Father, Mother and I (and Miriam, when she reached the age of two) would have a six-thirty dinner by ourselves, and then Father would leave for the theater alone. Sometimes Mother would go with him, but only if she didn't have to see the show.

She had seen *Cocoanuts* and *Animal Crackers* performed every night during their Boston and Philadelphia tryouts, and many times more after they had opened in New York, and an alarmed look would cross her face at the mere suggestion that she sit through either one of them again.

"I don't blame you," Father would say. "If I were in your shoes, I wouldn't see it either. And I wish I were in your shoes. I'm getting pretty sick of this turkey myself. I'd like to stay home once in a while, too."

Mother wasn't fond of staying home alone. Great Neck wasn't very built-up in those days, it was especially lonely at night, and the house seemed large and frightening to her.

There was nothing Father could do about that, but to make Mother feel a little more secure, he bought a .32 caliber pistol and kept it in the top drawer of his dresser, where it would be easily accessible.

82

A week after he bought the gun, Mother came into the bedroom and found Miriam, who was a toddler by then, standing on a chair in front of the dresser, with the gun in her hand. She retrieved the gun before Miriam could do any damage, but when Father came home she told him what had happened and ordered him to get rid of the gun immediately.

Father turned pale, but he said, "Why get rid of it? I paid a lot of money for that gun. We'll just have to find a place where Miriam can't get hold of it."

For about an hour, he went through every corner of the house, looking for a safe place to hide the gun. Finally, his expression brightened, and he walked to the wall safe in their bedroom and opened it.

"Why didn't I think of this before?" he said, putting the gun in the safe, closing the heavy iron door, and twirling the dial. "Miriam will never get at it in here."

"But, Grouch—" protested Mother. "The safe's the first place a burglar will go. How will I ever get the gun out if I need it?"

"We won't use that gun for burglars," replied Father. "We'll get another gun to keep in a handy place!"

Father realized that being the wife of a legitimate stage actor could be an awfully frustrating existence six nights a week, if she didn't go out once in a while without him. So generally he was cooperative about whatever Mother wanted to do while he was at the theater. And if she didn't have any ideas, he'd more than likely suggest something himself.

"Why don't you call Max Gordon?" he'd say. "He can probably get you a ticket on the cuff for *The Band Wagon*. Or would you rather see that new revue at the Music Box? I hear that's pretty good. Sam Harris can get you in."

If Mother didn't want to go out by herself, it would be perfectly all right with Father if one of his bachelor friends, like Sam Behrman or Morrie Ryskind, took her to a show—or even to a nightclub.

It wasn't any problem getting escorts for Mother in those days, even on a platonic basis. She was one of the prettiest women around Manhattan, and no one could do the Charleston better than she, nor was anyone more willing.

Father didn't mind—just as long as *he* didn't have to do the Charleston. He hated any kind of night life himself, and if he could get his friends to take her dancing, it relieved him of the duty.

On Wednesdays and Saturdays, Father stayed in town after the matinee, and Mother, whether she had any after-dinner plans or not, always drove in and ate with him at Dinty Moore's or Sardi's, between performances. It was usually Moore's, because in addition to having good food and being handy to the theater, it was the most brightly lighted restaurant in New York.

Sometimes, at Father's suggestion, I would go along and have dinner with them. I always considered this a great treat—not only because Father would take me backstage before the performance and let me play with all the props and scenery, but because it was fun eating in Dinty Moore's—even for a child of six.

"There's Jack Dempsey," Father would say. "He's champion of the world. You'd better behave yourself, or I'll have Jack come over here and knock you out."

Or, "You see that fellow over there? That's Will Rogers. I taught him to play the guitar when we were on the bill together in Grand Rapids."

Father knew everyone, from Eddie Cantor to Mae West, and at some point during the evening he'd table-hop and take me along, and then I'd know everyone.

But the main reason I liked to eat with Father after the matinee was because I'd get a chance to see my uncles.

Almost always Harpo, Chico, Zeppo and their wives would be at the table with us, and I enjoyed that immensely, because no child could have more doting uncles than they were. They'd shower me with expensive toys, slip ten-dollar bills in my pockets when Father (who disapproved) wasn't looking, and spoil me in every way possible.

Aside from presents, the Marxes were a hilarious group when

84

they were together. They were loud, raucous, and never took any-thing seriously. The jokes would fly back and forth across the table so rapidly you couldn't keep up with them. And all the brothers except my father were accomplished at the art of doing table tricks. They'd be spring-boarding silverware into glasses of water, making rabbits out of napkins, pulling cards from their sleeves, and perhaps shooting dice with the sugar cubes.

It was that way whenever they'd get together, which in those days was still fairly often. Usually they'd come to our house—in addition to the restaurant gatherings—because Father was the only one of the brothers who owned a house. And besides, we had a pool table, and they loved to play. But sometimes we'd go to their apartments in New York, and about once a week there would be a family gathering at Sam and Minnie's house in Little Neck.

My grandparents were in their middle sixties then, and Minnie's health was failing rapidly, but they were happy at last in the re-flected glory of their famous sons, who were doing everything possible to make them comfortable. They bought them a house, gave them a car and a chauffeur, and saw to it that they'd never again have to have another financial worry. In return for this, Sam and Minnie were always eager to cook a stuffed miltz for them, or some other German dish they constantly craved.

Undoubtedly, it was Minnie, whom they loved dearly and who unquestionably was responsible for some of their success, who kept the brothers together as a social group, because it wasn't very many years after she died in 1928 that they started to drift apart. Of course they still saw a good deal of each other, since they worked together and were constantly being thrown into one an-other's company whether they liked it or not. And as individuals, it wasn't unusual—and still isn't—for one Marx brother to enter-tain one of the other brothers. But it's been at least fifteen years since I've seen the five of them assembled around the same din-ner table. I've often regretted this, because not only did they seem to have fun whenever they were together, but it was fun being with them.

Their growing apart was inevitable, I suppose. Outside of their careers, they've always had completely divergent interests and ideas of how they wanted to live.

Chico, for instance, has been a heavy gambler from the day he first started making the kind of money that permitted him to wager two and three thousand dollars on everything from the turn of a card to the outcome of a girls' softball game.

He has tapered off some in the last few years, but basically he's still the same. If you want his company at dinner, and you're not a gambling man yourself, you can get him, but immediately after the meal he'll excuse himself and head for the nearest card game —not only card games, but any place where he stands a reasonably good chance of losing his money.

Harpo was a gambler, too, but of a different sort. With him, it was an avocation. For many years he was a bachelor, and he went around with a group of bachelors that idolized the late Alexander Woollcott, who was their unofficial leader. This was a more sporting group. They played expert croquet on Bucks County lawns, no-limit poker, and championship bridge for a dollar a point. Occasionally Harpo and Chico would team up together at bridge, and when they did, they were a formidable combination.

"If Chico had stuck to bridge," my father once told me, "he could have been a rich man. But unfortunately he felt his skill at the game gave him an unfair advantage over his opponents. He'd rather play something where the opposition has a more sporting chance—like betting on horses."

Since his marriage to Susan Fleming in the mid-thirties, Harpo has done practically no gambling at all. Age and four children have mellowed him and curbed his gambling instincts.

Father was a family man who could play neither bridge nor croquet, and who didn't care to learn. He despises cards in particular, and he's always looked with good-natured disdain upon people who jump up from dinner and rush right to a card table. "Cards are for people who don't want to talk to each other," he's often said. "If I don't want to talk to people, I'd rather not see them at all."

Once after we moved to California, Father, in an unwitting

moment, let Norman Krasna talk him into taking bridge lessons. Krasna couldn't play either, and he thought it would be nice for the two of them to learn together. So they hired a bridge teacher, who came out to our house in Beverly Hills one evening after dinner.

The teacher was a prim, middle-aged woman. She sat down at the table with Krasna and my mother and father, and started out by saying, "Now, the first thing we do is deal thirteen cards to each person." She dealt the cards. "Now we arrange the cards in our hands according to suits—hearts, spades, and so on."

"What does a spade look like?" asked Father, completely deadpan.

Very patiently, the teacher explained to him about the different suits.

"Why do we have to call a spade a spade?" asked Father. "Why can't we call a diamond a spade for a change? That's the trouble with this game. It's too reactionary. What this game needs is young blood!"

The teacher cleared her throat. "As I was saying, the first thing we do is arrange the cards according to suits."

"Why do we have to do that?" asked Father.

"Because that's how you play the game."

"That's how *you* play the game, you mean."

"No, but those are the rules."

"Whose rules?"

"Well, we're going to play the Culbertson system."

"What right does he have to dictate to me how we're going to play bridge?" asked Father indignantly. "This is my house. Let him play the Culbertson system in *his* house if he wants."

"Grouch—" said Mother. "We're paying this lady for lessons. Let's listen."

"How much are we paying?" asked Father suspiciously.

"Five dollars an hour," announced the teacher.

"It's too much," said Father. "We could have bought Culbertson's book for a buck and a quarter."

After about an hour of suffering through Father's interruptions, the teacher thought they knew enough of the fundamentals to try playing a hand. At this point, they recessed while Mother went into the kitchen to get a pitcher of ice water and Krasna excused himself to go to the washroom.

Alone with the teacher, Father leaned over to her and said, "How about you and me blowing this joint and heading south over the border? I know a nice litle motel in Tijuana. Of course, we won't have enough people for bridge, but we can play two-handed strip poker."

The lady collected her things, streaked for the door, and was never heard from again.*

* That's not true. She sent me a bill. GROUCHO

CHAPTER 11

WHEN HE WAS in a show, Father's free nights were too precious to waste on indoor sports he wasn't interested in.

There were too many books he hadn't read, too many authors he was just discovering: Priestley, H. G. Wells, Somerset Maugham, Arnold Bennett, Huxley, and even Tolstoy.

He read most of their works, and everything else that was in the large library he was swiftly accumulating in Great Neck. He was even interested in the children's books that he had bought for me which he hadn't had the opportunity to read when he was a child.

He was particularly delighted with the *Winnie the Pooh* stories of A. A. Milne and *The Swiss Family Robinson*.

After he read the first chapter of the latter one Sunday night, he sent me to bed and stayed up until dawn, finishing the book. The next time he was going to read aloud to me, I brought out *Swiss Family Robinson* again. But Father returned it to the shelf and selected *Jack the Giant Killer*.

When I asked why, he said, "I've already finished *Swiss Family Robinson*. I'll tell you how it comes out. You wouldn't like the middle part anyway. It's too good for children."

So he gave me a quick synopsis of it, and we were on to *Jack the Giant Killer*. He didn't have time to waste reading the same book twice.

He could do some reading, of course, in his dressing room between acts, and occasionally if Chico was in the throes of a long musical number, Father would wander into his dressing room in the midst of the show and read a few lines from *War and Peace* or the *Journals* of Arnold Bennett.

But that wasn't the most satisfactory way of keeping up with what was going on in the world of literature.*

It wasn't too satisfactory for me, either, because even though he read to me as often as he could, he didn't have as much time for bedtime stories now that we were living in Great Neck.

Broadway was a good hour away by automobile, and Father, being a nervous performer, liked to leave himself plenty of time to eat and make the drive into town. Not only because he opened the show and had a fear of being stuck in a traffic jam on the Fifty-ninth Street Bridge when the curtain was going up, but also because he felt too logy and sleepy to give a good performance if he went on the stage immediately after a heavy meal.

He preferred to be made up and in costume by eight o'clock at the latest. That way he could spend a quiet half-hour on the cot in his dressing room, napping or reading, until the boy knocked on the door and yelled, "Overture!"

The revelation that the show was about to begin never failed to send a shiver up and down Father's spine and give him a momentary sick feeling in the pit of his stomach.

He just couldn't be casual about it—even after twenty years in the theater. Every time he walked out on the stage, he told me, he was firmly convinced that he was going to forget all his lines and that this particular performance was going to lay a big egg.

He was never to overcome this fear completely. Many years after *Cocoanuts*, while I was a student at Beverly Hills High School, the principal asked me if I wouldn't talk Father into making a funny speech at one of our assemblies.

I knew he didn't particularly relish the idea of appearing in public (especially when it wasn't in the line of business), but I didn't think he'd mind making a few funny remarks for a group of school children. After all, he was a professional entertainer, and Beverly High wasn't the Palace. But when I mentioned it to him,

* *I'll say it wasn't. I still haven't finished* War and Peace. GROUCHO

he immediately changed the subject, and when I brought it up again, he said, "Maybe next year. I'm busy now."

However, I kept after him for about a week, because the principal was hounding me, and besides I figured that if he did make the appearance, it would do a lot for my personal prestige on the campus.*

He remained stubborn to the last, and finally it became necessary for me to bring out my ace-in-the-hole. "Well, Eddie Cantor made a speech at school when Marilyn asked him to," I said one evening, after he had just turned me down for the seventeenth time.

"He would," said Father. "He'll go any place where he can make a speech—even if no one asks him to."

About two days later he came to me and said, "I'll make a deal with you. If you paint the porch furniture, I'll give a talk at your school."

He probably didn't think I would paint the porch furniture, but I did, and there was no way of his escaping.

He worked on the speech for days. He had trouble finding a suitable topic, he had trouble writing it, and he had more trouble memorizing it. Finally, on the night before his appearance at high school, he emerged from his study, looking worn and haggard and gripping a manuscript that had so many pencil notations on it you couldn't read the typing.

"I'm worried about this speech," he said. "I don't know if it's right for a high school audience. And I don't know it very well, either. Do you think it would be all right if I *read* it tomorrow?"

"Eddie Cantor didn't read his," I told him.

"I'm sure of that," replied Father. "He probably sang twelve songs besides."

"No, he only sang three!"

"Okay," said Father, in a doomed voice. "I won't read it. I'll stumble through it the best I can."

On the morning of the speech, while the principal was an-

* *Certainly your grades wouldn't.* GROUCHO

nouncing to the assembly that "Beverly Hills High was fortunate in having an honored guest with us," Father stood in the wings looking as pale and nervous as he must have appeared the night *I'll Say She Is* opened in New York.

I was sure he would do the speech badly, that the students wouldn't understand his humor, and that he would be hooted off the stage amid shouts of "We want Eddie Cantor back." But Father came through like a professional, didn't forget a word and, needless to say, was a big hit.

According to Father, it isn't uncommon for an actor to get a sinking feeling before he goes on the stage, "particularly if he's any good." But I believe Father was more apprehensive about facing an audience than most actors. Certainly more so than Harpo, Chico, or Zeppo ever were. Frequently they'd show up at the theater at the very last minute, coming directly there from various card games around town, slap on their costumes and make-up without even looking in the mirror, and stroll out onto the stage as unconcerned as if they were entering someone's parlor.

On several occasions their nonchalance was responsible for some pretty embarrassing moments. One incident in particular was, I'm sure, the most embarrassing of all. It happened during the first act of *Animal Crackers*, one night after the show had been playing on Broadway for about a year, and the cast was getting pretty sloppy, anyway.

The scene was in the palatial home of wealthy Mrs. Rittenhouse (Margaret Dumont), who was giving a formal reception in honor of Captain Spalding (my father), the great African explorer. As each guest arrived at the top of the marble staircase in Mrs. Rittenhouse's living room, the butler would take his or her coat, and the guest would be announced and proceed down the stairs to the reception. When Harpo was announced, the butler was to whisk off his cape, revealing that he had nothing on underneath but a pair of swimming trunks.

That's how Kaufman and Ryskind wrote it, and it usually turned out that way, but one evening Harpo was detained and didn't arrive at the theater until after the curtain had already gone up.

He hurriedly undressed and donned his cape and red wig, but in the excitement of trying to make his first cue, he completely forgot about putting on his trunks. The result was that when the butler relieved him of his cape, Harpo found himself in full view of the audience with nothing on but a very skimpy G-string.

Harpo was not easily embarrassed or flustered, but he was that night, and with a shriek he fled into the wings. As he left the stage, Father turned to the audience and said, "Tomorrow night he's not going to wear anything, so get your tickets early!"

Once the curtain rose—and in *Cocoanuts* it rose on Father clerking behind a hotel desk in Florida—his nervousness disappeared completely. He was as relaxed on the stage as he was at home in his study, and as uninhibited as the worst extrovert. He rarely forgot a line or a piece of business, and he was never at a loss for a funny ad lib to cope with an unexpected development on the stage. And if there were no unexpected developments, he would frequently stray from the original manuscript anyway, just to break the monotony of saying the same lines night after night.

The monotony was the only thing that occasionally tripped up Father. After playing the same show for two or three hundred performances, the lines would come so automatically to him that he wouldn't have to think about them. When he did think about them, he'd get in trouble. His mind would go blank for a moment.

"Would you mind giving me that cue again?" he'd have to say to Chico, if it happened while the two of them were doing a scene together. "I seem to have lost my place."

"No trouble at all," Chico might reply. "You said to me, 'Do you know what a blueprint is?' and I said, 'Sure, oysters.' Now do you know where you are?"

By that time, he would know, of course, but frequently he'd pretend that he didn't, just to confuse Chico.

"No, I don't know where I am," he'd say. "But I've seen you someplace before. Say, you aren't by any chance related to that red-headed moron I've seen running around here tonight, are you?"

"Sure, he's your brother!"

"Well, if he's my brother," Father would say, switching to a

93

Jolsonesque Southern accent, "how come you're an Italian and I'm from the deep South?"

While Chico was thinking that one over, Father would slip back into the show dialogue. "We're going to have an auction."

"Now I don't know where *I* am," Chico would reply. "Give me that line again."

"Oh, no," Father would answer. "You're getting the same cut of the show I am. You figure it out."

Eventually they'd get back into the dialogue, and the show would proceed. But it was rarely the same show twice. Father and his brothers were constantly striving for new lines and better pieces of business.

And it's a good thing for their shows and careers that they were adept at this; because no authors, not even Kaufman and Ryskind, who had no peers when it came to writing Marx Brothers' material, could sit down at a typewriter and knock off a perfect piece of material for them. Their humor was unique and too individualized.

Chico played an Italian; Harpo played a deaf-and-dumb blond chaser; and Father played a brash, wise-cracking charlatan who never stopped talking.

If an author could write Italian dialect material, chances were he couldn't write for my father. If he could write my father's dialogue, then he might not be good for Chico. And if he could write for both of them, he couldn't write for Harpo. No one, for that matter, could write for Harpo.

"How can you write for Harpo?" George Kaufman once complained when they were in the throes of putting *Cocoanuts* together. "What do you put down on paper? All you can say is, 'Harpo enters.' From that point on, he's on his own!"

Harpo, more than anyone, had to know how to devise his own material. It was either that or have no part when the show opened. And frequently he didn't have much of a part when a show of theirs opened out of town for the try-outs. All he'd have would be a trunkful of props, his harp and his Puckish sense of humor. It

94

would be entirely up to him to experiment with these ingredients in front of a live audience and find out what was funny and what wasn't.

As a result, their out-of-town openings were usually a shambles, with none of the brothers, authors or producers knowing what was going to come next. *Cocoanuts* and *Animal Crackers* died torturous deaths in Philadelphia and Boston. They were overlong, unfunny and appeared destined for failure in New York. But by the time they arrived on Broadway, they were transformed, as if by magic, into hilarious vehicles. The dialogue would be sharp, the situations airtight, and even Harpo would have a fat part.

It's a show business axiom that any show can be greatly improved by a few weeks on the road. But once it's a hit on Broadway the people connected with it are content to leave it alone. The Marx Brothers, however, never stopped tinkering with the material from opening night until the show closed—perhaps two years later. By the end of the run, the show would barely be recognizable—even to its authors.

One night, during the last few weeks of *Cocoanuts'* two-year run on Broadway, George Kaufman and Heywood Broun were watching the performance from the standing-room section. They weren't actually watching; they were just killing time by talking. But at one point, Broun noticed that Kaufman was ignoring his conversation, and in an annoyed tone, asked, "What's the matter with you?"

Kaufman, whose attention had been directed toward the stage for the past several seconds, turned back to Broun and said, "I may be wrong, but I thought I just heard one of the original lines!"

Many people would be so fascinated by the flexibility of the Marx Brothers' performances that they would come back and see the show half a dozen times or more. Still others would return to catch the parts of the show they missed the first time because the audience's laughter had drowned out so much of the dialogue.

Bobby Jones, the golfer, once visited Father in his dressing room after the performance and said, "I just had to come back and meet you, Groucho. This is the twelfth time I've seen *Cocoanuts*, and there are still a few lines I'm not sure of. I thought maybe you could tell me what they are right now."

Father was always particularly delighted if an outstanding figure in some other field dropped by his dressing room after the show to pay him a compliment. And there were a number of them, including Calvin Coolidge, Al Smith, Jimmy Walker and even the Prince of Wales (now the Duke of Windsor).

Father would deny that he was ever impressed with meeting this kind of person. But he was. I remember his coming home and telling me with great enthusiasm that he had spent an hour with the Prince of Wales in his dressing room, that they had got along famously, and that the Prince had invited Father to drop in on him at Buckingham Palace, if he were ever in the neighborhood.

The Marx Brothers were great favorites with politicians and royalty alike—probably because it was a refreshing change for them to meet someone like Father, who showed them anything but proper respect. If he knew, for instance, that an important personage was in the audience, you could count on him, at some point in the performance, to throw in a few impudent ad libs especially for that person's benefit.

"I see we have the Honorable Mayor Walker with us," he announced to Chico while they were giving a show one election eve. "I wonder why he isn't home stuffing ballot boxes."

The night Calvin Coolidge came to see Cocoanuts, Father stepped to the footlights, eyed the President for a moment, and then said, "Aren't you up past your bedtime, Calvin?"

But of all the people who saw Cocoanuts, the one who made the greatest impression on Father was Herman Schroeder.

He and Schroeder had been school chums back in the days when the Marx clan was hiding from the landlord on Ninety-third Street. But twenty years had elapsed since then, and Father barely remembered his old playmate when he presented himself at his dressing room door one night after the show.

Schroeder had always been a stodgy, humorless fellow, even as a child. He had been an honor student at P. S. 86, and had been very serious about becoming a lawyer. But now he appeared stodgier than ever. He was thick around the middle, with an elk's tooth dangling from a chain on his vest, pince-nez, and a homburg hat.

"I saw the show tonight, Julius," he said. "I thought you were quite good."

"Glad you liked it," said Father, starting to remove his black mustache with cold cream and a towel. "What are you doing these days?"

"I'm doing very well," said Herman, clearing his throat. "I'm a lawyer. I'm a junior partner with Handel, Grossmeyer, and Handel."

"Glad to hear it," said Father politely.

"My annual income is nine thousand dollars," announced Herman. "And in two years, when they make me a senior partner, it will be twelve thousand dollars a year."

"That's nice," said Father.

"I also have nineteen hundred in the bank and a twenty-thousand-dollar endowment policy for the wife and kids, and we live in a nice apartment up in the Bronx. Yes, sir, I'm really doing well."

"Herman—I'm proud of you," said Father, playing it perfectly straight. "I always knew you'd come through."

Herman beamed. "It's just like my mother used to tell me. If you work hard and go to church, a person's bound to be successful. Do you go to church, Julius?"

"Well, I haven't been yet today," replied Father.

"Maybe that's your trouble," said Herman.

"Trouble?" Father looked at him curiously. "What kind of trouble?"

"Well—the reason you're not doing any better."

"I thought you liked the show," said Father. "Didn't you just finish telling me how good I am in it?"

"I meant no reflection on your ability as an actor," said Herman. "What I mean is, this is no way for a man of your age to have to earn a living—smearing black grease-paint on your face and cavorting around the stage every night like a lunatic."

97

"No, it isn't very dignified," admitted Father.

"You're not a boy any longer," pointed out Herman. "It's about time you settled down."

"Do you really think so?"

"I certainly do. Besides, what can a job like this pay? Not very much, I don't suppose."

"Oh, the pay's pretty good," said Father. At the time, his share of the profits amounted to approximately two thousand dollars a week.

"Tell me, Julius, what do you make in a job like this?"

"Well at the moment I'm getting fifty a week," said Father. "But when my brothers make me a full partner, I'm going to get raised to fifty-five."

"That's what I mean," said Herman. "This is no business to be in."

"What do you suggest I do?" asked Father.

"I'd start looking around for another line of work," Herman advised him. "Before you're too old to get into anything else."

"Herman Schroeder," said Father, "you're perfectly right. But what kind of work do you advise me to get into? I don't know anything but show business. I didn't even finish grammar school."

"You could go to night school until you get your diploma."

"How could I live?"

"You could get a temporary job in the daytime."

Father shook his head. "No, if I'm going to make a change, I'd like to get into something where I could make some money right away."

"Have you ever considered selling?" Herman asked. "You're a glib talker. You'd probably make a good salesman."

"I've considered it," replied Father, "but I don't think it would work out. You see, most actors steal, and I'm afraid I'd always have my hand in the till."

"Not really!" exclaimed Herman.

"I wouldn't kid you," said Father, taking his gold watch off the dressing table and holding it up. "You see this watch? I stole it at the Ritz-Carlton in Boston. And that trunk over there in the corner? I picked it up right from under a redcap's nose at the Union depot in Philly."

Herman stared at him open-mouthed.

"As a matter of fact, I wouldn't get too close to me," Father went on. "I might steal your watch. And that gold chain, too! I've always wanted a gold chain with an elk's tooth on it."

"I'd better be going," said Herman, backing toward the door.

"So soon? We haven't decided on a business for me yet."

"I'm afraid it's getting late."

"Say—I've got an idea!" exclaimed Father. "How about taking me in with you and those shyster partners of yours? I could be a junior partner, with a little practice."

"Oh, we couldn't take in any more partners," said Herman nervously.

"Why not? I wouldn't ask for much at first. Say, five thousand a year and all I can steal."

"I'm afraid not," said Herman, turning to go. "Good-bye, Julius."

"Good-bye, Herman."

At the door, Herman turned around again. "Julius," he said, "you used to be a good boy. It's not too late to mend your ways. Think over what I told you. And do me a favor. Don't steal any more."

"I wish I could stop," said Father sadly, "but unfortunately, it's the only way I can make both ends meet."

CHAPTER 12

ALTHOUGH IT WOULD have taken a good deal more than a
Herman Schroeder to make Father quit the theater, he was never
so enamored of the life of a legitimate actor that it would have
broken his heart to give it up.

Typical of his attitude was the time he took sick during *Animal
Crackers* and Zeppo understudied for him. Father was so delighted
that his brother could handle the assignment competently that he
stayed out of the show for two weeks after he had completely recovered.

And only the fact that Zeppo—the only one of the Marx Brothers not working on a percentage basis—started hinting that he was
entitled to Father's share of the profits sent Father scurrying back
to his part. But he wasn't happy about it, for he had discovered,
while he was recuperating, how delightful it was to spend his
evenings at home, in a big chair in front of the fireplace.

Of course, he liked the money and the prestige that went with
being a Broadway star—especially the money. And I doubt if he
would have been happy, or even successful, in the pants business,
for example. But you could never say of him, as you can of so
many actors, that he has grease-paint in his blood.

"Show business" in his blood would be more accurate.* He'd
have to be in some branch of show business. If not acting, then
writing, directing or producing. He'd be reasonably satisfied doing

* No blood would be more accurate. GROUCHO

100

any of these things—just as long as he'd have some reason to read the weekly Variety, which has been his bible ever since it first started being published.

Many actors—especially comedians—live for that moment when they can be on the stage in front of an audience. Hearing laughter and applause gives them a lift that nothing else can give them.

For Father, all those needs are fulfilled in a once-a-week, two-hour workout in front of a very much alive television audience. Then it's an ice cream soda at Wil Wright's, and home to semi-seclusion until the next week.

But for most performers this isn't enough. They have to be "on" more. And if they have no reason directly connected with their business for appearing before an audience, they will go out of their way to find one.

The Hollywood chapter of the Friars Club is a notable example of this. Its members are constantly getting together at elaborately prepared ceremonial banquets to pay homage to someone. Occasionally they have a legitimate reason for giving one of these banquets—Jack Benny's silver anniversary in the theater, perhaps, or the dinner they threw for Al Jolson after his remarkable comeback a few years ago. But generally their dinners are just flimsy excuses to put on shows afterwards in which they all can participate.

One night it'll be in honor of George Jessel's impending trip to Palestine. Another night it'll be in honor of Jessel's return from Palestine. One night they'll be comemorating George Burns and Gracie Allen's seventh year with the same sponsor. One night it'll be to lionize Bob Hope for having flown his millionth mile to entertain servicemen, and still another night it'll be because "it was just forty-two and one half years ago today that Eddie Cantor sang his first song for Gus Edwards."

By the time they finish a round of these banquets, Jessel is due to go on another trip again, and the dinners start all over.

Father will go out of his way to avoid any of these dinners—in fact, any affair where there is even a small likelihood that he will be asked to perform. If someone from the Friars calls him up and asks him to attend one of their dinners, he's likely to say, "What's it in honor of this time? Lou Holtz's dog having a birthday?"

"No, Groucho—this is on the level. Milton Berle's fifth year on TV. We want to toast him."

"Why don't you guys get on to yourselves?" Father will say in a spoofing manner. "You don't really give a damn whether Berle deserves a dinner or not. You're a bunch of hams and you just can't wait to get up in front of an audience. Well, have a good time. I'll be thinking of you when you're eating that rubber chicken under glass."

Once in a great while he lets himself get roped into attending one of these banquets. The last one he attended was at the Coconut Grove, several years ago. The occasion was to honor George Jessel, and because he likes Jessel so much, Father agreed to be one of the after-dinner speakers. But his remarks on that occasion were pretty indicative of his whole attitude on the subject.

GENTLEMEN:

This is the first dinner I have attended in years that didn't celebrate Cantor's birthday. Cantor's birthdays are like the yearly anniversary numbers of Variety. They happen about every six weeks. I don't know how old Eddie is, but I would guess from the frequency with which these dinners are thrown that Eddie must be between three and four hundred years old. However, as one who has made a career out of ducking benefits, I want to take a deep bow in Eddie's direction. Eddie is a one-man Marshall Plan. He has never ducked a benefit. Last week he even offered to play one for the Bank of America.

I never thought the day would come when I would be forced to sit on a dais to honor a movie producer. It's a disturbing indication of how rapidly class distinctions are breaking down throughout the United States. Fortunately I don't regard Jessel merely as a movie producer. Jessel is an orator—a great orator. Georgie has done as much for Pico Boulevard as Patrick Henry did for the Thirteen Colonies.

102

I am constantly astonished at the facility with which Jessel tosses the English language around. This is even more astounding when one realizes that he doesn't know the meaning of half the words he uses.

George is unquestionably the most relentless speechmaker of our time. He gives of himself unremittingly. He speaks at weddings, funerals and bar mitzvahs. He speaks so often that sometimes he gets confused. On one occasion he married a thirteen-year-old boy to a woman who had been dead for three days.

If it's a noteworthy cause, Father will appear at a benefit—even go out of his way to do so. A couple of years ago he flew to Oregon to make a forty-five minute speech before a group of students at the University of Oregon. But he only agreed to do this on the condition that the admission price for each student be a pint of blood donated to the Red Cross.

And during the last war he made dozens of War Bond and USO tours. But very rarely will he appear in public just to satisfy his own ego.

Since Father quit Broadway, he's turned down at least a hundred good offers to return to the legitimate theater, and hundreds more to appear in nightclubs and vaudeville houses. I was with him one day when he received a telephone call offering him twenty-five thousand dollars for a one-week engagement at Glen McCarthy's Shamrock Hotel in Texas.

"No, I can't do it for less than fifty thousand," was his counter offer, and when they refused to give it to him, he hung up happily.

"Why did you do that?" I asked. "No one's worth fifty thousand for one week."

"No one's worth twenty-five thousand for one week," he replied. "I just told them that because I don't want to be bothered with any personal appearances."

About once every ten years he'll get a yen to return to the stage. In 1940 he read a book called *Franklin Street*, which he thought could be turned into a very fine stage vehicle for himself. He suggested it to George Kaufman and Arthur Sheekman, another old friend of his, and the two of them excitedly agreed to collaborate on it—if Father would promise to appear in it. He gave his word, but after they completed it, he bowed out of the production, saying he didn't think it was "right" for him. Father probably had a premonition of disaster, because *Franklin Street* folded in Baltimore. But even if it had been the finest play written since *Hamlet*, Father would have found something wrong with it, because when the chips are down, his yen for the bright lights of Broadway suddenly disappears.

It was the same thing with *Time for Elizabeth*, the play Father wrote in collaboration with Norman Krasna. It was Father's original idea to do a play about a businessman who retires and then finds out that a life of idleness isn't so much fun. It was also Father's idea to play the leading role himself. He figured he'd be perfect for the part, since he had tried retiring for about six months and discovered that he didn't like it at all.

This intrigued Krasna, and the two of them set to work on the play in the spring of 1941, and brought the completed manuscript to New York in the fall. He let several people read *Time for Elizabeth*, and he was advised by Kaufman, Max Gordon, and Owen Davis not to let it go into production the way it was. It needed more work, they said.

So Father and Krasna flew back to the Coast and decided to do another draft on *Time for Elizabeth*. They had just completed it when Pearl Harbor came. That ended the venture for the time being. It wouldn't be very patriotic, they felt, to do a play about a man retiring to escape income taxes when we were in the midst of a war.

After the war, they did three more versions of the play, and in 1948 finally decided that they had a draft that they were satisfied with.

"Who do you think would be good to play the lead?" Father asked his collaborator the day they finished the play.

"What do you mean?" asked Krasna, shocked. "I thought we wrote this for you."

"Well, we did," said Father, "but any good actor can play the part. Why don't we try to get someone else? As a matter of fact, it might be better with a straight actor in it. If I'm in it, the critics will expect a Marx Brothers comedy, and they'll be disappointed."

"What's the matter?" asked Krasna suspiciously. "Don't you think it's any good? Do you think it'll be a flop? If that's your attitude, let's just put it in a drawer and forget about it."

"I think it's very good," said Father. "I think it'll be a big hit. That's the trouble."

"What do you mean by that?"

"Well, if it's a hit," replied Father, "that'll mean that I'll probably have to spend a couple of years in New York—walking around in the slush in the winters, working every night, and living in that stifling heat in the summers. I don't want to do that any more. I'm very comfortable here."

As it turned out, he could have played the part himself, and been back in his home in Beverly Hills the following week. *Time for Elizabeth* took a panning from the critics, and folded after eight performances.

In spite of the critics, Father still had a soft spot in his heart for the play—and also a suspicion that *Time for Elizabeth* might have been a success if he had appeared in it. Norman Krasna had a similar hunch, and in the summer of 1952 he talked Father into appearing in their play at the La Jolla Playhouse.

Whether *Time for Elizabeth* was a better play with Father in it, or whether audiences just wanted to see him on the stage again is debatable. However, his one-week engagement there was the outstanding success of La Jolla's summer stock season. The management had to schedule two extra matinees to take care of all the customers who had been turned away from the regular showings.

Time for Elizabeth probably could have played to capacity all summer, if other shows hadn't previously been booked into the theater, and if Father had been willing, which he wasn't. He also received several offers to bring the show to Broadway again with him in it, but he turned them down, too.

I realized why, after watching him do the show every night in La Jolla. On opening night, he was keyed up and razor sharp. He obviously enjoyed appearing before a theater audience. On Thursday night his performance was still good, but it was no longer inspired, or sparkling. And on closing night—Saturday—he looked as if he could take the legitimate theater or leave it—preferably the latter. At one spot in the third act, the action called for Father to stretch out on the couch, say a few lines, and then stand up again. Father managed to lie down on the couch without any trouble, but when the cue came for him to get up again, he didn't budge. In fact, he remained on the couch for about five extra pages of dialogue, and for a moment I thought perhaps he was planning on finishing out the act flat on his back. He finally made it to his feet, and the play proceeded without any serious harm done to it, but I knew then that Father had had his fill. He'd proved that he could make an audience like *Time for Elizabeth*, and now he wished he were home on his own couch.

CHAPTER 13

IN HIS BROADWAY DAYS, of course, Father gave an energetic performance every night—and at one point in 1928 he not only was appearing in *Animal Crackers* on the stage, but he was making the moving picture version of *Cocoanuts* at the same time.

But he was young then, and anxious to hasten the day when he would have so much money in the bank that he would never have to work again if he didn't feel like it.

Cocoanuts was one of the first sound movies ever to be made. It was also the first of five pictures the Marx Brothers had signed to do with Paramount, which, very conveniently, had a studio in Astoria, Long Island, in addition to their Hollywood plant.

Astoria was on the way to New York from Great Neck. Father would leave for the studio early in the morning, shoot until six or seven in the evening and, after a hasty meal with his brothers, would go straight to the theater. It was hard work, for picture making then was even more arduous than it is now.

The technicians were as unfamiliar with working with sound as were the actors. The equipment was crude and constantly broke down in the middle of the scene. Simple scenes had to be shot over as many as twenty and thirty times. The slightest noise two blocks away could ruin a take.

I was at Astoria one day when Father was doing a scene in which he was showing Chico how to read a blueprint. It seemed like an easy scene to do, especially since they were so familiar with the

107

dialogue after doing it on the stage that they could recite it in their sleep. But every time they went through the scene, the crackling noise of the stiff blueprint paper came over so loudly on the sound track that it drowned out the dialogue. They had to take twenty-seven retakes before the director got the bright idea of soaking the blueprints in water. Then the excess water was squeezed out of the prints, and the scene was tried again. It worked. Handling damp blueprints didn't make any disturbing noises on the sound track.

There were dozens of other equally annoying problems that could only be worked out by the trial-and-error method. That's why it took them five months to shoot their first picture. That, plus the fact that on matinee days they couldn't work on the picture at all—except in the mornings.

"Sometimes I'd get so punchy," Father told me, "that I'd find myself spouting the dialogue from *Animal Crackers* in a scene I was doing in *Cocoanuts*, and vice versa."

But *Cocoanuts* couldn't have been made otherwise—at least not at the time. The Marx Brothers had a run-of-the-show commitment with Sam Harris, the producer of *Animal Crackers*. There was no telling how long *Animal Crackers* would be running on Broadway, and Paramount wasn't willing to wait. The picture studio wanted the Marx Brothers while they were hot. (After all, how long could comedians last?)

No one could have been hotter than they were after the opening of *Animal Crackers*. The critics' attitude seemed to be that the Marx Brothers could do no wrong, and evidently the theater-going public thought so, too.

Animal Crackers was a bigger hit than any of its predecessors, and the Marx Brothers were in their prime as a team. The book, by George S. Kaufman and Morrie Ryskind, was full of lines that are still being quoted; and the score, by Bert Kalmar and Harry Ruby, contained a comedy number that has since become sort of a classic. It was called "Hooray for Captain Spaulding," and Father sang it and did an eccentric dance to it after his first entrance—his arrival at the Park Avenue reception Mrs. Rittenhouse was throwing for him (the same scene I described earlier, when Harpo forgot to wear his trunks).

Father, dressed in boots, riding pants and a pith helmet, was supposed to be a famous explorer who had just returned from the wilds of Africa. He was carried into the reception on an African sedan chair, supported by four husky Nubian slaves. After alighting from the chair, Father reached into his pocket for his wallet and said to one of the slaves, "How much do I owe you?"

The slave mumbled the price, and Father replied, "That's an outrage. I could have got a Yellow Cab for a buck and a quarter. I *told* you not to go through the park."

After disposing of the slaves, Father turned to the assembled guests, and sang "Hooray for Captain Spaulding," which started out with:

> *Hello, I must be going.*
> *I cannot stay, I only*
> *Came to say,*
> *I must be going.*
> *I'll stay a week or two,*
> *I'll stay the summer through,*
> *But I am telling you,*
> *I must be going.*

Finally persuaded to stay, Father gave a resumé of the Spartan life he had led in Africa:

"Up at six, breakfast at six-thirty, and back in bed at seven. . . . One morning I shot an elephant in my pajamas. How he got in my pajamas I'll never know."

I remember *Animal Crackers* more vividly than I do their other shows—partly because I was older by then and could appreciate what was taking place on the stage, and partly because I was in it a few times myself.

I didn't have any illusions about becoming an actor, but I enjoyed watching the show from the wings, and I'd frequently be standing there when Father would be getting into his sedan chair.

To give me a thrill, Father, if he were in a good mood, would sometimes say, "Hop in, and take a ride with me," and then he'd pull me into the chair with him.

I'd ride out onto the stage and have to sit there while Father went through his routine with the Nubian slaves. Much to the audience's bewilderment, the routine would contain no reference to the little boy in short pants who remained in the sedan chair, gaping worriedly out into the sea of faces until he was carried back into the safety of the wings again.

Miriam received the same kind of treatment as soon as she was old enough to walk. I remember, in London, in 1931, Father interrupting Harpo in the midst of his harp number to have Miriam, who was then three, with Shirley Temple curls and blue eyes, sing "Show Me the Way to Go Home."

He didn't inflict this sort of thing on audiences very often, but sometimes he just had no will power. The odd part about it was that whenever one of us finished a stint on the stage, he'd say, "Well, how do you like being an actor?"

If I said I didn't particularly like it, he'd scold me for being too diffident, and if I said I liked it, he'd say:

"Well, don't ever let me catch you wanting to be an actor. You can be anything else—a doctor or a lawyer or even a garbage man —but if I catch you getting any ideas about the stage, I'll beat your brains out."

Despite his insistence that the life of an actor was a pretty horrible one, I wasn't quite convinced. And I don't think he was either.

He'd never had it so good—especially as 1928 progressed into the boom days of 1929.

Not only was he in a smash show on Broadway, but *Cocoanuts* was as big a hit with the nation's moviegoers as it had been on the stage, and *Beds* was being serialized in *College Humor* and about to be published in book form by Farrar and Rinehart. Money was pouring in from everywhere, and there was no income tax to speak of.

On the home front, everything was going well, too. Except for a few typical husband-and-wife arguments, all was serene between him and my mother, and if there was a hint of any serious trouble ahead, it was not noticed at the time. He had always wanted two children—a boy he could play baseball with, and a girl he could cuddle—and he had them. And his prized orchard was at last showing some signs of life. An apple was beginning to sprout on the cherry tree.

Father's had his share of good times since then, and he's making more money today than he was in 1929. But I think that was the happiest period of his life, as it was for many people.

It was a crazy, wonderful era. Babe Ruth, Bobby Jones, and Bill Tilden were still the Big Three of sports. Rudy Vallee in *The Vagabond Lover* was causing women across the nation to swoon. People were making gin in their bathtubs, and Anaconda Copper was selling at one hundred and seventy-five a share.

Getting into the spirit of the times, Father traded in the staid Lincoln sedan for a very flashy Packard convertible with red wire wheels and a rumble seat; he bought my mother a long sleek Cord —the first model put out; and he paid five thousand dollars to become a member of Lakeville Country Club in Great Neck.

Five thousand dollars was a lot of money to spend for the way he played golf, but Lakeville was one of the most exclusive clubs on Long Island. Many of his friends belonged, and besides, he had every reason to believe that he had the makings of a great golfer. He had only played a few times before we had moved to Great Neck, but even so, he could already boast of a hole-in-one—at the famed Brae Burn course in Boston.

All the Boston papers had carried the story of the hole-in-one and had printed pictures of Father holding up the lucky ball. Father insisted that it had been an accident, and that he wasn't really as good as Bobby Jones yet. But the next day, when he went out to tackle Brae Burn again, he found a number of sports writers and photographers waiting to catch him in action on the same three par hole.

111

"They didn't believe it was an accident," said Father afterwards, "but I certainly showed them. I got a fourteen on the same hole."

But even golfing greats had their off days, and that incident, far from discouraging Father, only made him more determined than ever to master the sport when he joined Lakeville.

In his case, determination was not enough. Nearly every afternoon he and my mother would play eighteen holes together. And whenever he was leaving for the club, he'd announce confidently, "I think I've got it today." But whatever it was he had, it disappeared by the time he arrived on the first tee, dressed in golfing knickers and argyle socks.

In all the years he played, he was never able to crack ninety, and usually his score hovered somewhere between ninety-five and one hundred. This was a constant source of annoyance to him, because all his friends, including his brothers, could shoot in the low eighties.

"Of course, they cheated," recalls Father. "They'd concede eight-foot putts, play winter rules in August, and if no one was looking when they made a bad shot, they wouldn't count it."

The odd part of it is that Father's a pretty good natural athlete. He used to play semi-pro baseball when he was in vaudeville; he could swim and ride horseback well; and later on, after we moved to California, he and I won the Men's Doubles Championship at the Beverly Hills Tennis Club.

But his golf game never improved; in fact, if anything, it grew steadily worse.

His main trouble seemed to be that the sight of a golf ball unnerved him. He had a perfect practice swing. No golf professional could ever find a flaw in it. But as soon as you put a ball down in front of him, his game fell apart.

Unlike a lot of golfers, he didn't have any one shot that gave him trouble. His short game was as bad as his woods, and his putting was especially atrocious. He could never be sure of sinking any putt over a foot long.

112

Once, the only time he ever had a chance to break ninety, he missed a two-foot putt on the eighteenth hole. He was so furious that he hurled his putter to the green, embedding it about a foot deep in the velvety green turf that had been brought over to Lakeville from Scotland.

Needless to say, the greens committee was not pleased, and instigated a movement to have this ordinarily mild-mannered actor tossed out of the club immediately. But they did give him a chance to defend himself at the expulsion proceedings.

"Sure, I have a terrible temper," he confessed, "and I wouldn't blame you no matter what you decide. But I don't think throwing me out is the answer. That's no punishment. Look how happy you'll make me. I won't have to play this confounded game any more."

In view of his testimony, the committee reconsidered and let him remain a member. To show his gratitude, Father, while playing Lakeville's water hole the next day, killed one of the club's tame swans with a wild two-iron shot.*

With his golf game in such desperate straits, Father was constantly on the lookout for some magic cure-all to lift him out of the ranks of mediocrity. He was beyond the stage where he thought lessons could help him. He was now spending his free time poring over all the how-to-play books by the world's best professionals, and eating up everything he read in the newspapers that might contain a hint on how to lower his score.

As a result, he didn't have to stick to any one method of playing. He had a number of different swings at his command.

On the first tee, he might start out by making an announcement like, "I think I'll use the *World-Telegram* swing today."

The *World-Telegram* swing was something he had read in a box called *Tips for Golfers* in that newspaper.

"All left hand. That's what the *World-Telegram* recommends,"

* You're wrong. It was a mashie niblick. GROUCHO

he'd go on. And then he'd take a vicious cut at the ball. If by some miraculous chance, the ball went straight and far down the fairway, he'd stick with the *World-Telegram* until he dubbed a shot, which would be almost immediately.

At this point, he'd switch to another swing—perhaps something he had read in Gene Sarazen's book. With Father doing it, Sarazen's swing looked exactly like the *World-Telegram* swing, which in turn resembled all the rest of his assortment of swings.

Even if the swings had been different, he never would stick with one long enough to find out whether or not it was practical. And sometimes he'd combine two or three of his favorite swings. For instance, "Today I'm going to try the *Evening Sun* swing on the backswing, the Gene Sarazen on the downswing, let the clubhead do all the work like Walter Hagen, and after I hit the ball, spit on the ground to keep my head down. Angus McTavish at the St. Louis Country Club told me I should try the spitting."

Ben Hogan couldn't play golf with all the things on his mind that Father used to try to remember. But even though Father couldn't actually play himself, he never hesitated to tell you how to play.

"Keep your head down and follow through," he'd say to my mother, whenever she missed a shot. "How many times do I have to tell you that?"

Mother, of course, would get highly indignant. "You're certainly a fine one to be telling anyone else how to play. You haven't made a good shot in three weeks."

"That doesn't mean I'm not a great teacher," he'd reply. "Just remember, the great virtuosos aren't necessarily the best instructors. What kind of a teacher do you think Rachmaninoff would make? Or Heifetz?" *

He also knew a number of annoying little aphorisms which he liked to quote at strategic moments:

"Never up, never in."

"Whom the Gods would destroy, they first make mad."

* *Especially at golf.* GROUCHO

114

And an old Scottish saying: "If the duffer would just remember that when he's off his game he's on, and when he's on his game he's off, there would be less grousing in the locker room."

Father can only concentrate on the game for a few holes. Once he has used up all his swings and he realizes that the whole thing is pretty hopeless—at least for the remainder of the day—the match quickly degenerates into a deliberate comedy of errors.

Anyone intent on breaking par will do everything possible not to get mixed up in a game with Father. For his attitude—in fact his whole game—is very contagious, and pretty soon everyone else in his foursome, threesome, or twosome will be playing just as badly as he.

But though Father still plays occasionally—he's using the Tommy Armour swing now—he actually retired from serious golf about fifteen years ago. The match that hurried this decision took place on the famous Cypress Point course in Del Monte, California.

His opponent was Ed Sullivan. It was a close match, with Father only seventeen down, when they arrived at the windswept sixteenth hole. The sixteenth is a water hole, and, though a three-par, you have to drive across a two hundred–yard gap of ocean to get to the green.

Father teed up breezily and with hardly any effort knocked five brand-new balls into the blue Pacific. But after many years of golf playing, he had at last learned to control his temper on a course. Very calmly, he removed the remaining balls from his bag, and stepping over to the edge of the cliff, dropped them into the ocean one by one. Then he hurled his bag of clubs over the cliff and went back to the hotel, as light-hearted as if he had just been reprieved from the gallows.

But Father was a more determined sportsman when we were living in Great Neck. All his friends were leading the sporting life, and he felt he was expected to do the same.

A number of Father's close friends had magnificent estates on the Long Island Sound, complete with private beaches and their

115

own yachts riding at anchor. When Father wasn't golfing, we'd frequently go swimming at Sam Harris' and at Herbert Bayard Swope's, and yachting with anyone who asked us.

Father wasn't too fond of life on the waves. He's always had a rather queasy stomach, and Dramamine hadn't been invented yet. But everyone was living dangerously in those days, and Father didn't want to be excluded. He even bought himself a yachting cap and a blue coat with brass buttons.

"If I'm going to throw up, at least I want to be dressed properly," he used to say whenever we were preparing for a cruise around Long Island Sound.

For a while we were giving most of our yachting trade to Larry Schwab, one of the producers of *Follow Through*, who was a good friend of Father's. Schwab had one of the prettiest and fastest yachts I've ever seen, but he was a madman at the helm. He liked to see how close he could come to other boats without actually hitting them. He also liked to criss-cross over the bumpy wake churned up by ocean liners and huge yachts like J. P. Morgan's *Corsair*.

This sort of recklessness could only end in disaster, Father often predicted while he was huddled up miserably in the boat's stern. And he was right. One day, when we weren't along, Schwab rammed a log, and his forty-thousand-dollar yacht went down to the bottom of the Sound.

There were no casualties, and Father was delighted. He figured that would put an end to his nautical activities. But his brother Zeppo crossed him up by getting a yacht of his own. Zeppo's yacht was the talk of the Marx family. No one could understand how *he*, the junior member of the team, could afford such luxury. Zeppo remained mysteriously mum on the subject, but years later it turned out that he had never owned the yacht. He was merely shilling for a company that manufactured yachts, and it was loaned to him so he could lure prospective customers out onto it and induce them to buy boats of their own.

Father was anything but a prospective customer, but we were

116

guests on Zeppo's boat frequently. Zeppo wasn't the wildman at the helm that Schwab had been, but that didn't stop Father from getting deathly ill every time he boarded the vessel.

"Why do you go out on it?" Mother asked him one day. "Why don't you stay home and stop spoiling everybody's fun?"

"I'd like to," replied Father wistfully, "but I've got too much money tied up in yachting clothes."

In addition to being a sterling seaman, Father was a pioneer in the air. One of our neighbors in Great Neck was a commander in the Naval Air Corps, and he used to take Father and me up for rides in an open-cockpit seaplane. The commander was pretty casual about his passengers. He never even suggested that we strap ourselves in, and we didn't have the sense to take the precaution ourselves. I remember Father standing up in the cockpit one day and leaning far over the fuselage as he pointed out with his cigar the Statue of Liberty and other interesting landmarks in New York harbor as we flew over them.

One good air pocket, and *Animal Crackers* would have been without a Captain Spalding.

Although, with the exception of golf, I'd usually be included in Father's activities, every so often he'd get the notion that maybe he ought to do something that would be of special interest to a boy of eight.

One day he took time off from his rich man's pleasures to take me and a small group of my friends to Coney Island. This was my first trip there, but Father was well acquainted with the place. Many years before he had worked as a boy soprano in some of the joints along the boardwalk, and he was full of nostalgia for it and determined that I should have as good a time as he remembered having.

"Wait until you taste those hot dogs with sauerkraut," he said as we were driving to Coney Island. "You've never had hot dogs until you've eaten them at Feldman's. And that roller coaster they have there is the last word."

But when we got there, I absolutely refused to go on the roller coaster.

"It's perfectly safe," said Father. "Go ahead. You'll love it."

"I don't want to."

"I know a lot of poor kids who would give their eye teeth for a chance like this," said Father, trying to conceal his annoyance and not doing a very good job of it. "I used to go on this roller coaster all the time when I was a kid, and nothing ever happened to me."

"Well, why don't you go on it now?"

"Because I'm a grownup, and I'm not supposed to be enjoying myself. Besides, it makes me sick. But I wouldn't be afraid. Now go ahead. Get on the roller coaster. Junior Hanft is on it, and he's not afraid. Do you think I made this trip down here because I enjoy driving through traffic on Sunday in the stifling heat?"

His words were futile, and what annoyed him even more was that when we got to Feldman's, I wouldn't eat a hot dog with sauerkraut on it. I wanted it plain.

"Don't be a schlemiel," insisted Father. "You've gotta have sauerkraut. That's what makes it good."

"I don't like it."

"Try it. How are you going to know that you don't like it if you don't try it?"

"I have tried it."

"I don't know what kind of a son I'm raising," complained Father bitterly. "First you don't want to go on the roller coaster. Now you don't like sauerkraut. Next I suppose you'll be wanting to go home. Well, you're not going home. We're going to stay here, and you're going to have a good time if it kills you."

After lunch I went on a few of the less breathtaking rides, which made Father feel that all was not lost. But even this minor victory was short-lived. It only lasted until we arrived at the fun house. This particular fun house contained a number of amusements like the revolving barrel that you had to walk through; a small, very fast-whirling merry-go-round that you were supposed to stay on if you

118

could; and a couple of huge slides that were approximately eighty feet high.

The slide looked like fun to me until I climbed the steps and reached the point of embarkation. The long descent seemed a hundred miles to the bottom and as steep as the side of the Empire State Building.

Children all around me were whooping and hollering with glee as they rushed up the steps and slid fearlessly down the long, slippery incline, but for some reason I sat frozen on the brink, unable to make myself take the plunge.

Father was at the bottom of the slide, looking up at me expectantly and urging me on with frantic hand motions.

"Come on already," he finally hollered. "Don't be a coward. Slide!"

I nodded obediently—as if I fully intended to do it, if he'd just give me time—but I knew in my heart I was not going down the slide, no matter how ashamed he would be of me.

I sat there, trying not to think of what he must have been thinking of me, and when I lost sight of him in the crowd below, I was quite relieved—in fact, rather pleased—because obviously he had become interested in something else and had decided to leave the decision up to me, as a wise parent should.

Suddenly, I felt a tremendous shove from behind, and the next thing I knew I was on my way down the slide. It was so unexpected that I didn't have time to be frightened. And when I reached the bottom, I glanced up at the top of the slide, and there was Father laughing uproariously.

"I had to do it," he apologized afterward. "It was a lousy trick, but I had to do it. No son of mine's going to make a bum of me in front of all those other parents."

CHAPTER 14

ALTHOUGH 1929 was a period of gay living and free spending, Father was not being too reckless with his money.

Other people could own yachts and strings of polo ponies, or go off for extended vacations on the French Riviera. But except for the five thousand dollars he had parted with to join Lakeville, Father was playing things very conservatively. He was preparing for that well-known rainy day.

By the autumn of 1929 he had accumulated a nest egg of roughly a quarter of a million dollars, and he was keeping it in a nice safe place—the stock market.

Knowing how wary Father has always been of schemes where you can make money without working for it, I'm amazed that he ever let himself get sucked into Wall Street.*

As I've mentioned previously, he has no gambling instincts, and never—even in the most prosperous times—did he stop looking for ways of keeping unnecessary expenses down around the house. He was as conscious of the price of pumpernickel in 1929 as he had been before *I'll Say She Is* put him in the high-income brackets.

Yet when it came to tips on the stock market, he was as gullible as everyone else. He'd accept without question the word of a total stranger and invest thousands of dollars in a stock that he knew absolutely nothing about.

And I'm not exaggerating. One morning, while he was in Boston

* *I'm amazed, too.* GROUCHO

120

breaking in *Animal Crackers*, he got into the elevator at the Ritz-Carlton Hotel to go down to breakfast. During the ride down, the elevator boy leaned over to him and whispered in his ear, "Union Carbide just dropped two points. Now's the time to load up on it."

"No kidding?"

"On the level, Mr. Marx. I just looked at the board." A Wall Street brokerage firm had its branch office in the hotel, and the elevator boy would poke his head in between trips to see how things were going.

Thanking him effusively, Father slipped a ten-dollar bill in his palm, went straight to the broker's office, and wrote out a check for nine thousand dollars. He also passed the tip along to Harpo, who put half his savings in that one stock. It dropped to twenty-five cents a share at the time of the crash.

Father received another good tip from Eddie Cantor. Cantor was playing at the Palace, and, after seeing the show one afternoon, Father called on him in his dressing room.

"Julius," exclaimed Cantor, "get yourself two hundred shares of Goldman-Sachs immediately. It's selling for one hundred and thirty-seven, and I just got word from Herbert Swope that it's sure to go one hundred and fifty by the end of the week."

Father hates to be called Julius by his friends, and Cantor never calls him anything else, but Father was so grateful for the tip that he overlooked it on this occasion, and promptly phoned his broker to buy two hundred shares of the stock for him. He paid over twenty-seven thousand dollars for Goldman-Sachs, and when it dropped to two dollars a share during the crash he was forced to sell his holding in the company for four hundred dollars.

"It cost me twenty-seven thousand dollars plus the price of a ticket to see Cantor at the Palace that day," recalls Father. "Believe me, Eddie's show wasn't worth it."

It would be an understatement to say that Father didn't realize playing the market was so risky. He was in it because, like everyone else, he was convinced that it was a sound, money-making venture. You were in partnership with big business. Financiers had been on

121

to this for years. Did J. P. Morgan, the Whitneys and the DuPonts bury their money in banks that only paid two and three percent interest? Of course not. They put their money to work for them. That's why they could afford yachts like the *Corsair*.

It was amazingly simple. Father could never get over the wonder of it.

Every morning, after he had eaten breakfast and read the newspapers, he would get in his car and drive down to Newman Brothers & Worms, his Wall Street representatives who had a branch brokerage office on Great Neck's main street. There he would solemnly study the ticker tapes and watch the boy marking the latest quotation on the huge board.

He would sit in the office by the hour, watching his stocks go up and up, and gloating over his good fortune. He was not alone. Newman Brothers & Worms' Great Neck branch was doing a land-office business. He'd meet all his friends and neighbors and the local tradesmen in the place, and they would exchange tips and discuss the latest financial trends, as if they really knew what they were talking about.

Very often, if I wasn't in school, he'd take me with him, promising he wouldn't bore me with it for long.

"I'll just take a quick look," he'd say, "and then we'll go home and play baseball."

His quick look would usually last for a couple of hours, by which time I would give up trying to persuade him to leave and walk home.

Or if we were driving through the village on our way to the beach or some other place, he'd have to park the car and dash into his broker's "just for a minute," to see how things were going.

"What an easy racket," he'd exclaim jubilantly, when he returned to the car, if he returned. "RCA went up seven points since this morning. I just made myself seven thousand dollars."

Although there was no one less qualified than Father to analyze the strength of the nation's economy, he must have had a premonition of disaster.

One day, in early October of 1929, he found himself standing in front of the ticker-tape machine with Mr. Green, who managed this particular branch of Newman Brothers & Worms.

"Wonderful times we're living in," commented Mr. Green, pulling off a piece of tape and showing it to Father. "Look at this, will you? RCA is up to five hundred and thirty-five a share. Have you ever seen anything like it?"

Father agreed that he hadn't, and then added: "There's just one thing I don't understand, Mr. Green. I own RCA, too. But how can it be selling for five hundred and thirty-five a share and never declare a dividend? If a company's sound and making money, it should declare a dividend once in a while. Doesn't that seem strange to you?"

Mr. Green shook his head sagely. "Mr. Marx," he said reassuringly, "it's different for the average man not schooled in high finance to comprehend what is going on today. But I can tell you this. Wall Street is no longer localized. We're now in a world-wide market. It's going to keep going up and up and up. Is that clear?"

"Well, I think I know what you're talking about," replied Father, "but I still don't understand why RCA doesn't declare any dividends."

"Look, Mr. Marx, this thing is bigger than both of us. Don't fight it. Just be assured that you're going to wind up a very wealthy man. And I know what I'm talking about. I'm in the market myself. I'm a family man, and I wouldn't take the risk if I didn't know the market is sound. I've invested my whole life's savings in it—eight thousand dollars. It's the only sure way to become a millionaire."

If Father had had any real doubts about the wisdom of entrusting his fortune to the financial geniuses of Wall Street, they were dispelled by his conversation with Mr. Green.

They were further dispelled by what happened while he was playing golf at Lakeville with Max Gordon later that same day. Gordon was in the market as deeply as Father—in fact, deeper because he had more money—and they both were huge shareholders in Auburn Motors.

When they returned to the locker room after the game, Father

123

picked up the phone and checked with his broker for any last-minute developments. He was greeted with the astonishing news that Auburn Motors had risen one hundred points—in the length of time it had taken them to play eighteen holes.

"A hundred points in one day," said Gordon. "It's hard to believe."

"No, it isn't," said Father, thinking of Mr. Green. "It's very easy to understand. Wall Street is no longer localized. We're now in a world-wide market. The possibilities are limitless."

"Wonderful!" exclaimed Gordon. "This is better than working. Why didn't we get in the market before?" And then, fixing his eyes on Father, he added in an ecstatic tone, "Tell me, Marx—how long has this racket been going on?"

The next day—it wasn't really the next day, but it makes a better story—the stock market began its historic collapse.

At nine in the morning Father was wakened from a sound sleep by an urgent call from his broker.

"There's been a slight break in the market, Mr. Marx. You'd better get down here with some cash to cover your margin."

"I thought I was covered."

"Not enough for the way things are going. We'll need more. And you'd better hurry!"

All was bedlam at Newman Brothers & Worms when Father arrived there. Ticker tape was knee-deep on the floor, people were shouting orders to sell, and others were frantically scribbling checks in vain efforts to save their original investments.

Father joined the latter group, but it was hopeless. He was in much too deep. He quickly went through his cash that wasn't already tied up in stocks, and then he left to borrow more.

In the next two days he borrowed money from the bank, he borrowed money on his insurance, and he even mortgaged the house. But soon all that was gone, too.

Three days after that first call from his broker, he knew the worst. Not only was he penniless, but he was in debt, besides.

Returning home after writing his last check and seeing it go down the drain along with the others, he walked through the front door just as the phone was ringing. Wearily he picked up the receiver, to find that it was Max Gordon, phoning from New York.

"Marx," said Gordon solemnly, "the jig is up!"

The jig was up, and there was nothing Father or anybody else could do about it. But like the criminal returning to the scene of the crime, Father paid a last visit to Newman Brothers & Worms, on the following evening about six o'clock.

The place usually closed at three, but since the crash it had been staying open late. No one was around except Mr. Green, and he was a pathetic sight. He was sitting in front of the now-stilled ticker-tape machine, with his head buried in his hands. Ticker tape was strewn around him on the floor, and the place smelled of stale cigars and looked as if it hadn't been swept out in a week.

Father tapped Mr. Green on the shoulder, and the man looked up.

"Say," asked Father, "aren't you the fellow who said nothing could go wrong—that we were in a world market?"

"I guess I made a mistake," said Mr. Green.

"No, I'm the one who made a mistake," said Father. "I listened to you."

"I lost all my money, too," replied Mr. Green.

Father suddenly felt as bad about Mr. Green's eight thousand dollars as he did about his own quarter of a million.

"Well, buck up," said Father. "Don't let it get you down. Just remember—twenty years from now you'll be looking back on these as the good old days."

CHAPTER 15

IT ISN'T LIKELY that Father will ever consider the autumn of 1929 "the good old days." Yet the picture wasn't as bleak for him after the crash as it was for some.

He was still making two thousand dollars a week in *Animal Crackers*, which continued to play to capacity business for some months to come. Following its Broadway run, the show had a long and successful tour on the road. And after it finally closed, in the summer of 1930, the Marx Brothers still had four more pictures to make for Paramount, at two hundred thousand dollars a picture for the team.

Father was in far worse shape mentally than he was financially. All his life he had been striving for complete financial security, and berating others—principally his brother Chico—for spending their money on ridiculous luxuries, instead of putting some away for the future, as he was doing. He had known the value of money. He had invested it—wisely, he thought.

Now it was gone. Those who had squandered their money foolishly were just as well off as he. Probably better off, because at least they had had the fun of spending it.

"There's no justice," he announced at the dinner table one night shortly after the crash. "Chico's got the right idea. He has no money either, but meanwhile he's had a hell of a time for himself —gambling, the best hotel suites, private schools for his daughter. Well, from now on, I'm going to live by his philosophy

126

—eat, drink and make merry. Ruth, run out and find me a girl named Mary!"

We knew better than to take this kind of talk seriously. He had said this same thing many times before the crash, but when it came to putting it into practice, it never lasted for more than a couple of hours. Father just didn't have it in his nature to live "dangerously," or to shrug off the loss of his savings.

While people all around him were selling their yachts and jumping out of windows, Father was worrying himself to the brink of a nervous breakdown. He never actually had a breakdown, but he was in a state of severe depression for many months afterwards.

"I've given some unfunny performances in my time," recalls Father, "but the one I gave the night of the crash would have depressed an undertaker. I just didn't feel like making people laugh. I wanted to cry."

The next night he was in even worse shape. He sat brooding silently in his dressing room before the performance, and when it came time for him to make his first appearance on the stage, he wouldn't move. He had never done anything like this before, and Harpo, Chico and Zeppo were sick with fear as they frantically ad libbed in front of the audience for fifteen minutes, while everyone, from the assistant stage manager on up to Sam Harris, tried in vain to get Father out of his dressing room.

Fortunately, Harry Ruby was backstage that evening, and when he heard about what was going on, he rushed into Father's dressing room.

"Listen, you can't do this," said Harry. "The audience is out there waiting for you. They paid to see you, and you've got to give them a show."

"What for?" asked Father. "What's the use of working and making money? I'll only lose it again."

"If you don't get out there," threatened Ruby, "I'll play the part myself."

He sat down at the dressing table, and started to paint a black mustache on himself.

127

"Okay. You win," said Father, grabbing his pith helmet from the hook and striding toward the door. "No audience deserves to have to look at you for a whole evening."

If his brothers were apprehensive about the kind of a performance he was going to give, they must have felt reassured by his first ad lib after alighting from the sedan chair. Indicating the sedan chair with his hand, he said to one of the carriers, "Take this out and sell it. I just got word from my broker that he wants more margin."

After that, he kept up a running fire of jokes about the crash that had the audience rocking. Many of the lines were so good that they stayed in the show permanently.

At home, Father was not so funny. He was more obsessed than ever with the idea of living economically. These were trying times, and the budget just had to be cut.

Unfortunately, it wasn't easy to cut our budget, for we didn't have any major evtravagances to eliminate. We had no yacht to sell. Our house wasn't too large for the size of our family. And mother had never been the type who ran wild through Bergdorf Goodman's and Hattie Carnegie's.

Nevertheless, the order of the day—every day—was to "conserve."

"All right," said Mother agreeably. "Where do you want to start economizing first? In the kitchen?"

"Yes, let's start in the kitchen."

"Well, we can let the cook go," suggested Mother. "That'll save a hundred and fifty a month."

"No, we can't do that," replied Father. "I like her cooking. Let's save somewhere else. What about food buying?"

"Well, we could buy hamburger instead of ground sirloin."

"I don't like it as well. It's too fatty."

And so it went, with Father overruling every cut that Mother suggested. They couldn't let the nurse go because cooking and taking care of the children would be too much work for the cook, and she might quit. They couldn't let the gardener go, because then Father would have to do the gardening, and that would leave him

128

no time for golf. And if he couldn't play golf, then it would be a waste of money to belong to the country club. And he couldn't resign from the country club, because then he'd have no choice but to do the gardening.

Father was in much the same fix as the Eighty-third Congress. He'd like to cut the budget, but there were no cuts he could make that would amount to anything.

As a result, he had to be content with ferreting out the smaller, inconsequential items—electricity, water, oil for the oil burner, and even toothpaste—and issuing daily ultimatums to conserve on them.

Sometimes he had to go to even more ridiculous extremes than that to make himself believe he was being economical. My grandmother used napkin rings at her table, and from her Father got the idea to do the same at our house. If each person used a napkin for a whole week, the laundry bills would be smaller. Father bought four of the most expensive sterling silver napkin rings you could buy, and had our names engraved on them. This came to one hundred and thirteen dollars, but in the long run Father figured it would be worth it.

In twenty years, he probably would have saved at least seven dollars by using napkin rings, but we didn't keep them twenty years. In fact, the napkin-ring regime lasted only until the third night, when Father unrolled his napkin and was shocked to find food stains on it.

"What's this?" he exclaimed indignantly. "Can't a person get a clean napkin around here?"

"Next Monday you'll get one," said Mother, "unless we have company before then."

"I want a clean napkin," demanded Father.

"Grouch," Mother pointed out, "there's no use in having napkin rings if you're going to use a clean napkin every night."

"Then let's get rid of the napkin rings," was Father's solution. "I don't like them. They're old-fashioned. Whose idea were they anyway?"

On another occasion, I remember Father getting very upset because of a slightly larger than usual gasoline bill that had come that day from Standard Oil of New York.

"How come it's so high?" he asked Mother.

"I don't know," she said. "I didn't do any more driving than usual."

"We'll have to cut down," roared Father. "That's all there is to it. This bill for gasoline is as much as the average family pays for food."

"I don't know what you expect me to do about it," replied Mother. "I can't tell the car not to use so much gasoline."

"No, but you can be more careful," Father told her. "You can do what I do—put the car in neutral when you're going downhill!"

But aside from the fact that his warnings to economize were a little more frequent after the crash than they had been before (though no more effective), there wasn't the slightest change in our mode of living, with the possible exception that we no longer had any friends who could afford yachts.

In short, we were a long way from the poorhouse, as Mother used to remind Father whenever he started complaining about the bills.

But this was small consolation to a habitual worrier like Father. Maybe we weren't in the poorhouse yet, but with his savings gone, what was going to become of all of us when he was eighty years old and too sick and feeble to work any more? Or supposing Paramount went under? Or supposing the public suddenly didn't want the Marx Brothers any more? Or supposing the Government collapsed, and the money he was making turned out to be worthless?

He'd ponder the pros and cons of these questions every night after he had gone to bed. And at six in the morning he'd still be awake, thinking about them.

Thus began his introduction to insomnia, and they've been constant companions ever since.

Even before the crash, Father was an exceptionally light sleeper. If a car backfired in Little Neck,* it would wake him instantly. Or-

* Or even Port Washington. GROUCHO

dinary household noises while he was still in bed in the morning—
a pan dropping in the kitchen, Miriam or I raising our voices, the
stairs creaking under someone's weight—would put him in a bad
humor for the rest of the day.

After the crash, while he was suffering from insomnia as well,
these same noises would send him forth from his room, ready to
commit mayhem—even if he were just lying in bed wide awake at
the moment he heard them.

"For heaven's sake," he'd yell, if he were in one of his milder
moods, "can't a man get a little sleep around here without you kids
raising the roof? Now shut up, or I'm going to take your bicycles
away from you."

Retreating to his room, he'd slam the door and lock it. When
he'd finally emerge for breakfast, dressed in a long bathrobe, he'd
be scowling at everyone—even those who had nothing to do with
waking him.

"We're going to have to do something about those kids screaming when I'm trying to sleep," he'd say to Mother ominously. "I
can't work all night and not be able to sleep in the morning. It'll
ruin my health. I won't be able to work."

"I don't know what I can do about it," Mother would reply
hotly. "The children are not being especially noisy. But this is not
the most well built house in the world. Every noise carries—you
know that."

"I don't know what the solution is, but we're going to have to do
something—or I'm going to start staying in town and sleeping in a
Turkish bath!"

He never quite reached the point where he carried this threat
out; * but occasionally, if we made enough noise, he'd forbid Miriam and me to get out of bed in the mornings before he did (school
days excluded, of course). This would usually last for one morning,
by which time he'd realize that it wasn't our fault that he had insomnia and the restriction would be lifted.

* *That's what you think.* GROUCHO

"But try and be a little quiet from now on," he'd say, and for the next few mornings we'd all be tiptoeing around the house in mortal fear of making the slightest sound.

We couldn't keep it up indefinitely, however, and eventually the cook would drop another pan in the kitchen, or I would yell out the window of my room to the boy next door, and the harangues would begin all over.

In the first month he was afflicted with insomnia, Father used up all the conventional cures. He tried reading himself to sleep, but that only made him more wide awake. He'd try drinking a glass of beer before he went to bed, and when that didn't work he switched to hot Ovaltine.* He read all the books on how not to worry, but of course there's never been a book written that could stop him from worrying.

He tried sleeping on his back, on his stomach, on his right side, on his left side; with one pillow, two pillows, three pillows, no pillows; with the windows open, with them shut; with the lights on, with them off; alone, not alone; sitting up in a chair; lying on the floor; with the radio on, with it off; with pajamas, with no pajamas; and with a night coat.

He finally settled for the bed, one pillow, a night coat and bed socks. (He had heard that no one could hope to fall asleep with cold feet, but in his case it didn't make any difference.)

After the bed socks failed to do anything more than keep his feet warm, Father was feeling pretty despondent about the whole situation. And one night, at a party with Bob Benchley, Father said glumly, "If I don't get some sleep soon, I think I'll kill myself."

An expert on insomnia himself, Benchley suggested to Father that he try taking a hot bath scented with pine needles every night before turning in.

Willing to grasp at any straw, Father bought a bottle of the pine-needle solution on the way home, and tried it in a hot bath before going to bed. This appeared to be the answer. Almost immediately, the soaking and the smell of the pine needles relaxed Father.

* *I also tried half beer and half Ovaltine.* Groucho

Within fifteen minutes his eyelids started to feel heavy, he became drowsier and drowsier, and finally he fell asleep in the tub.

When Mother heard a gurgling sound coming from the bathroom, she rushed in, pulled Father's head out of the water before he drowned and helped resuscitate him.

"What happened?" asked Father groggily.

"You nearly drowned," said Mother. "Don't you ever try this again."

"No matter," said Father. "At least I'm sleepy. Hand me a towel and my night coat. Quickly! I want to get to bed before I wake up."

But by the time he dried off and got into bed he was wide awake.

"That's a fine insomnia cure," Father told Benchley the next time he saw him. "I fell asleep in the tub and almost drowned."

"Who said it was an insomnia cure?" exclaimed Benchley. "You said if you didn't get some sleep you wanted to kill yourself. Well, I was just expediting things."

On a friend's recommendation, he started consulting with a psychiatrist. The doctor tried to convince Father that he really had no worries. He was doing well professionally, he was in good health physically, and he had a nice family.

"But I can't sleep," said Father. "That's what I've got to worry about. As soon as I get up in the morning, I start thinking about not being able to sleep when I go to bed at night."

"Exactly," said the psychiatrist. "That's why people have insomnia. You're pressing. You're trying too hard to fall asleep. Stop worrying about it. It's not injurious to your health. No one ever died from lack of sleep. As soon as your body is tired enough, you'll sleep. Forget about how many hours you've been awake. Take the clock out of the room, so you won't know. As soon as you attack it with this attitude you'll have the problem licked."

Father felt relieved of a great burden. He would do exactly as the doctor had advised. He would not worry about having insomnia any more. And he even took the alarm clock off the night stand next to his bed.

But his insomnia got no better.

133

"Did you do as I said?" asked the psychiatrist during the next consultation. "Did you remove the clock from the room?"

"Yes, but it didn't help," admitted Father. "I kept looking at my wrist watch. It has a luminous dial."

Father kept going to the doctor for about a year and finally admitted complete defeat. "There must be something wrong with me," he said. "That advice about not worrying may work with other people, but I don't sleep any better now than I did a year ago."

"Well, it doesn't always work," said the psychiatrist. "I can't sleep, either. But at least I don't worry about it."

The patient wasn't cured, but at least he went away with a better outlook on life. For if his consultations with the psychiatrist had done nothing else, they had helped him to acquire a certain philosophy about his insomnia that made the dark hours of the night seem a little less torturous.

Today Father is one of the best adjusted insomniacs I know. He's completely resigned to the fact that he's never going to sleep like a child, that when he goes to bed at night he's going to lie awake for a couple of hours or maybe three, and that he will probably wake up at five or six in the morning. He's so resigned to this that occasionally he relaxes enough in bed to get a good night's sleep.

In addition to the fact that insomnia is something he can complain about, which is in its favor these days when he has very little else to complain about, he makes a game of it. While he's lying awake, he has all sorts of time-passers which he has devised to keep him from fretting about the fact that he isn't sleeping.

For example, one night he might run through the alphabet trying to think of a baseball player's name beginning with each letter. A would be Grover Cleveland Alexander, B would be Home-run Baker, C would be Ty Cobb, and so on through the whole alphabet until he gets to the letter X. Though he's tried for many years, he has yet to think of a ball player whose last name begins with X.

"I've given up," confesses Father. "Now if I'm still awake when I get to X, I find it simpler to get up and take a Seconol."

When the baseball season is over, he switches to playing the alphabet game with football players. And in the spring and early summer he does it with golfers and tennis players.

"It keeps me from getting stale," he says.

He has many variations of the game. Sometimes he tries to think of an All-Star ball team whose names all begin with the same letter. This is a little harder than the straight alphabet game, and it's not unusual for him to come down to breakfast and still be mulling the problem over.

"Sarah," he might say to his housekeeper, "can you think of a shortstop whose name begins with Y?" And though Sarah usually can't, it no longer surprises her to be asked such questions while she's serving him his toast and coffee.

Besides making up new games to play while he's trying to get to sleep, Father keeps his bedroom well equipped with all the latest sleeping gadgets.

His greatest source of delight is his electric blanket, because with it he doesn't need more than one. He can't stand the weight of having two ordinary blankets on him, no matter how light they are—"They make me feel as if I'm in an iron lung," he claims.

He also wears a mask to keep out the light, puts wax in his ears so he won't hear any noises, and he keeps a BB gun next to his bed so he can take pot shots at the neighbors' dogs if they start barking in the middle of the night. Since he is an even worse marksman than he is a golfer, the dogs are perfectly safe.*

When he is ready for bed, dressed in his sleeping coat, and black mask, and gripping his BB gun, he resembles a man from outer space.

Last year he took a trip to Palm Springs with his friend Irwin Allen, the producer of the movie version of *The Sea Around Us*. They didn't go to a hotel, but instead rented a small bungalow

* *One night I almost got a cat.* GROUCHO

135

near the Tamarisk Golf Club, a new club which Father and his brothers and a group of his friends had invested money in. The purpose of the trip, as a matter of fact, was to celebrate the opening of the Tamarisk, and the first night Father was in Palm Springs, he and Allen went to a party at the club.

As usual, Father got tired of the festivities around eleven o'clock and had a yearning to get back to the bungalow and the latest copy of the New Yorker. Irwin Allen had no such yearning, however, and at Father's suggestion, decided to stay at the party.

Taking the only key, Father returned to the bungalow, read in bed for a little while, then carefully stuffed the wax plugs into his ears and turned out the lights. But he had forgotten to leave the door unlocked.

When Allen returned a couple of hours later, he practically knocked the door down pounding on it, but he got no response. Thinking perhaps Father had gone out again, he peeked in the window, which was also locked, and saw Father in bed, sleeping blissfully. Allen yelled at him and banged on the glass, but it was no use. Father didn't stir. The ear plugs were working like a charm, and Allen had to spend the night sleeping in his car.

"That'll teach you to make a trip with a man who wears ear plugs," said Father when a bleary-eyed and bedraggled-looking Irwin Allen presented himself at the door the next morning.

"Why didn't you come looking for me?" asked Allen, annoyed. "Didn't you think it strange when I didn't come back to the bungalow by morning?"

"Strange? Not a bit," replied Father. "With all those pretty girls at the party, why would you ever want to come back to little old me?"

CHAPTER 16

TRAVELING WITH FATHER, with or without ear plugs, has always been somewhat of an ordeal, though a pleasant one.

One of the things that makes it an ordeal is that there is no known method of transportation that he doesn't have a strong aversion to. Ships, of course, make him seasick. He isn't afraid of flying, but he can't stand the food served on airplanes. Trains are out of the question, because he can't sleep at all in a Pullman berth. He claims Pullman blankets are made in an iron foundry. And traveling by automobile is too slow, and usually very uncomfortable and tiring.*

Secondly, he's highly suspicious of hotel managers, room clerks and anyone else who has anything to do with establishing room rates. He somehow seems to feel that all people in the hotel business, from the keeper of the smallest roadside motel to the manager of the Savoy in London, have banded together in a common conspiracy to bilk him of his last dollar.

When Miriam and I were in our teens, Father and Mother took us on a number of week-end trips around Los Angeles—to Palm Springs, Lake Arrowhead, Coronado and other resorts. The pattern for these trips would always be the same.

None of these places is more than three hours away from Los Angeles for the average driver. But with Father driving it always took us six, partly because we made so many stops for cokes, rest

* *Except in a De Soto.* GROUCHO

rooms and flat tires, and partly because he would never heed Mother's warnings that he was on the wrong road.

We never seemed to arrive at a resort until dinner time. This is sort of a drop-dead hour for Father, anyway. He's nervous, irritable and in need of that one drink he usually has before dinner. After a six-hour drive, he'd be even more irritable because he wouldn't have had his afternoon nap.

But no matter what time we arrived, or how many times previously he had stopped at this hotel, he'd always be surprised by the rates—even if they had been quoted to him when he made his reservation by phone.

"Too much," he'd say. And then we'd pile our mountain of luggage and our weary bodies back into the car, and we'd drive all over town, while he checked the rates at each hotel and inspected the rooms.

And we'd always wind up slinking back into the lobby of the hotel where he had originally made his reservations, and he'd have to say to the room clerk, "I've changed my mind. Do you still have those rooms?"

The first major trip I remember taking with Father saw the four Marx Brothers and their wives bound for London during Christmas week, 1930.

It was a combination business and pleasure trip. *Animal Crackers* had finished touring the country and had been made into a hit picture by the fall of 1930. The Marxes' next picture for Paramount—no one as yet knew what it would be—was not scheduled to go before the cameras until the following spring, in Hollywood, which they had decided to make their home, having no further plans for any legitimate productions on Broadway.

In the meantime, since they were technically unemployed, they allowed themselves to be booked into London's Coliseum Theater for a six-weeks' vaudeville engagement, starting the first week in January.

But though it was business that took Father to London, I don't think he would have accepted the engagement if he hadn't been in dire need of a change of scenery and some relaxation. Despite the

138

fact that he hadn't suffered any actual hardships as a result of the stock-market crash, the past year had been a strain on him in other ways. His mother had died of a heart attack very unexpectedly, and it had been a severe blow to him as well as to his brothers.

At first, Father and Mother planned to go to Europe without Miriam and me. Father seemed quite enthusiastic about making the trip. But as their sailing date approached, he became more and more sullen, as though he wasn't really looking forward to it for some reason.

Then one night at the dinner table, he turned to me and said, "How would you like to go to Europe?"

I was delighted. But Mother was a little more reserved in her enthusiasm.

"I thought this was going to be a pleasure trip," she said.

"It is," replied Father. "But I can't have a good time if I have to be away all that time without seeing the children."

"Children?" Mother was horrified. "Don't tell me you want to take Miriam, too?"

"Of course. We can't take Arthur and leave Miriam behind. It would be unfair."

"Chico and Betty aren't taking Maxine," said Mother, referring to my fourteen-year-old cousin.

"That's their business," said Father. "I like to be around my children."

"I like being around them, too," said Mother. "But I'm going to be the one who'll wind up sitting in a hotel room with them nights, while you're out seeing the sights."

"I've thought of that," said Father. "We'll take the nurse along, too."

"What about Arthur's school?" asked Mother. "You can't just yank him out of school in the middle of the year."

"Why not?" said Father. "Going to Europe will do him as much good as sleeping in a classroom."

"I know, Grouch, but he'll get behind the other children in his studies."

"Tell his teacher about the trip," Father advised her. "She can

139

give you some school work for him to take along. You and I can tutor him."

"It's going to be awfully expensive taking five people to Europe," she reminded him. It was an unfair blow, hitting him in the pocketbook.

But Father was not vulnerable. "Who cares how expensive it is?" he said. "What good is money if you don't spend it?"

"Are you sure you're feeling all right?" asked Mother.

"I'm feeling fine now that the kids are going along," said Father.

Whether or not we would accompany them on trips was always a good starting place for an argument, for as devoted a parent as my mother was, she usually preferred to leave us at home.

Now that I'm a parent I can see Mother's point, but when Miriam and I were children, we naturally looked at it selfishly and were always on the sidelines rooting for Father in these arguments.

In this case he made it up to her—not only by taking along a nurse, but by booking the most luxurious steamship accommodations the French line had to offer. We had the royal suite on the *Paris*—which consisted of three bedrooms, two baths, a dining room, a butler's pantry, and a large living room complete with a gold-inlaid upright piano.

Our accommodations were the envy of the rest of the Marx family, who had to make the voyage in ordinary staterooms without pianos. No one could understand why Father, of all people, and in the midst of the depression, had suddenly turned into a Diamond-Jim-Brady–type spender. Had he really stopped worrying about money, or was he a little bit off his rocker from having insomnia night after night? But there was no explanation. It was just another example of Father's inconsistent spending habits.

We sailed from New York on December 23, a wintry white day with a wind of gale proportions howling off the Hudson River.

The *bon voyage* party for the Marxes was held in our suite because of the lavishness of it. A great many of Father's friends came down to see us off, including Harry Ruby and the whole New York Giants football team. The team presented Father with an autographed football. Dozens of people were milling around, the champagne was flowing like champagne, and I remember a great many choruses on the piano of Harry Ruby's latest hit song, "Three Little Words."

In the midst of the festivities, Sam Harris shouted, "Where's Groucho? We can't let him go without a chorus of Captain Spaulding."

It was then noticed that Father had disappeared. A searching party was sent out for him, but they came back without him. Finally, about fifteen minutes before sailing time, the door to one of the bathrooms opened up, and out staggered Father, his face absolutely green.

"What's the matter?" asked Mother, rushing up to him.

"I'm not sure," moaned Father, holding his stomach, "but I think I'm getting seasick."

CHAPTER 17

FATHER AND MOTHER made three ocean trips together during their marriage—twice to Europe, and once to Honolulu—and on none of these voyages were they ever on speaking terms by the time they reached their destination.

They got along well enough to stay married for twenty-two years, but there was something about shipboard life that magnified their incompatibilities as nothing else ever did.

Shipboard life represented all the things that Father disliked and Mother loved: gay parties, with the women in long dresses and the men in white dinner jackets; dancing until the late hours; convivial companionship; and organized play.

Added to this was the fact that Father never felt physically up to par with the unsteady motion of a deck beneath him. He'd only be in bed, actually seasick, for a day or two, but even after he was up and about, he'd always be on the verge of seasickness, and that would keep him in a continually grumpy mood.

What's more, he got very little sympathy out of Mother. She had a wide streak of Nordic blood in her and a very strong stomach. She had never been seasick in her life and could not understand how anyone else could be made ill by the rocking of a ship. In fact, it was always her opinion that Father was malingering to avoid participating in the ship's activities.*

* *And don't think I wasn't.* GROUCHO

142

French liners, in those days anyway, were noted more for gaiety and rich cuisine than for seaworthiness, although they usually reached their destinations. But the *Paris* had the worst reputation of them all. She floated high in the water and never stopped rolling even on calm seas.

Every time she rolled to one side in the mountainous seas, she'd lie there for several sickening moments, while everyone on board wondered whether she would ever right herself again. Then, with a convulsive groan, she'd start back, and the same thing would be repeated.

Father had put himself to bed even before the *bon voyage* party had broken up, and, much to Mother's annoyance, he refused to get up for dinner.

"How can you be seasick?" she asked him while she was getting dressed to take Miriam, Sadie, the nurse, and me to the dining room our first night out. "We've barely left the Hudson River. There's no motion to the boat."

"It isn't just the motion," groaned Father. "It's these shipboard smells. As soon as I walked through the door, I knew I was gone. Why do ships have to smell this way?"

"It's all mental with you, and you know it," replied Mother. "You were already complaining of feeling ill when we were still in the taxicab on the way to the dock."

"Well, I don't like the smell of taxicabs either," said Father.

The *Paris* hit stormy weather the first night out, and Mother and Father were both thrown from their beds a couple of times. These were not ideal sleeping conditions for a man with insomnia, so by the time the day dawned Father had decided that bed was not for him. He got up and stayed up, in spite of the fact that he didn't feel well.

Mother was pleased to see that he was no longer pampering himself, but the stormy weather frightened her. Mother had a strong stomach, but a faint heart. The way the ship was rocking and pitching, she was convinced that we would all wind up in watery graves. Because she had shown him no sympathy about his seasickness,

Father did not bend over backwards to ease her fears about our safety.

We had a steward named Henri, who brought us our breakfast in our private dining room that morning.

"It's kind of rough out today, isn't it?" commented Father.

"It's smoooooooooooooooothe," said Henri, making a motion with his hand to show us how calm the ocean was.

"That's your story," said Father. "What's tossing this boat around?"

"It's smoooooooooooooooothe," said Henri.

"If this is smooth, what's it like when it's rough?" asked Father.

"The same," said Henri, darting into the passageway.

"See," said Father, turning to Mother, who was extremely pale and frightened looking. "You don't have a thing to worry about. Henri says it's smoooooooooooooothe."

"I don't care what he says. This ship isn't safe."

"It's smoooooooooooooothe," said Father reassuringly.

"Grouch, please don't joke. I'm worried."

"I thought you were such a great sailor," said Father. "Aren't you the same person who was kidding me about being seasick? Well, who has the last laugh now?"

"Please, Groucho, this ship frightens me."

"For God's sakes, Ruth, stop being a coward. Eric the Red would be ashamed to see a countryman of his acting this way. Besides, this ship's been making this crossing for years, and she's still afloat. Stop worrying. Would I take you on a ship that isn't safe?"

"I guess not," she admitted reluctantly.

"Well, that shows you how much you know," he said. "I happen to have made a very good deal on the price of these accommodations—much better than I could have made on a seaworthy liner."

Christmas on the *Paris* wasn't too unlike our previous ones, except that we had no tree of our own, and we had to hang our stockings from a porthole instead of on the fireplace. There was a mammoth Christmas tree in the main lounge, however, and Mother and Father had come aboard well supplied with presents.

Miriam and I ripped open our packages in record time, with Mother and Father looking on, and opening a few of their own. With each present he opened, Father would exclaim, "Just what I needed!" and toss it carelessly back in the box.

"Did you like the presents I gave you?" Mother asked Father, after the last package had been opened.

"Very much," said Father. "There's just one thing that worries me. How am I going to take them back and exchange them if we're in the middle of the Atlantic Ocean?"

Father's attitude about Christmas has always been the same—on land or on sea. He believes that the Christmas spirit is commendable, but that the holiday itself has become much too commercialized.

However, he accepts Christmas with good-humored resignation, and he was always a very generous Santa Claus. But at Christmas time, the most thankless job I can think of is trying to buy Father a present that he won't exchange on the following day.

The big difficulty, of course, is that he has every earthly belonging a man could want.* Unless you should be fortunate enough to hear him mention ahead of time that he is in need of a certain item, there is absolutely no danger that you will buy him a present that he will keep. And even then it's extremely doubtful.

I once heard him mention casually that he would like a corduroy loafer jacket. I filed it away in my head for future reference, and on the following Christmas I bought him a corduroy coat.

"Merry Christmas," I said, handing him the package.

"Just what I needed," he replied, giving the package a perfunctory glance and leaving it unopened on his lap.

"Don't you want to see what it is?" I asked.

"Oh, do you want me to open it, too?" he said. "I thought it would be easier to take it back this way."

He feigned enthusiasm as he unwrapped the jacket.

"Thanks," he grumbled, carelessly throwing the jacket back in

* Except Marilyn Monroe. GROUCHO

the box. "But what did you have to go and buy that for? I'm too old for Christmas. Next time save your money."

The day after Christmas he returned the jacket to the store, credited it to my account, and took nothing in exchange.

So on the following Christmas I purposely showed up empty-handed.

"What's the matter?" he asked. "Don't I get a present?"

"I took your advice," I said. "I didn't buy you one this year."

"A fine thing," he complained. "Well, that's the thanks you get for raising children. You feed them, clothe them and send them through school. And what happens? The one day of the year when they can show their appreciation, they don't even bother to buy you a present. That's children. As soon as they don't need you any more, they desert you."

Last year, I believe, Father established some sort of a record. He received a present from a close friend and he had already opened it and exchanged it three days *before* Christmas.

That same Christmas my wife and I and our two children ate Christmas Eve dinner with him, and afterwards he opened his presents. He received seven pairs of cuff links from various people around town. After he had opened all of his packages, he remained sitting in front of the Christmas tree, looking extremely despondent.

"Why so glum?" I asked.

"You'd be glum too," he answered, "if you had to spend all day tomorrow going from store to store, exchanging cuff links." And a little while later he added, "Wouldn't it be better if everybody gave everybody else money? Not only you wouldn't have to waste your time exchanging presents, but you'd know exactly how much your friends were spending on you."

One year I managed to give him a present which he kept and was actually pleased about. It was a plum tree, and it's growing in his back yard today. But how many plum trees can a man use?

On the *Paris*, of course, Father was stuck. There was absolutely nothing he could do with his presents but keep them. "It was the most frustrating Christmas I've ever spent," recalls Father.

On the third day out from New York, we had the usual "abandon ship" drill up on "A" Deck, alongside the lifeboats. Most of the passengers, including Father, turned out for it wearing their life jackets. Father stood with us in the center of the group and listened with studied seriousness as one of the mates explained the abandon ship procedure.

"Any questions?" asked the Mate, when he had finished.

"I have one," said Father, raising his hand. "Is it true what they say about French liners—that if anything should really happen, it's women and children *last?*"

Having thus insulted the entire French nation, Father next proceeded to go to work on the Captain. When the Captain sent word down to our suite that afternoon that he would like Father and Mother to have dinner with him at his table, Father said to the messenger, "Tell the Captain he's a lousy driver. He has no right to leave the bridge just to have dinner."

"Did you have to say that?" asked Mother, extremely annoyed, after the messenger had left to deliver Father's message. "It's supposed to be an honor to eat with the Captain."

"Why do I have to eat dinner with a total stranger, just because he happens to be Captain of a leaky scow? I'd rather eat with the kids. Besides, the Captain'll expect me to be funny. I don't want to have to be funny if I don't feel like it. I paid for my passage. I just want to be left alone."

"Well, I'm tired of eating with the children. Why can't we do something gay for a change?"

"All right, you eat with the Captain, if you think it's going to be so much fun. I'll eat with the children."

"It's too late now," pouted Mother. "You've already insulted the man."

But apparently it wasn't easy to insult the captain of a French liner. A little while later there was a knock on the door, and Father opened it up to see the messenger standing there.

"You again?" said Father. "I thought I got rid of you."

"The Captain says you are a very funny man," said the grinning messenger. "He would like you at his table at eight o'clock."

147

"Eight bells, if you don't mind," Father corrected him. Then, turning to Mother, he added indignantly, "See, what did I tell you? The Captain says I'm a funny man. That means he expects me to crack jokes all evening. The nerve of him. Do I ask him to come down here for free and tell me what he knows about seamanship?"

"Go ahead," whispered Mother. "Accept!"

"All right," said Father. "Tell the Captain to meet me in the children's dining room at seven o'clock sharp."

Father preferred the children's dining room because there were few other children besides Miriam and me on board, and it was fairly quiet in there.

"No, no," said the messenger. "At the Captain's table."

"Tell him we'll be there," said Mother, taking the bull by the horns for a change.

Father seemed fairly resigned to his fate until it came time to dress for dinner, and he discovered that the Captain's guests were required to wear evening clothes.

"I won't wear a tuxedo," said Father. "I'm supposed to be having a good time on this trip."

"All the men wear tuxedos in the main dining room," said Mother. "Even your brothers."

"Just because they're foolish enough to do it is no reason I have to wear one," said Father. "Tuxedos are too uncomfortable."

"You're just being stubborn. With that soft collar you wear, a tuxedo is no different than any other suit."

"That's your story. You don't have to wear one. You'll be in a very comfortable dress. Well, I'm going to be comfortable, too. I'm going to wear an ordinary blue suit. And if the Captain doesn't like it, let him keel-haul me if he can."

"Well, I won't be seen with you if you don't wear a tuxedo."

As I mentioned before, giving Father an ultimatum will get you nowhere.

He said, "All right, don't be seen with me. You eat at the Captain's table. Tell the old boy I'm under the weather."

At dinner that evening, Mother told the Captain that Father

148

sent his "regrets," and that he was in his cabin, seasick. If the Captain believed her then, he certainly didn't after Father, looking unusually fit, showed up in the main dining salon a short time later, and sat down alone at a small table. He was attired in an ordinary business suit.

Mother was furious, and as she danced by Father's table with Harpo, she leaned over and whispered angrily, "Why did you have to embarrass me by coming in here? I told the Captain you were sick in bed."

"If you must know, I was too late for the children's dining room," replied Father. "And if you'd stop talking to me, maybe the Captain wouldn't know I'm in here."

"Everyone knows you're in here. You stand out like a sore thumb in *that* suit."

"If you want me to, I can square it with the Captain," said Father, softening.

"You'd better," said Mother. "I certainly don't know what to tell him."

So when he had finished eating, Father walked over to the Captain's table and introduced himself.

"Mrs. Marx told me you were under the weather," said the Captain. "I'm glad to see you're feeling better."

"I wasn't really sick," explained Father. "I just told her to tell you that because I didn't feel like putting on a tuxedo. I was told I couldn't eat with you unless I came formal." Then, as if noting the Captain's gold-braided uniform for the first time, Father said, "Tell me, Captain, how come you're not wearing a tuxedo?"

Mother didn't speak to him for the remainder of the evening.

Once, on the trip across, Father decided that it was about time I did some studying, despite my protests that it was still technically Christmas vacation.

"You're getting enough vacation," he said. "Bring your arithmetic book. I'll tutor you."

Reluctantly, I dug out my math book and handed it to Father. He opened the book to the first lesson. "I'll start out with an easy problem," he said. "If you have five apples, and ten people to eat them, how would you divide them so everyone could have the same amount?"

Even I knew that. "I'd cut them in half so there would be ten pieces," I said.

Father shook his head gravely.

"What's the matter?" I asked. "I know that's the right answer. I can show it to you in the book."

"I don't care what the book says," replied Father. "The right answer is—you'd make applesauce. I know that because we had the same problem in 'Fun in Hi Skule.'"

A group of English newspapermen and women boarded the ship when we arrived at Southampton, and before we debarked, there was a welcoming party for Father and his brothers. The champagne must have been pretty strong, because Father gave out interviews and entertained the ladies and gentlemen of the press as if they were old friends.

He generally isn't available for interviews until he has arrived at his hotel and has had a night's sleep. Even then he won't be too cooperative, but if a reporter is persistent enough, in a polite way, of course, Father will finally give in and talk freely.

At any rate, he was exceptionally cooperative with the English press. Mother was so pleased to see him being garrulous for a change that she made up with him, and by the time we boarded the train for London they were as friendly as man and wife.

In London, we stopped at the Savoy Hotel. We didn't arrive there until two in the morning, but except for the fact that we were very tired, everything appeared to be going smoothly—until the room clerk quoted the price of our accommodations, that is.

I don't remember what price he quoted, but I do know that Father considered the room rates "outrageous." His first thought, naturally, was to tell off the management and go hunting for a cheaper hotel. But because we were in a foreign city, and he was unfamiliar with the hotel situation, Mother was able to persuade Father that it would be foolish to spend the rest of the night tramping the streets of London, in a very heavy fog, in order to save a few dollars.

"All right," said Father, after giving it considerable thought. "We'll stay here tonight, but tomorrow we're going to find an honest hotel—one where they don't charge you according to WHO you are."

But once we were settled in our rooms, Father was so pleased with them that he wouldn't dream of moving. We stayed there the entire six weeks we were in London.

However, to make up for the fact that the room rates were high, Father forbade us the use of "room service" in the mornings.

The vaudeville show that Father and his brothers presented at the Coliseum Theater was a sort of potpourri of the best comedy routines they had done in the past. It was very popular with English audiences, and this time there were no penny-throwing incidents.

Father was very much impressed with London—much more so than he was with Paris—I suppose because London really is a man's city, as they say. He liked the English people and their customs, the men's shops and even the sight-seeing. "There's only one thing wrong with England," he said. "You can't get a decent cup of coffee. But I suppose I shouldn't complain about that. I can't get a decent cup of coffee at home either."

He felt that the British were a more civilized people on the whole than Americans. To him this has always been exemplified by an incident that took place one morning in Hyde Park, where we had gone to play two-handed soccer.

Father and I usually played some kind of ball together whenever we were traveling, and since he was so enthusiastic about England, he had bought a soccer ball.

There was only one trouble with soccer, as we found out: it was an unhandy game to play in an alley in back of the hotel. Father looked around for a better playing field, and finally hit upon what he thought was the perfect solution—Hyde Park. So we went there one morning and started kicking the ball around on a grassy spot beside a herd of grazing sheep—the King's sheep, no less.

We had been there about five minutes, when Father kicked the ball with a little too much gusto, and it landed in the sheep herd, frightening the animals and causing them to scatter. At that moment a bobby happened along and hurried over to us.

"I'm awfully sorry, sir, but rugby isn't permitted here," the bobby told us.

"This isn't really rugby," replied Father. "We're not even keeping score."

"It's against the rules and regulations to play rugby here," said the bobby. "This is reserved for the King's sheep."

"Sheep can't play rugby," said Father. "I just kicked the ball over to them, and they didn't even kick it back."

"I'm sorry, sir," said the bobby, "but I just can't allow it."

"Well, where can we play?" asked Father in a pathetic tone. "We've been looking all over town for a place to kick the ball around."

The bobby told us the name of a playground where we could go, apologized very effusively for breaking up our game, and then strolled off.

"What a wonderful place this England is," said Father, as we were walking back to the hotel. "If this had happened in Central Park, the cop would have said, 'Get the hell off the grass before I turn you in.' In England you can't play on the grass either, but they're so nice about telling you, that it's a pleasure to get thrown off!"

Father was also very much impressed with all the pomp and pageantry in London. His usual attitude is that when you've seen one parade you've seen them all, but in London he never got his fill— either of parades or of watching the Changing of the Guard ceremonies at Buckingham Palace.

One afternoon when he didn't have a matinee he took Mother, Miriam and me to the Tower of London. He thought it would be a good opportunity to teach me history first hand, to make up for the fact that I was missing so much school.

"This is where Henry the Eighth had all his wives' heads

chopped off," explained Father when we were going through the grim-looking building with one of the guides.

"Why did he do that?" I asked.

"Because it was cheaper than paying alimony," answered Father.

Another morning, when we were walking by Buckingham Palace, I remembered that Father had promised to introduce me to the Prince of Wales, and I reminded him of it.

"Good idea, as long as we're in the neighborhood," he said.

He walked up to the sentry box in which the guard was standing, and knocked on the side of it.

"Anybody home?" he asked.

The guard ignored him.

"How do I get in this joint?" asked Father, indicating the Palace.

"What do you want?" asked the guard.

"I've come from across the sea," said Father in a mock-serious tone, "and I have business with Edward, Prince of Wales."

"Who are you?" asked the guard.

"My name is Julius H. Marx," replied Father, "and the Prince told me to drop in on him when I came to London."

The guard informed him that royalty didn't cater to drop-in business.

"All right for you," said Father, shaking a warning finger under the guard's nose, "but the next time I see the Prince I'm going to tell him to get rid of you. Turning away good customers is no way to run a business."

Later, Father tried to get in touch with the Prince through official channels, but he was told that the Royal Family was in mourning for a distant relative who had just died, and that they weren't seeing outsiders.

However, the Marx Brothers were invited to spend an afternoon and have dinner at the Duke of Manchester's estate, and at the last minute Father wangled an invitation for me, too.

The duke was a big, affable man and a charming host, with a reputation for being somewhat of a playboy. He lived in a huge

153

stone mansion surrounded by acres of beautiful grounds. He had dozens of servants, and a stable that was larger than our whole house in Great Neck.

But it was a damp, miserable day in January when we went out to Manchester, and the house was freezing. There was an enormous fireplace in the living room containing a very small, ineffectual fire, and unless you stood directly in front of it, you felt no warmth.

"Say, can't you turn the heat on?" Father finally asked the duke. "It's like the North Pole in here."

"I can't afford to burn any more fuel," said the duke, with a sad smile. "I'm flat broke."

"In a place like this?"

"Because of it."

"Can't you sell it and get a smaller place?"

He shook his head. "We dukes have to keep up a front, you know. Why don't you wear a sweater? That's what my other guests do."

The following Sunday we were invited to the duke's again. On our way out to the duke's estate in a rented car, Father spotted a place by the side of the road that sold firewood. Ordering the driver to stop, he alighted and proceeded to buy as much firewood as he could get into the trunk (and part of the back seat) of the automobile.

"I couldn't find a sweater," Father explained, when he presented the firewood to the duke, who was delighted. "So I brought some fuel for you instead."

By his standards, Father was quite active socially when we were in London. He and Mother attended a number of formal dinner parties, and he got to meet some of his favorite authors—J. B. Priestly, Noel Coward, A. P. Herbert and Somerset Maugham.

But the thing that impressed him the most was how British men, even at the most informal dinners, thought nothing at all of wearing evening clothes. He grew so used to this that he actually reached the stage where he would put on his tuxedo without pro-

154

test. Sensing that he was weakening, Mother gathered up her courage one day and suggested that he have a new tuxedo made.

"As long as you're in London, you might as well," she went on. "They know how to make them right here. And if you had a really good one that you could be comfortable in, you wouldn't mind wearing a tuxedo."

He surprised her by having not only a new tuxedo made, but also a full dress outfit with tails, white tie and even a silk hat. "I'll be the talk of the Cliveden Set," he said.

It was the kind of progress Mother hadn't dared to hope for. And they were on such good terms by the time we left for Paris that they were speaking to each other nearly all the way across the English Channel. But eventually the choppy seas got the best of Father, and a few minutes before we landed on French soil he and Mother got into a slight altercation about whether or not we would accept an invitation extended by a wealthy Dutchman to spend a few days in Holland after our sojourn in Paris.

Mother was in favor of accepting.

"The trouble with staying at Van Shruger's house is we'll have to see Van Shruger," Father said. "And I don't want to see Van Shruger. He's a damn bore, and besides, I can't understand a word he says."

"Well, who isn't a damn bore in your opinion—besides yourself?" asked Mother.

"Nearly anyone but Van Shruger."

"Well, I'd like to see Holland."

"Well, I wouldn't. In fact, I'm not dying to go to Paris either. I'm sick of Europe. I'm just going for your sake. But we're not going to stay long—just long enough to take a quick ride up the Eiffel Tower and then home!"

Mother got over her disappointment about Holland as soon as she saw Paris, and Father liked it well enough to stay there for two weeks, despite the fact that the rates at the George V Hotel were "outrageous."

In the first two days we were there, he methodically whipped us

155

through all the main tourist attractions—the Garden of Versailles, the Notre Dame Cathedral, the Thieves' Market, the Louvre, and the Eiffel Tower, where he got sick going up in the rickety, glass-enclosed elevator.

Then, while Mother spent the rest of her time in Paris shopping, Father whiled away the days hunting for a restaurant with American home cooking. The snails and the French sauces were getting him down. "I just want a plain meal," he kept complaining. "Isn't there some place in Paris where I can get a meal that isn't cooked in wine?"

One day Father took me to a Punch-and-Judy show in the park along the Champs-Elysées. He left me in the audience while he went out and took a walk through the park. When the show was over and he hadn't returned, I went out to look for him. I found him on the boulevard rolling hoops with a group of French children and apparently having the best time he'd had since we'd arrived in Paris.

Except for the night life, which he deplored, the main thing Father didn't like about Paris was the language barrier. Father, more than anyone I know, is dependent on the spoken language for his fun. If he can't get into ridiculous conversations with people, he feels that there's not much point in living.

Father can speak German but not French. And German got him nowhere in Paris.

One afternoon he and Chico decided to go to the horse races, but they couldn't make the cab driver understand this. Desperate because he'd already missed two races, Chico finally got down on his hands and knees on the sidewalk, and motioned Father to climb on his back.

"Make like a jockey," said Chico.

Father jumped on Chico's back, and started whipping him with a newspaper.

"Now do you know where we want to go?" Chico, still on his hands and knees, asked the driver.

"Oui, oui," said the driver, motioning them into the cab.

156

As they drove away, Chico was rather pleased with his inventiveness. But his confidence in himself was shaken after the cab driver dropped them off in front of a large building a little while later. They found that they were at a wrestling arena.

We sailed home from Le Havre on the German ship, the *Europa*.

Mother wanted Father to put on his new tuxedo to go into the dining salon the second night out, but he balked.

"You promised things would be different after you had a new tuxedo made," she reminded him.

"I only promised that I'd get a new one," he said. "I didn't promise that I'd wear it."

By the third night out he was even refusing to wear a necktie.

Fortunately, it was a short trip. The *Europa* was one of the two fastest ships afloat, and she made the crossing in four and a half days. If the voyage had taken any longer, Father would probably have wanted to go into the dining room in shorts.

The night before we docked, Mother and Father held a confab to discuss the strategy they would employ for getting through Customs.

They hadn't made a great many expensive purchases while we were in Europe, but they had exceeded the limit. Father had spent five hundred dollars on a single item—a combination lighter and watch—which he had bought at Dunhill's in London.

The duty on our excess, if it had all been declared, probably wouldn't have amounted to a great deal. But Father was in a gambling mood.

"I'll just put this lighter in my vest pocket," he announced, "and even if they should frisk me and find it, who'll be able to prove that I didn't buy it in the States before I left?"

"Just as a precaution," said Mother, "you'd better slip the Customs man a few bucks when we get on the dock, so he'll overlook some of the clothes in our trunk we're not declaring."

"Oh, no," said Father, "I won't resort to bribery."

"But, Groucho—everybody does it," protested Mother.

"Bribery is crooked," roared Father. "I'll have no truck with it."

157

"I suppose sneaking that lighter in isn't," said Mother.

"That's different," said Father. "I'm simply matching wits with them. But it's not crooked like bribery."

Father remained adamant. There would be no bribing the Customs men.

Nevertheless, everything probably would have gone smoothly— if there hadn't been a Declaration of Purchases Form to fill out. But given a blank questionnaire, Father can't control his comic tendencies, and this was the result:

NAME: *Julius H. Marx*

ADDRESS: *21 Lincoln Road, Great Neck, L. I.*

BORN: *Yes*

HAIR: *Not much*

OCCUPATION: *Smuggler*

LIST OF ITEMS PURCHASED OUT OF THE UNITED STATES, WHERE BOUGHT, AND THE PURCHASE PRICE: *Wouldn't you like to know?*

When we finally arrived at the pier, the other passengers went through Customs without much delay, but we were detained for several hours while the Inspector carefully examined every inch of our baggage.

Mother, who hadn't seen the form after Father had filled it out, couldn't understand why the Customs Department was singling us out for a close inspection. And with each new piece of undeclared clothing the Inspector discovered, Mother would whisper irately to Father, "It's all your fault. I told you you should have slipped him something. And look how he's messing up my new dresses!"

"It's just routine," Father assured her. "Everyone goes through this."

"This is the last ocean trip I take with you," she said at one point.

"Never mind that," said Father, in a whisper just loud enough for the Inspector to hear. "What did you do with the opium? Do you still have it on you?"

That was all the Customs Inspector needed to hear. We were

158

promptly taken to the Customs Office on the pier, segregated by sex, and made to undress. Then they searched through our clothes.

Father hadn't counted on his practical joke getting so far out of hand, and he was nervous and pale for fear that they would discover the lighter. But somehow he managed to conceal the lighter (he later confessed to me that at one point he had it in his mouth), and eventually we were released.

About six months later, after we had moved to California and were living in a hilltop home in Hollywoodland, there came a knock on the door one afternoon. Father opened the door.

Standing there was a fellow in a gray suit and a fedora. He had that unmistakable look of a Government man about him. His manner was polite, but at the same time a trifle ominous. He introduced himself, and said he was from "Customs"—and quickly got to the point.

"We're interested in a little item you didn't declare when you returned from Europe last February," he said.

"What kind of an item?" asked Father innocently.

"A lighter, Mr. Marx."

"That's absurd," said Father.

Ignoring his protest, the Customs man went on resolutely, reading from a notebook:

"A combination cigarette lighter and eighteen-jewel watch. According to our records, you bought it at Dunhill's London store on January 16. Salesman: John Winston, third floor. Purchase price: five hundred and twenty-eight dollars, American money."

In the face of such incriminating evidence, Father had no choice but to confess, agree to pay the duty, and also an additional penalty charge.

But he was filled with admiration for the Customs Department.

"You boys certainly are thorough," he said. "How did you find out all that?"

"We have our ways," smiled the Customs man.

"Well, it certainly teaches me a lesson," said Father. "That's the last time I buy anything at Dunhill's in London. The place is obviously full of stool pigeons."

CHAPTER 18

IN HOLLYWOOD, the Marx Brothers continued as a team for nearly twenty years. They made eleven more pictures together, and Father has appeared in three without his brothers in recent years. Two of them—*A Night at the Opera* and *A Day at the Races*—were, in the opinion of nearly every critic, minor classics.

Although they were box office favorites for many years, Father has always felt that if they had fallen into the hands of Irving Thalberg earlier in their picture careers, and if he had lived longer and continued to guide them, as he did with *A Night at the Opera* and *A Day at the Races*, they would have had more films of that caliber to their credit. But their association with Thalberg lasted only a short time.

The Marx Brothers' early pictures in Hollywood—*Monkey Business*, *Horsefeathers*, and *Duck Soup*—may not have been great pictures. But they were successful in the eyes of the public. And they've held up surprisingly well over the years. Exhibitors apparently think so, too, for there always seems to be at least one of their old pictures playing around in the big cities, and audiences still enjoy watching them.

Father never enjoyed watching himself, however, even in his very best pictures. At previews, he'd sit slumped down in his seat, usually with his coat collar turned up, so he wouldn't be recognized as one of the perpetrators, and afterwards he'd slink out into the lobby as if he were some criminal. His face would be a sort of off-white color, and his comment would always be the same:

160

"Gee, I gave a bad performance. I'm certainly not the actor I used to be."

This wasn't just false modesty, either. He believed it. He'd be depressed for several days, and he'd be convinced that he was "washed up." And during this period of depression, he'd pay particular attention to the ads in the magazines telling how a man could retire on two hundred a month and spend his "sunset years" sword-fishing off the coast of Florida.

But when we first arrived in Hollywood, shortly after our European excursion, Father was pretty enthusiastic about the moving picture business. The Marx Brothers already had two successful pictures to their credit, and he saw no reason why they couldn't continue to turn out more like *Cocoanuts* and *Animal Crackers*, especially if they made them at the leisurely pace of one a year, which they had insisted on in their contract with Paramount Studios.

Father, especially, was very firm on this point, even though it was hard to resist the temptation to make pictures more frequently, and therefore earn more money in a shorter space of time. But if he knew nothing else about picture making in those days, he was wise enough to realize that the quickest way to end a movie career, particularly a comedian's movie career, was to saturate the public with too many films.

"Never give the public a chance to get sick of you," he used to say. "It's hard enough making them laugh without having them say, 'God, do we have to see them again?' Better to give them too little than too much."

He stuck to this belief throughout his years in the picture business. And the fact that he lasted so long, while many of his contemporaries have disappeared from the public eye, is fairly conclusive proof that it is a good theory to abide by.

Actually, it turned out to be quite a struggle for the Marx Brothers even to make one picture a year in Hollywood. And this came as quite a shock to Father.

He had quit Broadway mainly because he was looking for a more

161

comfortable way of life, or "a softer racket," as he phrased it. He was in good health, but as he used to remind us often, he wasn't getting any younger. He was in his early forties, his hair was graying to the point where it needed to be touched up for public appearances, and he wanted to spend what he called his "declining years" in front of a fireplace in the evenings instead of in front of footlights.

He accomplished this by moving to Hollywood, but in return for the comforts of a more normal home life, he discovered that there were certain disadvantages to being a picture actor that he hadn't anticipated.

Aside from the mechanical aspects, there had been no problems in connection with putting *Cocoanuts* and *Animal Crackers* on film. The important ingredients—the story, the jokes and the comedy routines—were all sure-fire. There had been few changes to make. In fact, they had practically photographed the shows exactly as they had been on the stage.

But in Hollywood they had to start from scratch, and this turned out to be exceedingly difficult. True, they had to start from scratch when they were preparing a Broadway show, too, but there was one important difference. If they were not satisfied with a scene after an opening, they could tinker with it until they got it right. Lines that didn't get laughs would be thrown out, and they'd keep trying new ones until they found lines that did get laughs.

But in the movies, once a picture was on film, they were stuck with it, good or bad. There was very little that anyone could do to improve it, beyond cutting, or perhaps shooting a scene over, if it were exceptionally bad.

Jokes that didn't get laughs at the preview had to stay in the picture, nevertheless. And there were plenty of lines that looked like sure laughs on paper that didn't even get a snicker from audiences.

"The trouble is," claims Father, "you just can't tell what an audience will laugh at, and what it won't unless you try the mate-

162

rial out in front of an audience. No one can tell this. Some people are better judges than others, but in the final analysis, it's up to the audience to decide. I'll bet we had fifty jokes in our first few pictures that I thought would get screams that got nothing. It was very discouraging."

At the time, Father and his brothers saw no way that they could solve this problem satisfactorily. The only thing they could do was try to see that their scripts were as funny as possible before they went before the cameras, and hope for the best.

And in those days it wasn't easy to get Marx Brothers scripts that even looked good on paper. Most of the writers around Hollywood were left over from the silent days, and the few who could write good dialogue weren't particularly suited for originating Marx Brothers material.

As I mentioned before, writing for them was a very special proposition. An author not only had to write a story conducive to comedy, but he had to dream up one containing parts for comedians with three totally different styles, plus a love-interest role for Zeppo, the straight man.

Probably the hardest one to write for was Father. "Writers thought because they wrote long speeches for me and had me talking fast and using a lot of non sequiturs and silly puns that was all there was to it," explains Father. "That's my style all right. The trouble is, a lot of writers forgot to be funny along with it."

His fast-talking style had its origin back in his "Fun in Hi Skule" days, when he was just blossoming into a comic. He had had no confidence in himself as a comedian, and he was never sure whether his material was any good or not, so he decided that if he talked very rapidly, there would be less chance of the audience getting bored.

His off-stage character—which is essentially the same one you see on television today—also stems from the time when he didn't have much confidence in his ability to cope with people. Inherently shy, he discovered early in life that if you insult someone right off the bat or make a wisecrack there is a good chance that the other person will be so taken aback that he won't make any remarks about you or notice your shortcomings.

"It's the same principle they use in sports," maintains Father. "You know—the best defense is a good offense."

When he became successful, he realized that fast talking by itself was not enough to keep an audience from being bored. But many of the men who wrote for him didn't realize this, and what they turned out was usually a very bad carbon copy of the Groucho Marx they had seen on the stage.

Father believes that the writer is the most important person in the entertainment business, and he's very outspoken on the subject. He's also pretty disdainful of the performer who, with a stable of high-priced writers, likes to give the illusion that he is the sole creator.

Father, in contrast, has never taken a writing credit on any movie or any radio or television show he's ever appeared in, and very often he's been responsible for enough of the material to be entitled to a credit.

That's one of the reasons writers like to work for him, even though he is an unduly severe critic at times. The other reason is that he can be extremely helpful when it comes to revising scripts, writing jokes and suggesting story ideas.

Father always contributed a great deal to the Marxes' picture scripts. He'd sit in on all the story conferences, work right along with the writers, if need be, and he'd occasionally take a script home and toil away on it by himself.

He was also responsible for a couple of changes that hurt their first few pictures. One was the elimination of Harpo and Chico's musical solos. It was difficult finding spots for the harp and piano solos in the scripts, and Father didn't want to slow up the action just to drag them in. So he convinced his brothers that it would be best to forget about their specialties.

He was influenced, of course, by his own personal feelings about the harp and piano solos. Father had always been a music lover, and he realized that Harpo and Chico were quite accomplished on their respective instruments. But after listening to them hacking away at the harp and the piano nearly every night on the stage for the past fifteen years, he was, to say the least, no longer amused by this.

What he overlooked was how much their fans like the harp and piano solos—especially the piano. It's an odd thing about Chico's playing. He may not be a Rubinstein, but no one else has ever been able to master his one big forte—shooting the keys with his forefinger—and audiences eat it up. I've seen him play encores for a whole hour, and still the audience clapped for more.

But Father was tired of it, and besides he felt that maybe their fans deserved a change of pace. So the harp and piano were out.

The other change for the worse which Father suggested concerned Margaret Dumont. Miss Dumont is the big, dowager-type woman who spent a good deal of her acting career serving as Father's foil. She was in the movie and stage versions of *Cocoanuts* and *Animal Crackers*, and in all the pictures the Marxes made at MGM. But when they were casting *Monkey Business* and *Horsefeathers*, Father felt that they needed a change in that department, too. They got Thelma Todd instead, and while she filled the role competently, most dyed-in-the-wool Marx Brothers fans missed seeing Margaret Dumont. Many considered her a fifth member of the family, and set up such a clamor for her return that Father and his brothers were obliged to bring her back for *Duck Soup*, and never again thought of making a picture without her.

By the time the Marx Brothers finished *Monkey Business* and *Horsefeathers*, and were preparing *Duck Soup*, which Leo McCarey directed, Father was beginning to realize that making movies wasn't the soft racket he had imagined it would be. Not only was it becoming tougher and tougher to get good scripts, but he was already beginning to dislike movie-making in general.

First of all, he had no respect for most of the producers and front-office executives with whom he came in contact in those days. Many of them were businessmen and not good showmen. He was constantly fighting with them for script changes which they didn't feel were necessary. They were anxious to get the picture before the cameras, whether the script was good or not.

"It's like the story of the gashouse gang who went out to play football for the first time," Father used to tell us. "They had never played in their lives, and didn't know the first thing about the game. They lined up for the kickoff, but they had neglected to bring a football. When some wise guy mentioned this to the captain, the captain said, 'To hell with the ball. Let's get going!'"

He also didn't approve of the way many directors went about the business of shooting a picture. "Their idea of directing me in a scene was to say, 'Give 'em the eyebrows, Groucho,' or, 'When you come into the room, snap your fingers so the audience will know you just got an idea.' That idea of snapping your fingers went out with the Keystone Cops."

And he was rabid on the subject of directors who had to shoot simple scenes over and over again. "If the actors know their lines, there's no reason for this sort of thing," he'd say after a long day of shooting. "The trouble is, this jerk we've got for a director doesn't know what the hell he wants. So he shoots everything twenty times, and hopes there'll be something good in it."

Father always had more dialogue, and longer, trickier speeches than anyone in the picture, but he was very conscientious about learning lines and rarely flubbed one, even on the first take. So naturally it burned him up to have to do a scene over more than a couple of times—either because the director was unsure of himself, or because some other actor hadn't bothered to look at the script the night before.

Another thing that rankled in him was the working hours during the shooting of a picture. A movie actor has to be on the set, ready to begin shooting, at nine in the morning. Father can barely be civil at nine in the morning, much less get in the mood for cracking jokes.

"This is a hell of a time to have to be funny," he'd complain bitterly every morning when he was leaving for the studio. Ordinarily he rose at eight, so he didn't have to get up any earlier to be at the studio at nine. When he left the house he'd already have on his frock coat, striped pants and red tie. And he refused to bother with pancake makeup, claiming he looked just as grotesque with or without it, so when he arrived at the studio there was nothing left for him to do but slap on his painted black mustache.

However, when Father knows he has to be some place before noon, his insomnia gets worse. He'd be a wreck by the time he arrived on the set.

Father believes that picture studios would get much better performances out of their comedians if they wouldn't start shooting until noon, and everybody worked for a couple of hours after dinner, instead of quitting at six. It's impractical, though, because studios couldn't stand the expense of having to pay so much overtime to their union employees.

Much as he hated getting to the studio early, he'd usually be the first actor on the set in the morning, and if anyone showed up late, he or she would have to answer to Father.

When Father was working with his brothers, Chico very often would be late arriving on the set. Harpo deplored this practice as much as Father, so one day the two of them put their heads together to try to think of a way to cure Chico of the habit.

They finally decided that they would impose a fifty-dollar fine on Chico every time he showed up late, and to make it fair, the same thing would apply to themselves. Being a gambling man, Chico agreed to this, and Father was delighted with the whole arrangement.

The first morning that this new rule was going into effect Father rose at his usual time, ate a leisurely breakfast, and then walked out to the garage to get into his car.

We had a sliding overhead garage door that we had never had any trouble with before. But when Father went to slide it up, he found that he couldn't get it to move. Finally he called me out to the garage, and the two of us went to work on it—but with the same results.

167

"We have to do something," said Father, looking at his watch frantically. "I'm going to lose fifty bucks if I don't get to the studio by nine."

We entered the garage through its back door and discovered that a four-by-four board was wedged into the complicated spring mechanism that worked the overhead door. We tried to dislodge it, but it wouldn't budge.

"Why don't you take a taxi?" suggested Mother, who had come out to the garage to investigate the trouble.

"I don't want to waste money on a taxi, with two Cadillacs in the garage," he said. "Quick! Get me my saw!"

I brought him the saw, and after he had hacked away at the board for forty-five minutes, he managed to free the door. But he was late getting to the studio, for the first time in his life, and Chico was on the set waiting for him with palm outstretched.

"My garage door jammed," explained Father. "You're not going to count that!"

"Never mind the excuses," said Chico. "Hand over the dough."

"I don't have that much in cash on me," said Father, annoyed. "I'll write you a check later."

"No checks," said Chico. "I want cash—right now!"

"Me too," said Harpo.

Although Father never uncovered any evidence as to how the board got jammed inside the garage door, he has always suspected that there was foul play somewhere along the line.

CHAPTER 19

FATHER'S BEEN one of Hollywood's staunchest defenders ever since he first stepped off the Chief and settled permanently in Southern California, over twenty years ago.

By "Hollywood," I don't mean only the picture business or that famous piece of real estate in the vicinity of Hollywood and Vine. I'm referring to all of Southern California and the whole gigantic entertainment industry that has sprung up on the West Coast.

Father feels that Hollywood is the only place to live and to work, and at the first word of criticism from an out-of-towner, he'll rise to the community's defense more willingly than he'll come to the aid of a helpless lady.*

He fell in love with Southern California's temperate climate and informal way of life the moment he was exposed to them. And he still can't get over the fact that he doesn't need galoshes in the winter, or that sport shorts are acceptable most of the places he goes, summer or winter.

"Isn't this wonderful?" he's likely to exclaim suddenly when he's strolling along one of Hillcrest's fairways on a balmy day in the middle of December. "If we were in New York now we'd be kicking around in all that snow and slush, and freezing our tails off on Fifty-ninth Street."

Father gets particularly annoyed at the New Yorkers who would have you believe that there isn't an ounce of creative talent in the

* There's no such thing, and you know it. GROUCHO

whole movie business, and who are constantly taking pot shots at Hollywood because it seems fashionable and ultra-sophisticated to do so.

Dining at Chasen's recently, Father was invited over to the bar to meet a New York movie critic. This writer happened to be on the staff of one of Father's favorite magazines, but he's been highly resentful of its movie reviews since the time a former editor confessed to him that his policy was to slam every Hollywood product, good or bad, because it made more amusing reading.

This critic is also of the knock-Hollywood school of journalism, and Father could hardly wait to get at him as he strode over to the bar to meet him.

"Young man," said Father, shaking the reviewer's hand, "you're a brave man."

"Brave? In what way?"

"Brave to show your face around this town. If anyone recognizes you, you're liable to get lynched. You call yourself a movie critic? That's not reviewing, what you do. You're just writing funny pieces at someone else's expense. Why, to read your reviews, you'd think there hasn't been a good picture made in Hollywood in its whole history."

With that, he strode back to his table and finished his dinner. "Damned smart alecs," Father said to the other people at his table. "They turn on Hollywood every chance they get, and then they come out here and expect people to fall all over them, feeding and entertaining them."

And yet, with all his loyalty to the movie city, Father, over the years, has consistently rebelled against many of the things that Hollywood stands for—the phony glamour, the ostentatious living, the false adulation, in fact the whole social scheme as reported in the fan magazines.

For many years, for instance, he refused to have his own swimming pool. Aside from the initial installation cost and the upkeep, which he felt was an unnecessary extravagance, he believed that pools attracted too many uninvited guests. If there's anyone who's unwelcome in Father's house, it's an uninvited guest. He or she will get a greeting cool enough to freeze over Lake Arrowhead in August. But if you have a pool, it's practically impossible to keep friends from dropping in on you with their swimming suits and staying all day, no matter how frosty you are to them.

Father found this out back in 1932, when we rented, for the summer, a large Colonial house on Sunset Boulevard that had a swimming pool. So when he bought his own home in Beverly Hills a few months later, Father made sure that the back yard was bereft of any embellishments that would tend to make it a community playground.

Our new home was no slum. It had fourteen rooms, six baths and a three-car garage. And its grounds were spacious enough for a pool, and also a tennis court. But before Mother or Miriam or I could get any ideas, Father quickly filled up the back yard with citrus trees and a vegetable patch.

Without a swimming pool, we were definitely not part of the swimming-pool set. Now that I think of it, I'm not sure what set Father was a part of, or is a part of today. Certainly not the acting set. In Hollywood, just as in New York, he has never mingled very much socially with other actors and actresses.

Most of the people who used to come to our house, and who are still part of his crowd today, were a random assortment of writers, producers, composers and relatives. Some were important people in town; some were still struggling, or perhaps out of work altogether. But all were his friends for the same reason—because he liked them and considered them entertaining people to have around.

Father is very loyal to his friends. He's not the type who gets a whole new set every six months. Once he's made up his mind that he likes you, nothing anyone can say about you will change his opinion of you or your talents.

As a result, most of the friends he has today are the same ones he had twenty years ago. To name them all would take up too much space. His three closest friends and confidants since he moved to Hollywood have been Norman Krasna, Harry Ruby and Arthur Sheekman—all writers. He eats lunch a couple of times a week at Hillcrest Country Club, where he is a member. In a corner of the men's grill at Hillcrest is a large round table reserved for comedians and the show-business crowd. The group usually consists of George Jessel, Milton Berle, Jack Benny, George Burns, the Ritz Brothers, Danny Kaye, Danny Thomas, Lou Holtz and the Marx Brothers, and as a result the table is known as the Comedians' Round Table.

Father enjoys having lunch with this group. They discuss show business, world affairs, reminisce about the old Palace days, and try to top one another's jokes. Mostly the latter. No one in the crowd wants to be a straight man. No one even wants to listen to anyone else. If you hope to get a word in, you have to speak fast and loud. The only one who can hold an audience at the table for over twenty seconds is George Jessel.

"When he speaks, the rest of us shut up and just listen," claims Father, who'd rather hear Jessel talk than anyone else in the world. "He's the only one I won't heckle."

Coming from Father, that's quite a tribute.

Father is also very fond of Bing Crosby. The first thing they do, whenever circumstances throw them together, is organize a little barber-shop quartet group.

One of Father's favorite stories about Bing concerns the time they were on a war-bond tour together. They were in Milwaukee, eating dinner at a hofbrau-type restaurant. Jerry Colonna was also at their table, but they needed an alto to complete the quartet.

"I'll find one," volunteered Crosby, and he went to every table in the place, looking for someone who could sing alto. But everyone turned him down, and finally he returned to the table alone, and very disappointed.

"There's no big punch finish to the story," says Father, "but I don't think I'll ever forget that scene. There was probably the highest-priced singer in the world—one of the most famous personalities of all times—going through some dumpy joint in Milwaukee, pleading with people to sing harmony with us, and getting turned down. They didn't recognize him. They thought he was some screwball."

When we first moved out to California, Father used to see quite a bit of Charlie Chaplin, Will Rogers and W. C. Fields. He was very fond of Fields and Rogers. He had palled around with Will Rogers when they were on the Orpheum Circuit together. Rogers liked Father because he played the guitar. They used to sit in one another's dressing rooms and sing Western songs. And when Rogers thought it might be an asset for a cowboy actor to know how to play the guitar, Father taught him enough of the fundamentals to accompany himself.

Rogers had a big ranch out near Santa Monica, and Father was a guest there a few times. But Rogers played a lot of polo. In fact, he was more or less the kingpin of the Hollywood polo crowd, and if ever there was a sport that didn't appeal to Father, it was polo. It's too rich for his blood. Besides, Rogers did so much traveling that it was impossible to maintain any kind of a permanent relationship with him.*

Father first met W. C. Fields in his vaudeville travels. He considers Fields one of the all-time great comedians. He was one of the few people who's ever been able to make Father laugh out loud, and I'm sure they would have been closer friends than they were if Fields hadn't been such a serious drinker. But Fields was the top man in the drinking set, so Father only saw him sporadically.

One time Fields invited Father and Mother out to his house in San Fernando Valley, and I went along. It was a new house, and Fields was quite proud of it as he showed us through. Near the end of the tour he opened a door, and we passed through it into a high-ceilinged room that was about thirty by thirty. There was no furniture in it; just cases of liquor, from floor to ceiling, from wall to wall. It looked like a warehouse for a liquor concern.

* *Unless you were a polo pony.* GROUCHO

173

"What's all this for?" asked Father.

"It's in case prohibition comes back," explained Fields.

Father also had a tremendous amount of admiration for Charlie Chaplin, as a comedian. He feels that Chaplin was the greatest comedian of them all.

He first met Chaplin when they were playing the same vaudeville circuit in Canada, many years before his own first success in *I'll Say She Is*. "Chaplin was just another baggy-pants comedian at the time, recently immigrated from England, and he was making about thirty dollars a week," recalls Father. "But he had the audiences in the aisles, and I was among them."

Their tours brought them together again in Los Angeles, on Father's first trip to California. They were on the same bill at the Orpheum Theater, and there a movie producer spotted Chaplin and offered him one hundred dollars a week to work in pictures.

"I won't take it," Chaplin told Father.

"Why not?" asked Father.

"Nobody can be worth that much money," said Chaplin.

Years later, when he moved to Hollywood, Chaplin was one of the most famous men in the world, and extremely wealthy. He had a palatial home, with liveried servants, and his own swimming pool, tennis court, and projection room.

Father was a frequent guest at Chaplin's for a while. He liked being around his favorite comedian, and Chaplin enjoyed his company, too. Chaplin once told him, "Groucho—you're the greatest comedian of them all." It was sort of a mutual admiration society.

There are many things about Hollywood that Father doesn't like, and has tried to avoid.

He hates garish publicity stunts, like riding down Hollywood Boulevard in the Santa Claus Parade around Christmas time. He once got trapped into this ordeal, caught a cold during the long ride on a float through the streets of Hollywood on a foggy night, and wound up by calling Santa Claus an imposter in front of a group of small children.

He's never employed a press agent to plant his name in the columns, as so many Hollywood celebrities are wont to do. If he gets his name in a column it's either because he's said something amusing that's being quoted around town, or because one of the columnists has come to him and asked him for a few bright quips with which to liven up his copy.

When he first moved to Hollywood, he even balked at putting his footprints alongside those of the other stars in the cement in the forecourt of Grauman's Chinese Theater.

"What do I want to do that for?" he'd say, whenever the Paramount Publicity Department brought up the subject. "What good will it do me?"

Informed that any publicity was good, Father replied, "There are an awful lot of actors who have their footprints in there that can't get jobs any more. It's not doing them much good."

Under constant pressure, he finally consented, "But only one foot!" he stipulated. "If Paramount picks up our option, I'll give you the other foot."

The walls of the Hollywood Brown Derby, on Vine Street, are covered with autographed caricatures of famous people, past and present. It's considered an honor to get your caricature hung there, for it's a sign that you've really made the grade. And Father, too, was asked to pose for one of these drawings shortly after coming to Hollywood.

Father abhors posing—either for still pictures or drawings—and for months, every time the management asked him to sit for the caricature, he'd think of some excuse to duck out of the chore. But one day at lunchtime he agreed to go through with it, and for a couple of hours he sat very patiently, and only did a minimum of complaining.

After the caricature was finished, the manager of the Brown Derby handed it back to Father for the customary autograph. Father immediately dashed off the following inscription:

"To Al Levy's Tavern—the best restaurant on Vine Street! Groucho Marx."

The manager was so incensed at this tribute to a rival restaurant that he tore up the caricature immediately and stormed away from the table. "Obviously the man has no sense of humor," reported Father, equally incensed.

Father's caricature remained among the missing from the Brown Derby hall of fame during the various ups and downs of his career over the next twenty years. Finally, after television thrust a great deal of fame on Father once again, the Brown Derby requested another chance to do a caricature of him. Father said they could have another go at it, but only if they didn't censor his inscription. They agreed to his terms, and when it came time to autograph the drawing, Father wrote:

"To the Hollywood Brown Derby—the best restaurant on Vine Street, but only because Al Levy's has gone out of business."

Though he realizes that the time to worry is when no one wants his autograph, Father dislikes signing his signature for fans. He believes it's a lot of nonsense, and he's thoroughly convinced that anyone who goes around collecting movie stars' autographs is extremely hard up for amusement.

The two types of fans that annoy him the most are the ones who say, "Can I have your autograph?" but have neglected to bring either paper or pencil, and the ones who say, "Can I have your autograph? It isn't for me. It's for my grandmother. She's sick in bed."

On the subject of the latter, Father says, "Even the autograph hunters are ashamed to admit they want it for themselves. They have to say it's for someone else, who isn't there to defend himself."

Before he started wearing a mustache, Father wasn't even recognized by many autograph hunters. And to prove that they didn't know who he was, and that they didn't particularly care whose signature they were getting, as long as it was someone's, Father frequently used to sign Charlie Chaplin's name.

"Once I even signed 'Mary Pickford' and got away with it," claims Father.

Also high on Father's hate list is having to go dancing at Ciro's or the Mocambo, and attending picture premieres, the annual Academy Awards ceremonies, and the kind of large-scale parties that Louella Parsons and Hedda Hopper are always writing about in their columns.

Most of the people in Hollywood's upper strata jump at the chance to attend these affairs. It gives them the opportunity to dress formally and to be admired by a throng of milling fans as they alight from chauffeur-driven Cadillacs, amidst the glare of klieg lights and the popping of flash bulbs, at the scene of the event.

Mother enjoyed all this glitter, too, but unfortunately she was married to a misanthrope.

When she'd ask him to take her to Ciro's, he'd say, "Ciro's! Are you crazy? You have to be drunk to enjoy sitting in a crowded nightclub, watching Louis B. Mayer doing the rhumba. And even if I were drunk, I wouldn't like it."

When she was coaxing him to take her to a premiere, Father's answer would always be:

"What do I want to go to an opening for? It's just another picture. In two months it'll be playing at a neighborhood theater, with free dishes and bingo. And I won't have to put on a tuxedo or fight those crowds."

Occasionally, either to appease Mother, or for business reasons, Father would let himself get roped into one of these affairs. But he'd start feeling sorry for himself about a month prior to the impending event, and by the time the big night arrived, he'd either have a "grippy feeling" and be in a horrible mood, or else he'd be too full of life, which would mean that he'd probably wind up insulting everyone at the affair.

The first big event that Father and Mother attended in this town was a benefit thrown by the Wampus Club at the Biltmore Hotel. It was one of the most important social affairs ever to hit Hollywood. Ben Bernie's orchestra supplied the music, and every important star was there, including Greta Garbo, Charlie Chaplin and Mary Pickford.

A floor show was part of the festivities, and as a finale they had about an hour's worth of so-called ad lib entertainment, with many of the stars participating. Father was asked to emcee this part of the show, and he was quite put out about it, because he hadn't prepared any material—and he isn't the type of entertainer who keeps a routine up his sleeve for just such emergencies. But as Father well knew, many of the stars who were going to be called upon had come prepared. And it burned him up because they were pretending that everything was going to be strictly ad lib.

However, he couldn't escape, and the first person he had to introduce was Nora Bayes, the singing star of the twenties.

"And now," began Father, "Miss Nora Bayes. I hesitate to call on her, but if you give her enough encouragement, I think we can get her to do a number for us. I say I think we can, because Miss Bayes just happens to have brought her music and her accompanist along with her."

That got a laugh from everyone but Nora Bayes, and after that there was no holding Father. According to Mother, there wasn't a person there that night whom Father didn't insult during his stint at the microphone. Not only that, he got roaring drunk for one of the few times in his life, and he later wound up under the table, singing harmony with John Gilbert and Russ Columbo.

The odd thing about Father's insults is that he can make the bitterest, most caustic remarks imaginable and get away with it because, coming from him, people think it's funny. Someone else, saying the same things, would probably wind up with a black eye.*
To my knowledge, Father has never had a black eye, nor has he ever been involved in any kind of a fracas where he's had to resort to fisticuffs. However, he once was the cause of an incident that nearly succeeded in landing himself, Miriam and me in jail.

A few months after we had moved into our new home in Beverly Hills, Archie Mayo, a prominent Hollywood director, built a house with a swimming pool directly across the street from ours.

As frequently happens, the pool was completed and filled with

* I'm no Zsa Zsa Gabor. GROUCHO

water before the house was quite ready to be moved into. One hot day, while the house was still in the wall-papering and painting stage, Mayo happened to meet Father on the sidewalk in front of his place, and, being a very friendly fellow, issued him and the rest of the Marx clan a carte blanche invitation to use his pool.

Father didn't want to appear too anxious—after all, he was an important star, even if he didn't have his own swimming pool—so he waited until Mayo had driven off down the street before he told Miriam and me to get our bathing suits on, and that we were going for a swim.

Thirty minutes later the three of us were lolling beside Mayo's opulently tiled pool, thinking how fortunate we were to have such wealthy friends, when we heard the back door slam. We saw, coming toward us, a rather nice-looking, matronly woman, who seemed quite incensed about something.

"Who are you?" she demanded of Father. "What are you doing here?"

"I'm swimming," replied Father. "What are you doing here?"

"It so happens I have a right to be here," she answered, with indignation. "I'm a relative of the man who owns this house."

"In that case take off your clothes and come on in for a swim. Maybe I'll take mine off and we'll have a nude party."

"Don't you know this is private property?" she said, ignoring his invitation. "Who gave you permission to swim here?"

Miriam and I were a little nervous by this time, and we hoped he would tell her the truth and vindicate all of us. But Father had no such intentions.

"No one gave us permission," he said, looking her straight in the eye.

"Then what are you doing here?"

"Swimming, I told you," said Father.

"That's not what I mean. Who said you could swim here?"

"No one. The kids and I just happened to be loitering in the alley when we saw your pool, so we thought we'd go for a dip. After all, no one else is using it. It's silly to have it going to waste."

She was livid. "Well, you just pick up your things and get out of here before I call the police," she threatened.

"We're not hurting anything," said Father. "Why should we?"

"That's not the point," she snapped. "This is private property, and we won't have just anyone off the street dropping in here."

"That's the trouble with you rich," said Father. "You get a little money and right away the people off the street aren't good enough for you. Well, we're not budging. This is a free country, and I insist on standing up for our rights."

With that, he removed his glasses, put down his cigar and nonchalantly swam three lengths of the pool, as the woman watched, transfixed. Then he climbed out again and started to dry off.

"As long as I'm going to swim here," he said in a complaining tone, "I wish you'd see that the water is heated. It's a little too cold for my blood."

She bridled indignantly, and stormed off in the direction of the house next door, announcing that she was going to phone the police.

"Do you think she will?" asked Miriam.

"Probably," said Father, stretching out on a towel, unconcerned.

"I'm scared," said Miriam, who was only six. "I'm going home."

"That's right," said Father. "Desert your father when he's about to be thrown in the jug."

He finally persuaded the two of us to stick around, and then, when he saw her return from making the call and go inside the Mayo house, apparently to wait for the police, he stood up and beckoned us to follow him.

He sauntered inside the house, and found the offended lady admiring the freshly painted and papered living room. It was really a beautiful room, the last word in luxury, despite the fact that it still contained no furniture.

Father cast an appraising eye around the empty room, then turned to her and said, "That's Hollywood for you! People can't even afford furniture, and they have to have a swimming pool."

She turned so white I thought she was going to have a heart

attack, but two policemen arrived at that moment, and she managed to pull herself together.

"Here they are," she said. "I want you to arrest these people for vagrancy."

I was sure that Father would divulge his identity then, and tell them how we happened to be swimming there, but he double-crossed me by pulling the Julius H. Marx routine again, and stuck to it until they were actually herding us into the squad car. Then he glanced down at his bathing trunks and said:

"Would you mind terribly if I ran across the street and changed into something more formal?"

The officer looked at him as if he were out of his mind, and stiffly informed him that Groucho Marx lived in *that* house.

"I know," said Father. "Sometimes I go by that name, too."

CHAPTER 20

THOUGH FATHER spent considerable time poking fun at Hollywood and its customs, he was no jokester where vital matters were concerned. He played an important role in the formation of the Screen Actor's Guild at a time when championing the rights of his fellow actors was extremely hazardous.

The Screen Actors Guild was formed in 1933, but its bargaining power with the movie companies was practically nil—mainly because most of the important names in Hollywood were afraid to join it, after the failure of the Actors Equity Strike a few years earlier. Besides, most of the important stars felt they had no need for a guild; they were doing all right without it.

But a small group of stars, of which my father was one of the ringleaders, felt that the "little" actor had to be protected—even if it meant risking the disfavor of the movie moguls, who were against the formation of any kind of an actors union. They decided to reorganize the guild, and get all the stars in Hollywood to join. Father was the one who was responsible for arranging the first meeting of the new guild, which took place in the home of the late Frank Morgan. Among the stars who were present were Lee Tracy, Frederic March, James Cagney, Charles Butterworth, Jeanette MacDonald, Robert Montgomery, Boris Karloff, Ann Harding, George Raft, James Dunne, Chester Morris, Paul Muni, and of course Groucho Marx. With that lineup as the nucleus of

182

the new organization, the Screen Actors Guild soon blossomed into a powerful and respected union.

Father was the Guild's first treasurer. "And I'd still be Treasurer," he maintains, "if they hadn't started getting some money in the till."

This took place around the time the Marx Brothers were filming *Duck Soup*.

Duck Soup, which was about a mythical kingdom and a satire on war pictures, was the last of the five films the Marx Brothers made for Paramount. It was the last because even though it was the funniest of the three pictures they had made in Hollywood, it did not do too much business.

Father and his brothers felt that this was mainly due to the fact that *Duck Soup* was released in 1933—probably the worst of all the depression years.

But the Paramount front-office executives, under the new leadership of Emmanuel Cohen, who had recently taken over the reins from B. P. Schulberg, had another theory. They felt that the Marx Brothers' popularity was on the wane.

While Emmanuel Cohen was trying to decide whether or not to re-sign them, Father and his brothers got wind of a possible deal in the offing with Irving Thalberg.

Thalberg, who was producing under the MGM banner, was supposed to be one of the true geniuses of the motion picture industry. And any performer who could get Thalberg for a producer was considered to be fortunate indeed.

Oddly enough, it was through Chico's bridge playing that the Marx Brothers first got together with Thalberg.

It seems that Chico's bridge playing crowd consisted mostly of MGM executives, and Irving Thalberg was one of them.

One night, as their bridge game was breaking up, Thalberg said to Chico, "What are you fellows doing now?"

"Loafing," replied Chico. "Between pictures."

"Your contract's up at Paramount, isn't it?" asked Thalberg.

"Well, we haven't signed a new one—yet," said Chico.

"Before you do anything," said Thalberg, "I'd like to get together with you boys and talk. I'm forming my own company at MGM. Of course, it won't be for a while yet, but as soon as I know something definite, I'll call you and we'll have lunch together."

That conversation was the only assurance that they might go to work for Thalberg, but since Emmanuel Cohen didn't seem overly anxious to re-sign them, they decided to leave Paramount of their own accord and take their chances.

That was in the fall of 1933. When they still hadn't heard from Thalberg by the following January, Father was becoming a little panicky. That was the longest he'd been out of work in thirty years. He started looking around for another deal.

But the only deal he was able to come up with at that point was a job for him and Chico to do a coast-to-coast, half-hour radio show for the Esso Oil Company. This wouldn't have been so bad, except for the fact that it meant moving back to New York again. No national hook-up radio shows were being broadcast from the West Coast in those days. The facilities were too poor, and sponsors insisted on big shows emanating from New York.

Since they had nothing more promising to look forward to in Hollywood, Father and Chico went East and made their first plunge into radio in February of 1934. The show was called "Flywheel, Shyster and Flywheel," and, of course, was about a couple of shyster lawyers.

Father and Chico played essentially the same characters as they had been portraying on the screen and, as I recall, the show was extremely funny. But I was only thirteen at the time, and apparently a very easy audience, for the sponsors dropped "Flywheel, Shyster and Flywheel" after the first twenty-six weeks.

While Father was alienating his first sponsor, we'd been living in an apartment on Park Avenue. After "Flywheel, Shyster and Flywheel" went off the air in June, Father decided he'd had enough of civilization for a while. He wanted to "rough" it, so he packed up the family, and we moved to Skowhegan, Maine, for the summer.

There we roughed it in an eight-room cottage on Lake Wes-serunsett, with our own motor boat and two servants. Father likes to be comfortable, even though he's unemployed.

Directly across the lake from our cottage was the Lakewood Playhouse, one of the better known theaters on the straw-hat circuit, and probably the chief inducement for spending a summer in Skowhegan.

Father hadn't intended to participate in any of the shows, but when the director of the company asked him to play the leading role in Ben Hecht and Charlie MacArthur's *Twentieth Century*, he decided he would.

He was curious to see how he'd do in a play that wasn't a slapstick comedy. He hadn't appeared in anything but a Marx Brothers vehicle since he had become a successful comic.

The show was a big hit, and Father surprised many people, not only by being good in it, but also by being able to stick to a straight part without playing it any broader than Hecht and MacArthur had intended it.

"What a racket this straight acting is!" said Father, coming home after the first performance. "Anyone can do it. It doesn't take any talent at all." This bore out a theory that he'd had for a long time —that being a slapstick comic was the toughest work of all.

"When you come out on the stage in funny clothes and funny make-up, the audience unconsciously sets up a resistance to you," claims Father. "Right away their attitude is: 'So you're a comedian? Well, let's see how funny you can be. Go ahead. Make me laugh. I dare you to.'

"But when you come out in street clothes and look like a normal human being, they don't expect to be in the aisles at the first word you say. When you do say something funny they're pleasantly surprised and laugh all the harder."

The ease with which Father got big laughs in *Twentieth Century* started him thinking, and quite seriously, too, that possibly he ought to abandon his career as a Marx Brother and strike out on his own, without a painted black mustache. Maybe Emmanuel

Cohen was right. Maybe picture-goers really were tired of the Marx Brothers. Maybe their type of comedy was getting old-fashioned.

At any rate, there didn't seem to be any great rush on the part of the studios to sign the Marx Brothers up again.

Before we had left for Skowhegan, Father had told Chico, who was departing for the Coast, to be sure to let him know if anything was cooking for them in Hollywood. Chico had promised to keep his eyes and ears open, and assured Father that he would phone him long distance at the first indication that there was interest in the Marx Brothers at any of the studios. They had long since given up on Thalberg. They were ready to settle for any studio.

But now it was the middle of September. The leaves were turning brown and yellow. The other summer residents were beginning to move away from the lake. And the only time our very primitive six-party phone had jingled all summer had been when our landlady had called up to say that if our dachshund didn't stop eating her chickens, she would let him have both barrels from her shotgun.

Then one night, just as Father was getting into his sleeping coat and was preparing for bed, the phone rang eight and a half times. That was our ring, and Father rushed to answer it.

"Hollywood calling," said the long distance operator. "Just a minute, please."

"This must be Chico," Father said gleefully to Mother and me. "I guess he's heard something."

After a pause, Chico got on the other end of the wire. "Groucho?" he said.

"Yeah, this is Groucho," said Father, tense with expectation.

There was another pause, and then Chico said, "What's new?"

After he got over the shock, Father replied, "You're a hell of a businessman. You're in Hollywood, supposed to be arranging a deal. I've been in the woods for four months, with a six-party telephone and a bunch of farmers. And you have the nerve to call me up and ask me what's new!"

Chico hung up, very much chastened, and Father took two more sleeping pills and went to bed.

186

But things were not as dark as they seemed. When we arrived in Hollywood two weeks later, Chico did have news for Father. Thalberg had phoned him and was anxious to have lunch with the Marx Brothers, presumably to discuss a deal.

They met with Thalberg at the Beverly Wilshire Hotel on the following day.

Only three Marx Brothers—Harpo, Chico, and Father—were at the table, and this was to become a permanent condition. After seventeen years of being a relatively unimportant member of the team, Zeppo had decided that he was a better businessman than actor, and had opened up a theatrical agency on the Sunset Strip. The break was completely unopposed by his brothers, who wished him good luck and agreed to become his first clients.

It turned out to be a very astute move for the whole Marx family. The Marxes functioned as a better comedy team without Zeppo, and he wound up making more money as an agent than he ever could have made as an actor. Moreover, after he'd been in business for about a year, Zeppo took in Gummo, who'd been in the dress business in New York, as a partner, and the two of them built the agency into one of the biggest in Hollywood. Clark Gable, Robert Taylor, Carole Lombard and Barbara Stanwyck were just a few of their clients.

But getting back to the Thalberg deal, it didn't appear too promising the way the lunch at the Beverly Wilshire started off.

Father asked the producer what he thought of *Monkey Business* and *Horsefeathers*, and Thalberg replied:

"Not bad. Not good, either."

This criticism just about coincided with what Father thought of those two pictures, but he resented it coming from a comparative stranger—even if he was a prospective employer.

"What was the matter with them?" shot back Father indignantly. "I thought they were pretty funny myself. And I think I'm as good a judge of comedy as you are."

Harpo and Chico were writhing in their seats. This was no way to talk to a man who seemed to be the only one in Hollywood even remotely interested in hiring them.

"They were very funny pictures," answered Thalberg. "The trouble was they had no stories. It's better to be not so funny and have a story that the audience is interested in. I don't agree with the principle: anything for a laugh. For my money, comedy scenes have to further the plot. They have to be helping someone who's a sympathetic character. With a sound story, your pictures would be twice as good, and you'd gross three times as much."

"What about *Duck Soup?*" asked Father. "Didn't you like that?"

"It's just like the others," replied Thalberg unenthusiastically.

"Well, I didn't come here to be insulted," said Father. "If you just want to knock our pictures, I'd rather have lunch by myself, somewhere else. If you want to talk a deal, that's something else again."

Ultimatums, yet!

Harpo and Chico exchanged nervous glances, and wished their brother would keep his big trap shut for a change.

But, fortunately, Thalberg was more interested in signing them than he had let on. "No offense," he said to Father, with an apologetic smile. "I just thought it would be better for the four of us to understand each other before we actually started working together. If you're willing to go along with my theories, I think it can be very profitable for all of us."

From that point on, there was never any question about whether or not Father was willing to go along with Thalberg's theories. Now that it had been pointed out to him, he could see for himself what had been wrong with *Monkey Business*, *Horsefeathers*, and *Duck Soup*. The only thing that annoyed him was that he had been too stupid to realize it himself.

Father came home that day, enthusiastic about making pictures for the first time in five years. "I finally met a Hollywood producer who knows what he's talking about," he said at the dinner table that night. "Were we lucky to get out of Paramount's clutches!"

"Do you really think Thalberg is the genius everyone says he is?" asked Mother.

"If he isn't, he'll do until one comes along," replied Father.

Father was so elated over signing with the Thalberg unit at MGM that he had an addition built on to our playroom so we'd have space in the house for a regulation-size pool table.

Father had good cause for elation, for not only was he employed again, but he and his brothers had somehow managed to negotiate for themselves one of the most fabulous percentage deals in the history of Hollywood.

Percentage deals, where the participant gets a share of the net profits, are not uncommon. This sort of thing is done all the time. But the Marx Brothers had signed to do two pictures for fifteen per cent of the *gross*. There's a big difference. A picture can gross two million dollars and wind up showing no profit at all, if it was expensive to make and exploit. A percentage of the net profits will do you no good at all, in that case. But if your cut is off the top, the only thing that matters is how much business the picture does when it's released.

Soon after the Marx Brothers moved into their office on the Metro lot, the phone rang and it was a secretary, requesting that they be in Thalberg's bungalow for a story conference at three o'clock. Promptly at the appointed time, the three of them trooped into Thalberg's reception room, only to be told by the secretary that the producer wouldn't be able to see them until he had finished reading the script of another picture he was making.

"But we have an appointment," complained Chico.

"You'll just have to wait," said the secretary.

When a half-hour had gone by, and Thalberg still hadn't asked for them, Father and his brothers were fuming.

"How do you like that guy?" said Father. "Who does he think he is—Irving Thalberg?"

"I could have had a bridge game this afternoon," said Chico wistfully.

"We've got to do something," said Harpo.

After a hurried conference, they took out big cigars, lighted them and started blowing clouds of smoke under Thalberg's door. Pretty soon Thalberg noticed the smoke and rushed to the door to investigate. As Thalberg opened it and peered out, Father and his brothers stuck their feet in the door and wouldn't budge until the producer consented to let them in immediately.

Another time, they had an appointment with Thalberg for three o'clock and were still waiting at five-thirty, when even the secretary was preparing to leave.

"Just be patient," were her parting instructions as she left the bungalow. "He'll see you any hour now."

But their patience was exhausted. As soon as the secretary was out of sight, they shoved her desk in front of Thalberg's door, collected all the heavy, steel filing cabinets in the room and piled them on top of the desk. Then they went home.

It took Thalberg an hour to escape, and after that he always took care to be punctual when he had an appointment with the Marx Brothers.

Once they settled down to work, however, there were no more pranks, and Father and his brothers were amazed at how methodical Thalberg was about making a picture, even a slapstick comedy.

The first thing he insisted on was that their new picture have a dignified background. Upsetting dignity, he felt, was one of the basic musts of making a good comedy.

"Hit a fellow in old clothes with a snowball, and it won't mean a thing," explained Thalberg. "But dress a man up in tails and a silk hat, and then knock his hat off with a snowball, and you'll get a laugh."

After wracking their brains, they decided on grand opera. There couldn't be a more dignified background than that—and where else could you find so many silk hats to knock off? Secondly, their new picture had to have a believable love story. It didn't have to be as good as *Romeo and Juliet*, but it had to have some heart, nevertheless. Thirdly, the harp and piano solos had to go back in. Audiences loved them, even if they did slow up the action. And last of all, to put all this together, they needed writers who not only knew comedy, but who were good story constructionists, too.

"Well, when you find a good place to get those," said Father, "let me know. I'd like to buy half a dozen myself."

"What's the matter?" asked Thalberg. "You don't think there are any writers around who are any good for you boys?"

"I know two writers who are very good for us," said Father, "and their names are Kaufman and Ryskind."

"Let's get them," said Thalberg.

"We've tried," said Father, "but it's no dice. Kaufman says he won't go any place where he can't be in Times Square in twenty minutes."

"Let me try," said Thalberg, and within an hour he was on the long distance phone with George S. Kaufman and had persuaded him to tackle the job in collaboration with his old partner, Morrie Ryskind.

In addition to Kaufman and Ryskind, they also were fortunate in securing the services of a gag man named Al Boasberg. It was Boasberg's job to punch up the script and to originate sight gags for Harpo and Chico. Boasberg was no ordinary gag man. Many people, including Father, feel that he was probably the funniest man who ever lived. Whenever a group of comedians get together they get stars in their eyes at the mere mention of Boasberg's name and start regaling one another with Boasberg stories by the hour.

Boasberg had a rare gift. He wasn't much of a story constructionist, but no one could touch him when it came to dreaming up comedy routines or writing single jokes. Jack Benny used to pay him a thousand dollars a week just to look over his completed radio script and add a few jokes here and there. Benny felt that the quality of Boasberg's material was so good that even one joke a week from him was well worth the thousand dollars.

Like most big talents, Boasberg was what is known as a character. He was a large, heavy-jowled man—well over six feet tall and weighing about three hundred pounds—and he had an affinity for bathtubs and bathrooms.

He did about eighty per cent of his writing in the bathtub, immersed in hot water up to his neck. He kept a dictaphone by the tub, and another one next to the toilet. He also had a bookshelf filled with books in the glass-enclosed shower stall.

Father, Mother and I once spent a week with Boasberg at a dude ranch in Victorville. He spent the whole week in the bathtub, and only came out for meals and to sleep.

Because the stable was close by, there were hundreds of flies swarming around the ranch house. Outside Boasberg's window was an electric fly-killer that knocked off a fly about every five seconds. It made a buzzing sound with each fly that bit the dust.

After our first night there, Father asked Boasberg how he had slept.

"Not so good," replied Boasberg. "Every time I was about to drop off, the Warden would lead another condemned fly up the thirteen steps, and I'd hear the fly saying, 'You've got to believe me. I tell you I'm innocent. Don't send an innocent fly to the hot seat.'"

Boasberg could be very bitter about people he wasn't especially fond of, and he'd spend hours in the bathtub, thinking up stories to put them in a ridiculous light.

Once, after he'd had a fight with Joe Penner, for whom he'd been writing, he called up Father and said, "Groucho, I just bought a new radio that's the last word in radios. It's only been on the market a week, but it's so great the factory can hardly fill the orders."

Knowing how gadget-minded Boasberg was, and being that way himself, Father said, "Tell me about it. If it's so good, maybe I'll buy one myself."

"They're pretty scarce," said Boasberg. "Everyone is trying to buy one because it's got an amazing new gadget on it."

"What's it got that's so great?" persisted Father.

"I'll tell you what it's got," announced Boasberg. "It's a Joe Penner ELIMINATOR. No matter what station he's on, this radio won't pick him up—even if he's just doing a guest shot."

As talented as he was, Boasberg could not stand to be rushed. As soon as a producer tried prodding him into turning in more pages a day, Boasberg would purposely slow down. If the producer kept it up, there was no telling what Boasberg would do.

Once, after Thalberg had been hounding him for a couple of weeks to hurry up and finish a certain scene for *A Night at the Opera*, Boasberg phoned the producer and said, "Okay, Mr. Thalberg, I've got that material you wanted. But if you want it, you'll have to come over to my office and get it. I'm going home and leaving it here."

Father and his brothers were just as anxious to see the new material as Thalberg was, so the four of them walked over to Boasberg's office to pick it up.

But when they got there, they couldn't find the script anywhere. After considerable rummaging through desk drawers and filing cabinets, Father happened to glance up, and he saw some suspicious looking objects overhead.

Further investigation disclosed that Boasberg had torn the script into tiny pieces—each just large enough for one line of dialogue—and had tacked them all to the ceiling.

"It took us about five hours to piece it together," recalls Father. "But it was worth it, for it turned out to be the nucleus of one of the most famous scenes we've ever done—the stateroom scene!"

With all due respect to Kaufman, Ryskind and Boasberg, *A Night at the Opera* probably wouldn't have been a very good picture—much less a small classic—if Thalberg and the Marx Brothers hadn't hit upon a very revolutionary way of making comedies.

It came about one afternoon during a story conference in Thalberg's bungalow. The final version of the script was completed, they had all read it, and now Thalberg was asking Father what he thought the chances were of their having a hit.

Father gave the question considerable thought, and then said, "Frankly, Irving, I think the chances are pretty slim."

"What makes you say that? I think the boys did a pretty good job on the script."

"I think so, too," replied Father, "but somehow I just don't have any confidence in any comedy that hasn't been broken in on the road first, in front of a live audience. You just can't sit in an office in Culver City and know what they're going to laugh at in St. Louis. When we were on Broadway, we'd try a show out on the road for weeks before we'd bring it in to New York. Why do you think *Cocoanuts* and *Animal Crackers* were such good pictures? Because everything in them was sure-fire."

"Why can't we do the same?" asked Thalberg.

"You're joking, aren't you?" said Father. "How can you try a picture out on the road?"

"You don't have to take the *picture* on the road," said Thalberg. "You simply take what you think will be your five big comedy scenes, and put them together into sort of a vaudeville show. And play them in a few cities for a few weeks."

"How will the audience know what's going on?" asked Father. "The comedy scenes are part of the story. They'll be meaningless unless the audience knows what the story's about."

"Very simple," said Thalberg. "You just flash some narrative on a movie screen before each scene. In a few words, you can tell the audience which way the story is going at that point."

Father doesn't know whether this was a stroke of genius or not. In retrospect, Thalberg's idea seems like a pretty obvious solution to their problems—one that anyone could have thought of. But anyone didn't think of it. It was Thalberg's idea, and for that Father will always be grateful to him.

After a month of rehearsing on an MGM sound stage, the Marx Brothers struck out for the Northwest, to do six weeks of personal appearances in a cheaply produced vaudeville show called "Scenes from *A Night at the Opera.*"

They opened in a movie house in Seattle, and laid one of the biggest eggs in the history of the Marx Brothers, if not all show business. In their most pessimistic dreams, they had never imagined that the five best comedy scenes from the picture, as originally written, could be so far off the track, that they themselves could be so unfunny.

"But it proved my point—that our stuff just had to be tried

out," claims Father. "If we had shot A Night at the Opera with the material we opened with in Seattle, it would have been the end of all of us. Even the MGM lion wouldn't have been able to get a job."

Practically everything that had been written at the studio, except the basic story, had to be thrown out.

Today many people consider the stateroom scene from A Night at the Opera to be one of the funniest pieces of business ever shown on a screen. And it was one of the few scenes from the picture that Father had confidence in even before they worked it over on the road. Certainly it had all the basic elements of a good comedy situation—twenty people squeezed into a four-by-four cabin on an ocean liner, with Father trying to order dinner from room service, a plumber trying to repair some leaky pipes, and Harpo and Chico getting a manicure, all at the same time. But at the Seattle opening, it flopped along with the rest of the show.

Evidently it wasn't the kind of scene that could be written. Like most of their famous routines, it had to be worked out by the trial-and-error method, on the stage, in front of an audience. "That was the trouble with being a Marx Brother," says Father today. "We weren't like other comedians. We had to try everything out first. Otherwise we didn't work well together."

But as gloomy as their prospects for getting a good picture out of A Night at the Opera seemed in Seattle, there was one comforting thought. They could still save the picture by working hard on the road. For the next six weeks, they worked with beaver-like energy revising scenes and rehearsing. Morrie Ryskind and Al Boasberg made the trip with them, and they would sit in the audience with a secretary at every performance, making notes of the jokes and pieces of business that didn't get laughs, and trying, with considerable success, I might add, to think of new ones to take their places.

For a performer, this is the hardest work imaginable. There would be major changes in the dialogue to memorize and rehearse before every show, and they were doing five a day.

I wasn't along with Father on the *Night at the Opera* junket, but I have accompanied him on subsequent tours for other pictures, and I've always been amazed at the facility with which he can learn a big chunk of new dialogue on such short notice. Except for Harpo, it was hectic for the other actors in the cast, too, but since Father always had the most lines, the main burden of all this fell on him.

And he did plenty of griping about it. He was always saying during these tours, "Well, this is the last time I let myself in for anything like this. I'm getting too old to lead this kind of a life. If you have to go through this routine to make a good Marx Brothers picture, then I'm getting into another racket."

"Scenes from *A Night at the Opera*" wound up its tour at the Golden Gate Theater in San Francisco. Closing night, the Marx Brothers were in a state of great anxiety, for Irving Thalberg was in the audience to give his verdict, and if he didn't approve of their offering—after he had let them have their way about breaking in the material on the road, at considerable expense to the studio— he might not feel too kindly towards them. Conceivably he could even find a loophole in their contract and wiggle out of his commitment with them.

There was no reason, however, for such dire pessimism. The show had improved steadily since their Seattle opening, and the stateroom scene was now getting bigger laughs than anything they had ever done on the stage previously. During their first six days at the Golden Gate Theater, they had broken every existing house record.

"Nevertheless, that was the most nervous I've ever been in my life," recalls Father. "Facing Thalberg was worse than going up against all the New York critics."

Thalberg sat in the first row, and Father kept an eagle eye on him all through the performance, to see how he was reacting. Thalberg didn't crack a smile once—not even during the stateroom scene, which got yells from the rest of the audience. Father was sure that this was his swan song as a comedian. If not that, at least the Marx Brothers' finish with the Thalberg unit.

But when Thalberg came backstage after the show, he was all smiles. "You were right about playing the material on the road," he said, shaking hands with all of them. "What a difference! Now we're going to have a great picture."

"I don't get it," said Father. "I watched you tonight. You didn't laugh once."

"Well, this isn't the first time I've seen it," admitted Thalberg, with a grin. "I've been out front watching you for the past four days. But I didn't want to tell you I was here, for fear I'd make you nervous."

CHAPTER 21

THERE ISN'T much more to the story of *A Night at the Opera.*
Sam Wood directed the picture. Allan Jones and Kitty Carlisle
played the romantic leads. Margaret Dumont was back in the
line-up as Father's straight woman. And the Marx Brothers, after
their workout on the road, were again displaying the kind of form
that had put them on top on Broadway.

The picture, needless to say, was an immediate and huge success.
It got raves from most of the critics, it broke many a house record,
and it even contained a hit song, "Alone." It was the first time a
hit song had ever emerged from a Marx Brothers vehicle, another
tribute to Thalberg's producing talents. He had insisted that the
picture have something in it for everybody—even female picture-
goers.

Father had always felt that it was pointless to try to make a
broad comedy that would appeal to women, too. From past experience, he had found out that it was mostly men who enjoyed
the Marx Brothers. In fact, from time immemorial, it had been the
men of the world who enjoyed slapstick. Women preferred the kind
of picture where they could take out their handkerchiefs and have
a good cry.

But thanks to the Thalberg formula—road tour, songs, love
story and comedy—*A Night at the Opera* not only grossed more
than their earlier hits, but it was popular with women movie-goers,
too. And *A Day at the Races,* using the same formula outgrossed
its predecessor by more than a million dollars.

A *Night at the Opera* grossed over three million dollars, and it's still making money. As recently as 1949, Father and his brothers received a check from it for over thirty thousand dollars. A *Day at the Races*, using the same formula—road tour, songs, love story and comedy—grossed nearly four million dollars.

Two things happened while the Marxes were preparing A *Day at the Races* that made it extremely difficult for Father to be funny. While they were on tour in the East, breaking in the new comedy scenes, their father, who was living in Hollywood, suddenly became ill. The seriousness of his illness, however, had been underestimated by the doctors with the result that Father and his brothers felt that there was no necessity for leaving a company of forty-five people stranded in Cleveland just to come out and sit by Sam's bedside. So when the end came, very suddenly, only the four wives and Zeppo were with my grandfather.

According to the wives who made the bedside vigil, Sam was a true Marx up to the very end. Up to the day he died, at the age of seventy-three, he was still flirting with the nurses.

Father and his brothers were just getting over Sam's death, it seemed, when they received another blow. They were back in Hollywood by this time, shooting A *Day at the Races*, and everyone, including Thalberg, had high hopes that it would be another *Night at the Opera*.

The script, by Bob Pirosh, George Seaton, and George Oppenheimer, concerned the efforts of a certain Dr. Hackenbush (Father), who was really a horse doctor, and not a very good one at that, to save a ritzy sanitarium from going on the rocks. Horse racing entered into it because the sanitarium was close to a famous race track; and the hero, Allan Jones, owned the horse that won the big race at the finish (with Harpo in the saddle), thereby getting the money to pay off the mortgage.

The story was not quite the "natural" that the opera background had been, but the road tour had been a great success, and the Marx Brothers had come back from it with comedy scenes that were every bit as hilarious—if not more so—than the ones that had resulted from the *Opera* junket. So everyone had good cause to feel elated when they finally went into production.

They had been shooting for just three weeks when Thalberg came down with double pneumonia and died. He was only thirty-seven years old at the time, but he had always been a rather frail man, and he had worked much too hard for his own good. So when pneumonia hit, he just didn't have the strength to fight it off.

Father was really broken up—more so than I've ever seen him—for he was extremely fond of Thalberg personally, as well as a great admirer of his talents.

There were no jokes at the dinner table the night of the funeral. All Father had to say was, "Why is it the great men always have to go early? The schlemiels live to be a hundred."

Being human, Father was also upset about the loss for a very selfish reason. Thalberg had been the only one in Hollywood who seemed to understand the Marx Brothers. There was little likelihood that they would ever find another Irving Thalberg.

Actually, the production itself didn't suffer too much, for Thalberg had laid the important groundwork. The comedy scenes were solid from weeks of playing them on the road. And Sam Wood was again directing. But the completed picture lacked a certain indefinable something, and that something was undoubtedly the gifted touch of Irving Thalberg.

When they were deciding on a name for Father's character in *A Day at the Races*, they felt they should give him the most ridiculous moniker a doctor could possibly have—and one that would also imply "quack." After much mulling, they hit upon Quackenbush. It was so outlandlishly silly that it seemed as if there would be no danger of any real doctor having that name and taking offense.

But when it came time to shoot the picture, Metro's legal department informed them that there were dozens of real-life Dr. Quackenbushes throughout the country, any one of whom would probably sue at the drop of a hat.

"That's their hard luck," said Father. "Let them change *their* names if they don't like it. I've already got Quackenbush painted on my shingle."

Father's protests notwithstanding, the character's name had to be changed to Hackenbush. Since then Father has become so attached to the name that it's now replaced Jackson as his favorite pseudonym. He uses it all the time in everyday life, and has found that it comes in very handy when he's dealing with someone else's maid or secretary on the phone.

If he gets the usual, "Who's calling, please?" he's almost certain to reply:

"Who's calling? Why, Dr. Hugo Z. Hackenbush, of course!"

"I find I get a lot more respect when I pose as a doctor," maintains Father. "People who ordinarily wouldn't talk to me at all come to the phone right away."

Something else that didn't get into the released version of *A Day at the Races* was a song called "Dr. Hackenbush," written by Harry Ruby and Bert Kalmar. It's a satirical song, somewhat in the vein of "Captain Spaulding," and one of the funniest pieces of special material that I've ever heard. It got yells during the vaudeville tour, but the shooting script was much too long, and something had to go. Since Father is essentially a lazy fellow, and was not particularly anxious to go through the agony of shooting a musical number anyway, he saw to it that "Dr. Hackenbush" got the ax.

However, he has performed the number several times on various radio shows, and just last year he made a recording of it for Decca. "Dr. Hackenbush" is one of Father's favorite songs, and it's the number most often requested of him at parties.

Father is not a typical parlor entertainer. He's content to let others do the performing; he'd rather sit back and smoke his pipe, and make an occasional amusing remark. But if you twist his arm with enough diligence, he'll eventually agree to sing a song or two—especially if Harry Ruby is around to accompany him.

Once he gets to the piano, however, chances are he won't stop until he's exhausted his whole repertoire. And his repertoire is quite extensive. He has an unfailing memory for lyrics of old songs—some so old that even their composers don't remember having written them. One such song was a thing called "Down Below," a piece of anti-war propaganda that Irving Berlin wrote during the First

World War. Several years ago, Father exhumed it at a party where Berlin was also one of the guests. Berlin was so ashamed of it that he offered Father a hundred dollars if he'd promise never to sing it again. But Father wouldn't be bought off. He got too much fun out of heckling Berlin with it.

On another occasion, Father and Bing Crosby had a contest to see who could remember the lyrics to the most old songs. Crosby was forced to concede the match after the first hour, but during their musical interlude, Father came up with an old Berlin tune called "Play a Simple Melody." Crosby had never heard it before then, and he was so delighted with the song that he recorded it with his son, Gary, a few months later, and it turned out to be one of 1950's biggest hits.

But getting back to *A Day at the Races*, the last reel of the picture was shot at Santa Anita race track, shortly after the regular meeting was over.

The last sequence, naturally, was a horse race, with the hero's horse, High Hat, fighting it out neck and neck down the home stretch with the heavy's horse, Small Wonder. Of course, High Hat was to win by a nose, because the script said so.

Chico had read the script, too, but when he got out to the track he just couldn't control his gambling tendencies. Shortly before the race was to be filmed, Father caught him making a personal bet on the race with one of the extras—and Chico's money was on Small Wonder.

"I always thought you were crazy," said Father. "Now I'm sure of it."

"What's crazy?" shrugged Chico. "I just looked at the tote board and the odds on Small Wonder are 15 to 1."

With the success of *A Night at the Opera* and *A Day at the Races*, Father and Harpo were once again in extremely solvent financial shape. Father had learned his lesson in 1929. Since the crash he'd been entrusting his money to the care of a very wise and conservative Wall Street man named Salwyn Shufro. Harpo was also one of his clients, and Shufro had done very well by the two of them.

But Chico, though his share of those two pictures amounted to approximately three hundred and twenty-five thousand dollars before taxes, didn't have much more money in the bank than he did on the day, over forty years before, when he had lost his piano-playing job in a saloon.

Father considers anyone who gambles with big money extremely foolish, but he felt that Chico, of all people, had no business doing it, for Chico is probably the world's unluckiest gambler. He can bet on the surest thing on earth, and that will be the day that form will be reversed. The 1953 Kentucky Derby is the best example of typical Chico luck that I know of. Chico bought into a fifty-dollar pool at Hillcrest Country Club, and everyone congratulated him when he drew Native Dancer, who hadn't lost a race. But, as you no doubt know, the Kentucky Derby was the only race that famous colt lost in her first eighteen starts.

Recently a friend asked Chico how much money he has lost gambling during his entire career. Without stopping to think for even a second, Chico replied, "$1,232,147.62!"

"How do you know that's the exact figure?" asked the amazed friend.

"Because that's how much money Harpo has," answered Chico.

About the only one in the Marx family who was never too concerned about Chico's financial condition is Chico himself. But that didn't stop Father and Harpo from spending many a sleepless night worrying about it. If Chico wanted to throw his money away when he was young and had his whole career ahead of him, that was one thing. But now that they were all getting on in years, they told him that it was about time he started thinking about the future. Admitting they were right, Chico gave them his word that he'd save some money.

But when the financial returns from A Day at the Races began to pour in, and Father and Harpo saw Chico again letting the money slip through his fingers, they decided that there was little use in just telling him about it. Drastic measures would have to be taken—by them.

After *A Day at the Races*, Father and his brothers did one picture—*Room Service*—for RKO. In the meantime they had been negotiating a new deal with MGM. The MGM deal was all set but for the signing, when they finished *Room Service*.

However, for some strange reason, which Chico couldn't understand, Father and Harpo were taking their own good time about making an appointment at MGM to sign the contracts. Chico kept urging them to hurry and get it over with, but they continued their stalling tactics for three or four weeks.

By this time Chico was frantic, and finally he said to them, "What's the matter with you guys? Don't you want to sign?"

"Not particularly," answered Father calmly. "I'm in no hurry to go to work. I've got plenty of money, and we've been working pretty hard lately. I thought maybe I'd take a long rest."

"Me, too," echoed Harpo.

"How long?" asked Chico, worried.

"Oh, I don't know," answered Father casually. "Five or ten years, maybe."

"Me, too," said Harpo.

"Are you two nuts?" asked Chico. "We've got a great deal at Metro. Let's not fool around and lose it."

"Who cares?" said Father. "Now that Thalberg's gone, there's no one at MGM I'm crazy about working with, anyway."

"Yeah, I'd rather play golf," said Harpo. "My short game's not what it used to be."

"Come on, you guys," pleaded Chico. "What's the gag?"

"There's no gag," said Father. "We simply feel that there's no point in knocking ourselves out to make money when we already have plenty to live on very comfortably, and you just throw your share away, anyway. Of course, we might reconsider, provided a certain party, who shall be nameless, agrees to turn over at least half of his weekly earnings to us to save for him and invest as Shufro sees fit."

204

"Yeah, we don't want to wind up having to support you," added Harpo. "We have enough poor relations to support without taking you on. I agree with Dr. Hackenbush—no save your money, no deal."

"It's unconstitutional," screamed Chico.

"There's nothing in the constitution that says we have to work with you," said Father.

"You two are a cartel," protest Chico. "You're breaking the anti-trust laws."

Chico tried to argue them out of the scheme, promising that he would—and could—take care of his money without any help from them. But his pleas fell on deaf ears. In the end he had to capitulate and enter into the MGM deal on Harpo and Father's terms.

Salwyn Shufro has been handling their money ever since. When Father first met Shufro, he was a low-salaried investment counselor in a big brokerage firm. But Father had faith in him because he was both honest and cautious. He'd had his fill of sharp, go-getting characters who were only interested in speculation and a fast turnover so they could get more commissions. He liked Shufro's philosophy of only buying sound stocks for him—even if they never moved up or down.

In gratitude for what Shufro had done for them, Father, Chico, and Harpo bought him a solid gold watch, containing the following inscription:

From Groucho
to
Harpo
to
Chico
to
Shufro

Once a year, Shufro comes to Hollywood on business, and he always stays at Father's house. He's one of the few people Father will have as a house guest, for not only is he pleasant company, but it gives Father the opportunity to discuss Wall Street and to bone up on the world of high finance.

Father is no Henry Morgenthau, even after many years of association with his Wall Street friend, but naturally some of Shufro's knowledge has rubbed off on him, as you can see by the following letter, written to Shufro shortly after America entered the Second World War.

DEAR SHUF:

In view of the war—and the fact that generals are in such demand these days—I think it would be wise to invest in some generals—General Motors, General Electric and General Foods.

Sincerely yours,

HUGO Z. HACKENBUSH, M.D.

Father also always makes a point of dropping into Shufro's office, on Wall Street, when he visits New York. One day when Father was visiting him, Shufro suggested showing him the Stock Exchange. Father had never been there, and eagerly accompanied Shufro to the visitors' gallery. It happened to be the very busiest time of the day on the floor of the Exchange, and the trading that was going on was fast and furious. Father listened to the hubbub for a few moments, then stood up on a chair and in his loudest voice started singing "When Irish Eyes Are Smiling."

The trading stopped instantly, and all eyes suddenly were upon this lunatic in the gallery. No one recognized him, for he was still without mustache, but they all knew Shufro, and the Sergeant-at-Arms shouted to him to please quiet his visitor down. Being a very dignified gentleman, who wears a homburg hat and who has a respected position on Wall Street to uphold, Shufro was quite embarrassed.

"Groucho," he said, choosing his words carefully, "I'm afraid they don't appreciate clowning in the Stock Exchange."

When Father refused to be silenced by Shufro, the Sergeant-at-

Arms yelled up to him to pipe down or else he would call the police.

"Listen, you crooks," Father shouted back, "you wiped me out of two hundred and fifty thousand dollars in 1929. For that kind of dough, I think I'm entitled to sing if I want to."

CHAPTER **22**

AS MIRIAM and I grew older, it seems to me that life with Father got better. Or perhaps it wasn't really any better. Maybe I could just appreciate him more from a teen-age vantage point.

At any rate, the half-dozen years preceding World War II, when I was attending Beverly Hills High, Miriam was going to Hawthorne Grammar School, Mother was reading "Gone With the Wind," and Father was working at MGM and making occasional forays into the field of radio, were the ones I liked the best, because Father was at home so much.

Since Irving Thalberg's death, Father was taking less and less of an interest in going to the studio. He didn't like MGM without Thalberg, and apparently MGM was beginning to feel the same way about the Marx Brothers.

Father didn't approve of the studio's attitude which, to him, seemed to be: get the pictures made—it doesn't matter whether they are any good or not.

The Marxes would suggest what they thought were important and necessary changes, pertaining either to the script or the production of it, and the front office would come back with, "Why bother? We think it's okay the way it is." Or, "We've been in this business for years. We know what we're doing."

Coming on the heels of their very rewarding relationship with Thalberg, this made Father and his brothers pretty discontented. And they were fighting mad when the script of *A Day at the*

Circus was finished and the studio refused to let them try out the comedy scenes on the road.

"It's hopeless," Father would mutter, coming home from an irritating day at the studio. "They've seen what can be done when our pictures are made with some thought. And they've got the box office returns to prove it. And still they won't let us go on the road."

Father, as a matter of fact, was not very happy with his last three pictures at MGM, and he announced that when his contract was up he was going to quit.

"Why should I, at my age, let myself get upset over a movie—a movie that in three months will probably wind up on a double bill at the Oriental Theater, with bingo and free dishes?" he said one night. "It's not worth it. I'd rather retire than be constantly aggravated."

During his last year under contract to Metro, Father went to the studio as little as he had to, and spent most of his time around the house, supervising its management, writing an occasional magazine piece, and entertaining Miriam and me.

So what was bad for his career was good for us, for no adolescents ever had a better companion than Father.

There were some unhappy moments, too, for this was the period when the chasm between Mother and Father was beginning to widen quite perceptibly. The divorce clouds were only forming during these years. They didn't actually burst until I was twenty and living away from home. In the meantime, I enjoyed a pretty average American adolescence, complete with the regulation number of parents, a tomboy sister, dogs, report cards, braces on the teeth and no swimming pool.

Of course, it couldn't be completely average-American with a world-famous comedian as the head of the house. And Father realized this, too. In fact, he had long been aware of the pitfalls likely to be encountered by the children of celebrities, and he did his best to see that we had no more advantages or privileges than any of the other children in the neighborhood.

If anything, he leaned a little bit in the opposite direction. I know, for instance, that my allowance never kept pace with the weekly stipends my friends were getting.* He started me out in Great Neck with a nickel a week, and by the time I was a freshman in college I was getting a cool five dollars.† And all of this wasn't straight allowance. I had to work for half of it. I was supposed to dust Mother and Father's cars every morning before I left for school. I was supposed to, but I quickly discovered that the only time of the week when it was necessary for me to bother with the cars at all was on the morning of the day my allowance came due.‡

Actually, though my official allowance never reached the proportions I had hoped it would (if only for prestige purposes), I usually could get all the spending money I needed, within reason, by asking Father for it. He'd come through, but he liked to make me squirm for it. He wanted me to realize the value of money.

So if I were going to a movie in the middle of the week, and I had already spent my allowance, it would generally be with quite some trepidation that I'd approach Father in his study, where more than likely he would be reading or playing the guitar.

Perhaps, if I thought he was in a bad mood, I wouldn't even bring up the subject for five or ten minutes. I might just stand in front of the bookcase, with my hands in my pockets, nonchalantly looking over his books, or maybe I'd sit down at his desk and read over some of his more interesting mail.

"Well, what do you want?" he'd finally ask, peering at me over the rims of his glasses. "I know you're not just hanging around here because you're craving your old gray-haired father's company."

"I need some money to go to the movies."

"What?" he'd exclaim. "I thought I just gave you your allowance."

"Well, I spent it."

* Or even with the amount you spent. GROUCHO
† But don't forget—there was no withholding tax in those days. GROUCHO
‡ Don't think I wasn't on to what you were up to. GROUCHO

"On what?"

I'd tell him whatever it was I had spent it on, and he'd say, "Don't you know that money doesn't grow on trees? I have to work hard for every cent I make?"

I'd nod.

"Well, hereafter, see that you remember that," he'd say sternly, already reaching for the roll of one-dollar bills he generally kept loose in his pants pocket. "How much do you want?"

"Well, the show costs sixty-five cents, and I'll probably want to get a malt, and—"

"Here's two dollars," he'd say, not letting me finish, "and see that you go to the movies. Don't spend it on what I would have spent two dollars on when I was your age!"

Miriam had her troubles with her allowance, too. In addition to the fact that she seemed to have no difficulty at all going through her seventy-five cents a week, Father had discovered that the easiest way to keep her behavior in line was to take away her spending money. (He couldn't do this to me, because then there would be absolutely no chance of my dusting his car, and he was ever hopeful.) If it were an infraction of an important rule, like keeping quiet when he was sleeping, he'd simply take Miriam's allowance away for a week. But if she broke a piece of Meissen china, or an antique lamp, or something else around the house of any value, he'd make her pay for it out of her allowance, on the time-payment plan. The same thing applied to her own belongings that she happened to ruin through carelessness.

Since Miriam's allowance was even smaller than mine, it would frequently take her weeks to get out of the red. By then she would have demolished something else around the house, and the whole routine would have to be repeated.

Whenever Miriam had to go through these long financial droughts, Father would start to feel sorry for her around the end of the second week and let her borrow money on future allowances. But this required a good deal of bookkeeping and, as Father is easily confused when it comes to such matters, he'd eventually have to wipe out the whole debt and let her start over again with a clean slate.

When the subject of getting me my first car started cropping up at the dinner table with any regularity, Father was just as adamant against it as he was about letting Miriam and me have too much spending money. I was fifteen and had a driver's license by that time, but Father wanted me to wait until I was eighteen, for my own and other motorists' safety.

I couldn't see this at all. A car was a vital necessity, as far as I was concerned. The high school was a couple of miles from our house, the public transportation was very bad all over Los Angeles —and still is—and besides, a bicycle wasn't a very dignified means of transportation for a fellow who was already a varsity letterman and the heir-apparent to the captaincy of the tennis team.

But whenever I pointed these things out, Father's reaction was always the same:

"What do other boys do who haven't got rich fathers?"

It was an interesting question, but one which, at that age, didn't particularly concern me.

Knowing Father, I'm sure I could have broken down his resistance eventually, but fortunately I didn't have to go through the suspense of waiting very long.

In *A Day at the Races* there was a scene in which Dr. Hackenbush, the new chief of staff, was being introduced to the other doctors in the sanitarium.

"Johns Hopkins, '27," said the first bearded doctor, stepping forward and bowing to Dr. Hackenbush.

"Michael Reese, '22," said the second doctor.

"Mayo Brothers, '23," said the third doctor.

Then Dr. Hackenbush stepped forward and said, "Dodge Brothers, '29."

It wasn't a deliberate plug, but Chrysler Motors was so pleased that the company gave the Marx Brothers each a new Dodge. I wound up with the Dodge that had been given to Father, and his instructions were, as he turned it over to me, "Just remember that an automobile is a dangerous weapon in the hands of the wrong person. And if you must run over a pedestrian, be sure he's not in a crosswalk. Otherwise he can sue."

In some ways, Father was almost mid-Victorian in his thinking. He was always very strict about the time I went to bed. On school nights he'd hustle me off to my room sharply at nine, even when I was a senior in high school. On Friday and Saturday nights, he'd be a little more lenient. He'd let me stay out until ten or ten-thirty. But if I came in past then, he'd give me a long lecture the next morning on how a growing boy needed at least eleven hours sleep, and threaten to take my car away the next time it happened.

If he caught me, that is. Many nights he was out late himself and wouldn't know whether or not I came in a few minutes past the curfew. But on the nights he was home, it was very difficult to fool him, for his bedroom was right over the porte cochere, which you had to drive through in order to get to the garage, and Father, as you know, is a very light sleeper. He never failed to hear my Dodge roaring under his bedroom.

Deciding that something had to be done about this, I tried an experiment one night. I turned my engine off at the corner of our block and coasted down the hill, into our driveway and through the porte cochere and into the garage.

I was sure I had fooled him, but as I tiptoed toward the house, Father stuck his head out of the window, wiggled his eyebrows at me and said, "I still heard you."

In other ways, Father could be extremely modern and liberal-minded.

When I was eighteen I took up smoking a corncob pipe, unbeknownst to Father. One afternoon, when I was in my bedroom, puffing away on the pipe behind closed doors, I heard Father approaching down the hallway.

I quickly stashed the pipe, still lighted, in the drawer of my desk, and was sitting there with an innocent look on my face when Father opened the door and walked in.

He detected the smell of tobacco immediately and, without saying a word, turned around and walked back to his room. I was frightened, for I thought perhaps he had gone to get the snakewhip he kept in his closet (for what reason I never have found out).* But when he returned he was carrying one of his good Dunhill pipes and a can of tobacco.

"Here," he said, handing me the pipe first, "I think you'll like smoking this better than that cheap corncob you've been using. And here's a can of good tobacco. Now you can stop stinking up the house with that cheap stuff."

"Aren't you angry with me?" I asked.

"What for?" he said. "Smoking won't hurt you as long as you do it in moderation. And that goes for everything else you do, too. I've been smoking since I was seventeen, and except for the fact that I usually feel lousy, I'm fit as a fiddle."

"Moderation" is one of the inviolate rules governing Father's philosophy of life, and always has been. Many people think he is a heavy smoker because they see him with a cigar when he's performing. But actually he's one of the few people I know who has smoking completely under control. He never smokes before noon; he has one cigar after lunch and one after dinner; and after his evening cigar he'll generally puff on a pipe for a couple of hours. But that's the extent of his smoking.

He's just as moderate in his drinking and eating habits. An old-fashioned before dinner, and perhaps a glass of beer or wine with his meal will take care of him for a whole evening. If he drinks more he'll get a hangover. And he has never been a big eater. He can't be; he's too busy complaining.

In most respects, Father treated Miriam and me more like close friends than children. He confided in us about his business and matrimonial problems, we had private jokes that nobody else understood, and he liked to take us with him wherever he went, provided we wouldn't be too much out of our element.

* *It was a gift from a snake.* GROUCHO

214

And he'd be pretty disappointed if he wanted to take Miriam and me to a movie or to a ball game, and we chose to go out with people our own age.

"That's all right," he'd say. "You young folks run along and have a good time. Don't worry about me. I'll be dead in a few years." There's nothing Father enjoyed more than playing the martyr. It gave him an endless supply of household humor, even if there was no basis of truth to it. And usually there wasn't. If Mother, Miriam and I went out to the movies, and Father stayed home alone, it would be of his own choosing.

During our school days he'd keep Friday and Saturday nights open for movie-going with the family, and while he and Mother were having their dinner coffee, the four of us would sit around the table, with the paper open to the entertainment section, trying to find something that we could all agree on. Finding a movie to suit the tastes of four people is difficult enough for the average family, but with the restrictions imposed on us by Father, it was practically impossible.

"The new Humphrey Bogart picture is at Warner's Hollywood," Mother would say.

"I don't want to drive all the way to Hollywood," Father would answer. "It's too far."

"Well, what about the Fox-Beverly? Joel McCrea in *Union Pacific*.

"No good," he'd say. "You can't smoke there."

Father wouldn't—and still won't—go to any theater where you can't smoke, if he can avoid it. He'd rather see a bad picture and be able to smoke than a good picture and have to abstain from tobacco all evening. And since there are only a couple of theaters in Los Angeles where smoking is permitted, Mother would eventually have to remark, and with quite some indignation:

"Well, if you just want to smoke, why don't you stay home?"

"Good idea," Father would say. "You three go. I have a lot of magazines to catch up on anyway."

If, as we were rushing out the front door, I'd ask him if he minded staying home alone, he'd say, "No, don't worry about whether I have anything to do or not. I'm *only* your father."

Miriam came home from a matinee one Saturday, and Father asked her what she had seen.

"The Ritz Brothers," exclaimed Miriam. "Boy, they're *really* funny!"

"Well, if that's the way you feel about it," said Father, "let the Ritz Brothers buy you that new bike you want."

"Oh, Daddy, I didn't mean that you're not funny, too."

"That's all right. Don't bother to explain," said Father. "You've shown your true colors. Just don't come hanging around me the next time you want something. Ah, yes, 'How sharper than a serpent's tooth it is to have a thankless child.' *King Lear*, Act I, Scene 4."

"Oh, Daddy, don't be so corny."

"I used to have a line in *Animal Crackers*: 'You have to be a parent in order to find out how much your children hate you.' How true, how true!"

Father reveled in the disrespect of his children. He'd pounce on any innocent remark or incident around the house and build it up into a routine. And for my money, this was when he was at his funniest.

Being constantly around someone as amusing and stimulating as Father made it pretty difficult for us not to be bored with the company of children our own age.

However, I do know of one time when Miriam wasn't very happy about having a father who was so available. If he had gone to work during the day like other fathers, he never would have got the chance to damage her reputation by attending one of the PTA meetings at Hawthorne School.

Ordinarily, Father took great care to avoid school social affairs. So did Mother. Not that they weren't interested in our schooling; they both were a big help when it came to homework. Father, in fact, wrote two essays on Americanism for me that won prizes in school competition. Not only that, he wrote my graduation speech.*

But neither Mother nor Father was particularly willing to make the ultimate sacrifice of spending any afternoons at PTA meetings. Personally, I couldn't have cared less, but for some reason or other it annoyed Miriam that her family was represented at the meetings so infrequently. And one day she mentioned her gripe to Father, who said, "Well, if your Mother won't go to the next PTA meeting, I will."

It was a magnanimous gesture, even for as doting a parent as Father, and no one really expected him to keep his word. But at the appointed time he walked into the auditorium at Hawthorne and sat down in the front row among the other parents, mostly women. No one recognized him as Groucho Marx because he was clean-shaven, but Miriam, who was stationed at the refreshment stand in the back of the auditorium, was proud to see him there, anyway.

Father behaved himself astonishingly well from the time the president called the meeting to order until the treasurer of the PTA, an imposing-looking dowager in a flowered dress, started giving her report. He listened in martyred silence as the treasurer reeled off, in a high-pitched voice, page after page of dull facts and figures. But when she climaxed her report with the announcement that the PTA had spent eight dollars and ninety-seven cents for tea during the month of May, Father could no longer restrain himself.

Jumping to his feet, he shouted, "What kind of tea?"

Taken aback, but still in command of the situation, the treasurer said, "Why, orange pekoe, of course."

"Why wasn't I consulted?" exclaimed Father indignantly. "I happen to like Chinese tea!"

"We've always used orange pekoe," replied the treasurer, obviously wondering who this madman was. "And I think we all enjoy it."

* And as I recall, you got big laughs with it, too. GROUCHO

217

"Well, I don't," snapped Father. "And I'm not so sure the rest of these people do, either. They're just a bunch of sheep who'll drink any swill that's given to them."

"Please sit down," said the president, also getting into the argument.

"I will not," said Father. "I'm a citizen and a taxpayer and I have a right to drink the kind of tea I like for a change. I demand that we take a vote!"

This threw the meeting into an uproar, and before order could be restored, the president had to request Miriam to escort her unruly father home. Feeling completely humiliated, Miriam burst into tears the moment the two of them were outside, and didn't speak to Father again until the next time she wanted her allowance.

CHAPTER 23

A GOOD DEAL of our family life in those days revolved around the game of tennis. Everyone was playing—even Father.

Father had always been an ardent follower of the sport. He had watched Tilden and Johnson and Cochet and the rest of the greats of that era batting the ball around at Forest Hills, and he had also done some playing himself. Not at Forest Hills, but in Central Park.

Except as a spectator, he had given up the game during the years he was torturing himself on the golf course. And had I not shown an interest in tennis when I was in grammar school, I'm sure Father would have remained retired permanently. But I was swinging a racket every day, and by the time I was thirteen, professional tennis stars Ellsworth Vines and Fred Perry, who own the Beverly Hills Tennis Club, told Father that they thought I had a good chance of becoming a ranking player. This was all Father had to hear. His old enthusiasm for the game returned immediately.

Not only did he take out a family membership at the Beverly Hills Tennis Club, but one day, shortly afterward, he announced that he was coming out of retirement. (He had some free time on his daily calendar, right between lunch and his afternoon nap.)

Since amateur tennis was pretty much in the doldrums around that time—America hadn't won the Davis Cup in a number of years—Father's announcement that he was going to start bludgeoning the ball again naturally created quite a stir in the racket-wielding world.

Father had the "big game." It wasn't good, but it was big. His forehand, even though he frequently hit the fence with it, was probably his most formidable weapon, and it soon became known to the other club members as "Iron Mike." I'm not sure who first dubbed it this, but I think it was Father.

His other big forte was sitting on his racket between points, his legs astraddle, his racket propping him up, while waiting for his doubles partner to retrieve the balls, or his opponent to get into position. And sometimes, if he had a strong partner, he'd sit on his racket during the playing of a point. No other tennis player has ever mastered the science of racket-sitting to such a degree.

Because he played a scientific game, Father was extremely fussy about the kind of tennis racket he used. One day when Father was picking out a new racket the boy in the tennis shop handed him a Spalding–Bill Tilden model to try out. Father handed it right back.

"I can't play my best game with an American racket," he said. "They're too uncomfortable. Give me one of those Australian models, with the flat head. They're better for sitting."

Sometimes, when she couldn't avoid it, Mother would be Father's partner in doubles. But they were not a good team because she took her tennis too seriously.

"For goodness' sakes," she'd say to him when he was about to receive service, "will you please get off your racket and be ready, for a change? We need this point."

"Listen, Helen Wills, don't worry about me," Father would say, remaining calmly on his racket. "I can handle my side of the court. They don't call me the Old Gray Fox for nothing, you know. Just take care of your side of the court, Helen, and we won't have a thing to worry about. I'll give 'em Iron Mike."

He'd still be in the process of getting off his racket when the ball would fly past him for an ace.

"Some fox!" Mother would exclaim with a derisive laugh. "What happened to Iron Mike?"

"Never you mind, old girl," he'd say, nonchalantly propping himself up with his racket again. "Just remember, the race isn't always to the swift."

According to Mother, it would always be Father's fault when they lost a doubles match. He'd take this for a couple of weeks, and then his fighting blood would come to the fore, and he'd challenge her to a singles match. He heartily disapproved of men in their middle forties playing singles, but in this case he was willing to make an exception.

Actually, Mother was the better player, but Father, by some devious strategy, always managed to win. He'd lob her to death, which she felt was terribly unsporting. And if this didn't work he could talk her into submission.

"Well," Father would say to Miriam and me in a gloating tone at the dinner table, the night of one of these victories, "ask your mother how she came out against the Old Gray Fox today."

"You're certainly not going to count today's match," Mother would scoff. "You know I couldn't play up to my usual game with a blister on my hand."

"I don't know about that," Father would say. "All I know is that when the smoke cleared away, I was the victor. Thoroughbred blood. It always tells in the final analysis."

"Thoroughbred blood—that's a laugh. You were extremely lucky."

"Lucky?" he'd reply. "I prefer to think it was Iron Mike that made the difference. No human being can stand up against Iron Mike when I want to turn it on. And you know that, old girl, as well as I," he'd conclude, wiggling his eyebrows at her.

And after dinner perhaps he'd sit down at the piano and annoy Mother with ten or eleven choruses of a parody he had made up that was sung to the tune of "Just Break the News to Mother." I don't remember all of it, but the first two lines were:

> Just hit the ball to Mother,
> And you won't have to hit another.

No man, not even his idol, Charlie Chaplin, could emerge from a match with Father completely unscathed. The occasion for their match was the grand opening of the Beverly Hills Tennis Club's new clubhouse. The feature court attraction of the day saw the best that America had to offer pitted against the best of Great Britain. America was represented by Father and Ellsworth Vines, and Great Britain by Charlie Chaplin and Fred Perry.

The match had been given a good deal of publicity, so in addition to reporters and newsreel men, there was a large crowd of tennis fans on hand.

Chaplin played about the same brand of tennis as Father, but he took it seriously and was very jittery before the match. He wanted to win, and was scared to death of playing before such a large crowd.

Father had never played in front of that many people before either, but he wasn't a bit scared because, as he told Mother while she was giving him a rubdown before the match, "I've got Iron Mike on my side."

Not only Iron Mike, but, when he finally walked out on the court with Vines, Chaplin, and Perry, he was carrying twelve rackets and a large suitcase. To Chaplin's annoyance, he refused to divulge the nature of the suitcase's contents.

"Never mind what's in there," he told Chaplin. "Do I go around asking you what's in your suitcase?"

"I haven't got a suitcase," replied Chaplin, failing to see the humor in the situation.

"Well, why the hell haven't you?" asked Father in a loud voice. "What kind of a tennis player are you, going around without a suitcase?"

Father played the first two games of the match quite seriously, with disastrous results. Chaplin and Perry won both games. Then, with Perry about to serve, and Chaplin up at the net, Father, still sitting on his racket, held up his hand to stop the play.

"What's the matter?" asked the annoyed Chaplin.

"I just want to warn you that I'm going to give you Iron Mike," said Father, "so you'd better get down behind the net. I don't want to be responsible for hurting you."

The laughter of the crowd so unnerved Chaplin that he could hardly hit a ball in the court after that.

And just to make sure that there would be no more serious tennis play, Father got his suitcase from the referee's stand, brought it back to midcourt, opened it, and started spreading a picnic lunch out on a blanket.

"Have a spot of tea?" he asked Chaplin.

"Let's play tennis," demanded Chaplin. "I didn't come here to be your straight man."

"We're ready," said Father, munching on a sandwich. "Vines can do all my playing for me."

Needless to say, the match broke up a couple of games later, with neither side emerging the victor.

During the days when the Old Gray Fox was still prowling the courts of the Beverly Hills Tennis Club, he and I had a favorite match we liked to play. He'd take either Ellsworth Vines or Fred Perry as his partner, and I'd play with Mickey Levee, another junior tournament player, and the four of us would go to it.

When we first started playing these matches, my partner and I were about fourteen, and we'd get drubbed. As time went on and our games improved, it became increasingly difficult for either Vines or Perry to overcome the handicap of playing with Father, for he was without doubt the worst man player at the club. We were still losing, but every match would be very close.

Then one day, when we were about sixteen, Mickey and I beat Father and Vines.

"Don't get cocky yet," said Father. "Tomorrow I'll play you boys with Perry, and that'll be a different story."

So on the following day he played us with Fred Perry. Father was sure that he and Perry could turn the tables. After all, hadn't Perry wrested the world's professional title from Vines a few months before?

But when he lost with Perry too, Father realized that the whole

223

thing was pretty hopeless and decided that the time had come to hang up his racket for good.

"If I can't beat a couple of school boys with the two best players in the world as partners, then I think I'm definitely past my prime," muttered the Old Gray Fox, making the announcement that officially ended his playing days. "I want my fans to remember me as the great player I was—not the hollow shell of a man I am today. There's nothing more pathetic to see than the crumbling of a man."

With golf, tennis and yachting out of the way, Father was now free to confine his sporting activities to brisk walks around the block, rooting for the Hollywood Stars baseball team, and watching me play tennis.*

Father was as serious about my tennis as he wasn't about his own. When I was fourteen, I could beat most of the men at the Beverly Hills Tennis Club. The only two I couldn't beat were Gilbert Roland and Norman Krasna, who took turns at being at the top of the tennis ladder. Father didn't mind my losing to anyone else, but he couldn't stand it when Krasna would beat me because Norman would gloat about it when he came to dinner.

So one day Father asked Vines what would be the best thing I could do to improve my game, now that I was past the beginner's stage. Vines recommended tournament play, and since I was agreeable, I devoted the next six years of my life to becoming a tennis bum. I'd go straight to the tennis club from school. On Saturdays and Sundays I'd be at the club from nine in the morning until sundown. Our whole family ate, drank and talked tennis. And I played in all the tournaments.

From the first, this was quite a strain on Father, for even though I was starting out in the fifteen-years-and-under division, the competition was stiffer than any of us had bargained for. In addition to a number of other excellent boy players, Jack Kramer and Ted Schroeder were also in the fifteen-and-under division, and since

* And cleaning out the incinerator. GROUCHO

224

they had already been playing competitively for a couple of years, their games were considerably better than mine.

This was never more evident than on the day Father and Mother drove me to Long Beach where I was to play a second-round match in one of my first tournaments. Father was pretty elated that I had reached the second round, and since none of us recognized the name of the boy I was to play next—Kramer—it looked as if I had a chance to go pretty far in this tournament.

Before we knew it, we were back in Beverly Hills, licking our wounds. I had lost 6–0, 6–0.

"Well, Flatfeet," Father said after the match, "it looks as if your game needs a little more work. You kept rushing the net and the ball kept flying past you. What kind of business is that, after I've raised and supported you all these years?"

Though he frequently joked about my losses, he felt worse about them than I did, but thinking I needed comforting, he'd always wind up by saying, "Don't worry about it. It's only a game. It's not very important. Fifty years from now it won't make the slightest difference whether you lost to Kramer today or not."

But despite this false bravado, he'd get so nervous when he was watching me play that he couldn't bear to sit next to my mother, and eventually he'd have to move to another section of the grandstand.

Mother would become more overwrought than Father, and on top of this she was always moaning about the bad calls she thought I was getting from the referee or linesmen.

"For the love of Mike, keep quiet!" Father would say, if they were sitting together. "The bad calls even themselves up. Arthur is just playing like a schlemiel, that's all. Look at how he's rushing the net. He gets caught halfway in every time."

Although I was getting all kinds of professional instruction, there would be plenty of Monday-morning quarterbacking around our home after an important loss. After I'd been playing in junior tournaments for several years, there wasn't anyone in our house, with the possible exception of Duke, our police dog, who didn't know more about how to play Kramer and Schroeder and the rest of the boys than I did.*

But the only time Father would actually get angry at me for losing a match was when he thought it was because I had broken training. Then he'd really lay into me.

"Listen here, sonny boy," he'd say in his grimmest tone, "if you expect me to pay out good money for rackets and lessons and sending you around to all the tournaments, then you're going to have to take this thing more seriously. You can't stay out until twelve or one o'clock in the morning, necking in that little Dodge of yours, and expect to play tournament tennis. I'll bet you Kramer and Schroeder are in bed every night at seven o'clock."

My wife Irene, who was then my girl friend, still shudders when she thinks of one match I lost when she and Father were watching from the same box. Every time I missed an important point, Father would turn around and glare at her, as if to say, "It's all your fault —keeping my son out so late." And when we all drove home together, Father wasn't speaking to anyone.

After I had played in tournaments for several years, the gap between myself and the other junior players wasn't so wide. When I was seventeen, in fact, I was ahead of Ted Schroeder in the Southern California rankings, and had even beaten Kramer once.

By then, the strain on Father was beginning to tell. His nerves couldn't take it any longer. He retired from watching me play, except on rare occasions.

That left it strictly up to Mother to bear the Marx standard in the grandstand. Mother carried on for another year, loyally going from tournament to tournament with me, cursing out the linesmen under her breath and always insinuating that they were deliberately plotting against me.

At the dinner table, after an unexpected setback, Mother would usually exclaim: "Well, you should have seen that decision Arthur got in the second game of the third set. It was positively shameful. Van Horn hit the ball at least three feet into the alley, and the

* And I'm not so sure that Duke didn't, either. GROUCHO

226

linesman didn't open his mouth. And it was probably the deciding point of the match. Up until then it was very even."

"Unfortunately," Father would point out, "the only thing anyone is interested in is who won. When it goes down in the record book, they don't say 'Van Horn won the tournament, but Arthur Marx's mother claims he wouldn't have if her son hadn't got a bum call.'"

Pretty soon Mother couldn't take the nerve strain any longer either, and she, too, stopped going to tournaments. After that, the only time I ever saw either one of them on the sidelines was when I'd be fortunate enough to have reached the finals, or else when I was playing one of the big-name seniors against whom I wasn't expected to win.

Mainly because of me, all my uncles and their wives had become tennis-minded, too, and they would also come to the finals if I were playing. They were desperately anxious to see me win, for no other Marx had ever succeeded in distinguishing himself in any sports but the ones where cards and pool cues were the main weapons, and they wanted me to show the world that we were a family of athletes as well as comedians.

But I don't think they ever saw me win a finals. There was a period of about a year where I was runner-up in about nine different tournaments. In one of the tournaments I had scored a whole series of upsets to reach the men's singles finals of the Los Angeles Metropolitan Championships. With Harpo, Chico, Gummo, Zeppo and Father looking on, I failed to win more than a game a set against a man I was favored to beat. Every time I'd lose a few games, I'd glance over at the grandstand and one more Marx would be leaving in disgust.

When the match was over, only Father was left. "They were like rats leaving a sinking ship," said Father. "And boy, was it sinking! What happened? Out with Irene again last night?"

Devoting as much time to tennis as I did, I naturally found it very convenient to start neglecting my schoolwork, piano practicing, and reading. Father realized this, and it began to worry him.

227

One day, right after I'd lost another finals, I was with Father in his study, telling him what I thought was the reason for the loss—some flaw in my stroking—and adding that that afternoon at the club I had corrected the weakness. I thought he'd be pleased, and went on with considerable enthusiasm, but suddenly he drew me up short with a tirade I'll never forget.

"You're getting to be a real tennis bum, aren't you?" he said. "You don't think about anything else any more. To hear you talk, that's all there is to life. I don't think you've read a book in weeks or practiced the piano or done anything else that'll do you any good. And God knows how you're doing in school, though I imagine not very well. And what about your writing? You claim you want to be a writer, but do you ever write anything?"

I reminded him that I was one of the editors of the *Highlights*, the school newspaper.

"Only of the sports section!" he said. "Well, that's not good enough. Hereafter you're going to have to change your ways, and wake up to the fact that there's something else going on in the world besides tennis. I'd like to see you get to the top in tennis, too, and I'll do everything I can to help you, but not at the expense of everything else. Just remember, only one man can win at Forest Hills, and the odds are pretty long. There's probably not a hell of a lot of difference between the champ and the ones who don't quite make it. But only the very top can make a decent living out of the game. The rest, if they keep on playing, starve to death."

I told him I realized all that, that I'd try to change my ways.

"Okay," he said. "Now what was it you were saying about your backhand? You're going to try hitting it flat instead of slicing it? Maybe I ought to get Vines to work out with you again before you go East this summer."

It was an old trick of his in those days. He liked to make me feel as bad as he possibly could, so I'd remember his fatherly advice, and then he'd pick me right up again. He had no intention of making me quit. He was getting too big a kick out of seeing his son's name on the sports page. And as soon as I was ready to play in the more important grass-court tournaments in the East, he sent me to them without a moment's hesitation.

I spent the three summers preceding Pearl Harbor bumming around the Eastern tournaments. My tennis record was so-so, but the letters I received from Father, over those three summers, made the tours worth while, if for no other reason. They contain some pretty revealing glimpses of Father holding down the fort at home:

Summer of 1940
DEAR ART:

For a tennis bum, you're certainly leading a luxurious existence and I only hope you can keep it up. I see by the papers that it rained in St. Louis yesterday so that you had time to eat six meals in the hotel instead of the customary three.

Just came back from five days at Lake Arrowhead. It's a wonderful spot, and I expect to spend a good deal of time there in the future. We had a fine time on the lake, sailing. With the wind on my back, I was Sir Thomas Lipton, but when I tried to tack against it and into home plate, I botched it up completely and finally had to haul down the sail and suffer the humiliation of being towed back to port by a motor boat. This made Miriam very happy, for during the whole voyage she kept telling me that I didn't have the faintest idea of how to manipulate a sailboat and predicted that it would only be a question of time before I'd have to be towed back to shore. Anyhow, it was swell, and if I had a stronger stomach I would spend a good part of my declining years on the bounding waves. That's really the life. You require no golf ball, no caddies, no rackets or busted gut. All you need is a stout heart, a strong back, plenty of wind and a castiron stomach. Avast, mates! Yo-ho and a bottle of rum! Tonight I'll listen to Pinafore on the Capehart.

We expect to start shooting around July first, so for the next eight weeks you can reach me on the back lot at MGM. Please bring ice packs and menthol.

I'm brushing up on all the pictures. I saw Strange Cargo and was having a pretty good time until the head usher at the Marquis Theater tapped me on the shoulder and sharply told me that there was no smoking at that theater. He walked away and I began smoking. Again he tapped me on the shoulder—another warning. This time he didn't walk away—he just stood there, arms folded, and glared at the back of my head. Then my cigar went out, and then I went out. Sometime, I wish you'd let me know what happened in the last four reels.

Last night, I saw Waterloo Bridge at the Westwood Theater. It's quite a bit different from the old version. MGM, being a more leisurely studio, didn't make the girl a streetwalker until the fourth reel. In the other version, they went to bat with the little lady hustling on Waterloo Bridge. I liked it better that way—you can get home earlier.

I can't write any more at this time as I have to take dancing lessons for the next three days. Our friends, the Arthur Murrays, have bestowed the lessons upon us gratis, which, you can be sure, is the only reason I am submitting to them.

Saturday night, the Beverly Hills Tennis and Bad Food Club is throwing a barn dance and it's going to be a terrific sensation. How surprised we'll all be when we gather there that evening to see all of those new faces that we had left only an hour before on the tennis court. The food won't be served until midnight, so I've arranged with your mother to have mine brought up to my bed. Three dollars is a lot of money to pay for the privilege of eating stale delicatessen food and listening to Dave Fowler's wife, who used to be a showgirl, sing a medley of airs from The Chocolate Soldier. If this keeps up, I may take to drinking in a serious way. I've often wondered why people drink—now it's gradually beginning to dawn on me.

Last night the club threw its barn dance and surprisingly enough it was a big success. They had ninety people, a good band and open-air dancing around the pool. The catering was delegated to Levitoff, the demon pastrami prince, and the crowd ate like wolves and

230

drank like stevedores. If it weren't for the police the party would still be going, but at the fatal hour of two the cops arrived, brandishing their clubs, and announced that the band would have to cease firing or continue playing at the local jail. This sent most of the members and their friends to the bar, but the departure of the musicians dampened the ardor of the survivors and shortly after that they began wending their way homeward. This was quite a blow to many of them as home is something they don't like to contemplate.

The disturbing phase of the party is the fact that because of its success the girls are already beginning to discuss the next one, whether to have white tie and tails or have everybody come as coal miners. At any rate, the club cleared a nice profit at the bar. Many of the members, for example, decided to try to drink the club out of its deficit, and with the help of a few guests, who also gave up their kidneys for the good of the club, a healthy profit was cleared. It was heartening to see these members sacrificing themselves for good old Beverly, and I know they can always be relied upon in the future to do their bit to ward off the sheriff's writ of attachment.

I notice that you disappeared rather abruptly from the Baltimore Tournament and it must have been the day you played Elwood Cooke. There was no mention of it in the local papers. I've come to the conclusion that it's not so hot being the father of a tennis player. Hundreds of people, to whom I wouldn't talk normally, rush up to me and immediately begin a long, involved tennis conversation, explaining why you either won or lost in the last tournament. As you know, I'm deeply interested in your athletic progress, but not to the extent that I want to discuss it twelve hours a day. Now I have a new answer whenever anyone rushes up and asks me how you're doing at whatever tournament it happens to be. I say, "Don't you know? He's quit the game and taken up squash." This baffles them. A lot of people have only heard of squash in a cafeteria and they can't understand why anyone should want to stand in a restaurant and throw vegetables.

231

Go West has again been postponed. I don't know why the studio doesn't come right out and say they are afraid to make it. All I hear from the studio is an announcement once a week that I should come to the wardrobe department and be fitted for a pair of early American pants. They have been taking some big hacks at the story and from what I hear we should be able to shoot the whole thing in three days, once we actually begin. Irving Brecher (one of the authors) says this picture will be known as the longest short ever made. Well, it doesn't bother me. My attitude is, take the money and to hell with them. I had my hair darkened about three weeks ago, to match my grease-paint mustache, but it has been so long since we were scheduled to start that the dye has faded and I will have to go and have it done all over again. So you see my theatrical career has dwindled down to being fitted once a week for a pair of early American pants and having my hair dyed every three weeks. This is a fine comedown for a man who used to be the Toast of Broadway.

When I picked up the paper Tuesday morning, I read that you had been eliminated by Gilbert Hunt. A few moments later I discovered that you had been eliminated by Gilbert Mumps. We received your wire at eight Thursday morning, but since it was addressed to Mrs. Ruth Marx (why not the Groucho Marxes I don't know), I assumed it was a personal wire to your mother and therefore I didn't open it. Around eleven your mother arose, and then I found out that you were in the hotel at Seabright, swollen up with mumps, and I imagine pretty well disgusted with the whole thing. At any rate, that's life. You will encounter all sorts of these little upsets as you journey along, and you will have to learn to adjust yourself to them or gradually go nuts.

According to the wire, you are resting well and are being taken care of by a nurse. I hope she is beautiful and that she has red hair. I don't know why it is, but whenever I think of a nurse I always imagine she should have red hair. It makes a man want to recover his health quickly, so that he will have the strength to get on his feet and get her off hers.

Glad to hear from you this morning and to know that you are recovering your health. I am also pleased to learn that you have a rich dame who wants to put you up while you are recuperating. It's about time you got a rich gal. How does she have her money? In jewels or securities, or just plain gold? Some night, when you are sitting with her in the moonlight, you might find out. Do it discreetly, for God's sake. Don't come out bluntly and say, "How much dough have you got?" That wouldn't be the Marxian way. Use finesse. You wouldn't want her to think you were after her money. Well, I will leave the whole thing to you. I know you will be careful and get her bankroll without a disagreeable scandal.

I am sorry to hear that you haven't prettier nurses. I think they do the whole thing wrong. The patient should be permitted to have a test of the nurses, the same as Earl Carroll and George White have previews of their girls before they finally engage them. After all, it's the patient who has to look at the nurses, and I'm sure that the recovery would be much more pleasant, if not quicker, if the babe had soft hands and nice teeth instead of looking like that hag you've been describing.

I wish you would let me know about each letter as you receive it. I wrote you about this once before. For example, I sent you a check for a hundred dollars the other day and you have never even acknowledged it. Now I don't know whether you have it, or whether it is in Farley's pocket. What is this reluctance on your part to acknowledge the receipt of a letter? Is it the gamin in you? Are you just prankish and full of fun, or do you regard the whole thing as a game, and the winner the one whose opponent never finds out whether any of his mail has ever been received?

The house is pretty quiet these days. The cook is on her vacation, and your mother and sister are up at Lake Arrowhead trying to snare some unsuspecting males onto the dance floor. I have the

233

house to myself and for a change it's not bad. But I wouldn't like it permanently.

(The following letters were written in the summer of 1941, when Father was beginning to get ideas about quitting pictures after the termination of his MGM contract and branching out into radio.)

Gummo tells me that the Tommy Riggs show, which I spurned, now has a Crosley rating of seventeen. This will give you an idea of how little I know about audiences and what they want. I guess I missed the boat with that one. I am sure, however, that other radio shows will come along. Radio comedians die, I know, and they will need other comics to replace them. I am going to take good care of my health and when the next radio comic dies, I will go to the funeral, disguised as a pall bearer, and strike up an acquaintanceship with the sponsor who, I am sure, will have to attend the funeral, if only for appearances. Before you know it, I will be on the air, killing the audiences with my rapier wit and personality.

I feel pretty smart today. I just finished reading your Reader's Digest for July, and I know now why the Boston and Maine Railroad has had a comeback, why Japan is tiring of the war in the East, and the proper way to bring up a child. It also contains a condensation of Budd Schulberg's book, What Makes Sammy Run, and a very amusing portrait by Stephen Leacock of an uncle of his. So now you don't have to read the Digest for this month. In my next letter I will tell you all about the Atlantic Monthly.

I was hopeful of getting a letter from you today, but instead I got a letter from Standard Statistics showing me how I could clean up a fortune in the market if I only followed their sure-fire tips, a letter from an art dealer in Glendale offering me a solid-silver serving set for six thousand dollars, and a bill from Hokum the Plumber. One more batch of mail like today's and I will rip out the mailbox.

As a result, I don't know whether you are playing in a tennis

234

tournament in Cincinnati, or working in a brewery. The local papers carry no news of any tournament going on in the sleepy little village on the Ohio. They all carry big pieces about a collegiate tournament and also about some other meet where Kovacs and his inferiors are batting the rubber ball around, but nothing about dear old Cincy. I am going to stop guessing and this is the last mail you get from the good gray ghost until I hear from you, either by post, telegraph or Alexander Graham Bell.

I can't understand why you don't get any mail from us. Perhaps it's because we haven't been writing. However, now that you've broken your silence, I will do the same, despite the fact that you probably still wouldn't have written if you hadn't needed money. Well, that's one of the nice things about holding the purse strings. Eventually people come around to seeing things your way.

Since I had to stay in town to work with Krasna and couldn't get away for a vacation, your mother left today for a tour of the outlying hot spots with her sister Helen. Your mother was very vague about where they were going, but I have a hunch that they will wind up at Las Vegas with those nickel machines.

Miriam and I are alone. Tonight the Murrays are coming to dinner and tomorrow night, the Krasnas. Bertha is leaving for a vacation tomorrow, and her sister is coming into the kitchen to wreck my stomach for the next two weeks.

Krasna and I are working very hard on the play (Time for Elizabeth). We don't work long, but we work intensively each afternoon from 1:30 to 5. We've only been working for five days, but we have the entire play outlined, and we have very few problems that can't be ironed out. I think we have some very funny and human stuff, and we both feel quite good about it. I am not so keen about coming to New York in the fall, but if the play is a hit and I'm good in it, it won't be such a bitter pill.

Gummo is at Catalina under the delusion that he is going to catch a marlin or a swordfish. He's taken his wife and Bobby, and I can just see that scene in the boat, with the hook from Bobby's line in the rear end of Gummo's pants—a typical Marxian fishing expedition. He should have talked to me first.

Your mother was quite irritated over the fact that I quoted one of her sister's unpublished and very corny poems at a party the other night. I thought it was very funny but very few people have a sense of humor where their own family is involved. She said, "I don't see anything particularly funny about this poem. Helen labored over it for days!" I don't know. I'm not that way. I have always been able to laugh at my own family, but some people are touchy.

I took Señor José Iturbi to watch the Hollywood Stars win their third straight from Oakland. It was the first game he had ever seen, and we had gone to the Chianti Restaurant for dinner, along with Dick Mack, and between us we knocked off three flagons of red ink. Then we went to the ball park and attempted to explain the intricacies of the national pastime to a bewildered Hispano. He was pretty mixed up, but we had a lot of fun. After that, we went to Iturbi's house and he played some Bach recordings that he had just made with the Rochester Symphony Orchestra for the Victor people. I never thought it would happen, but I'm actually becoming a musical nut—I listen to about four hours of symphony music a day, and whatever time I have left over I run upstairs and rap out the Prelude in C Sharp Minor on the guitar.

Don't worry about whether you win or lose; we don't care. The main thing is to have a good time and keep your health. When you win we love it, and when you don't we love you just the same. Forgive me for becoming so sentimental, but I always have a feeling when you lose that you feel bad for our sake. But it's really unimportant, and with the whole world rapidly catching on fire, it's becoming less important by the day. I got my money's worth out of your game the day you beat Krasna, and anything you did from that point on was pure velvet.

I must close, as I have to go to the village to buy pumpernickel, which is now sixteen cents a loaf. When I was a boy, it was four

236

cents a loaf. That'll give you an idea of how times have changed, and also how old I am. Oh, well, you know what I always say— As pumpernickel goes, so goes the nation. I think pumpernickel is a better barometer for measuring the strength of America's economy than the Dow Jones averages.

I am enclosing a three-dollar dividend check which came for you today from General Motors. I think it's a pretty shabby act on your part to spend money earned from the sweat of the brows of thousands of workmen at the General Motors plant in Detroit and drive around in a Chrysler product. This is known in rural circles as absentee landlordship, and in recent centuries it has been responsible for many revolutions throughout Europe.

All of us are anxiously awaiting your return and knowing damn well Riggs is going to win, anyway, I hope that you aren't planning to hang around Forest Hills until the finals.*

Love,

PADRE

* And I knew what I was talking about. Riggs won the tournament, and your author suffered an ignominious defeat at the hands of Vic Seixas, and retired from the sport in utter disgrace. GROUCHO

CHAPTER **24**

MOTHER AND FATHER were rapidly approaching the parting of the ways by 1941, and everyone in our household was perfectly aware of what was happening and expecting the worst. We didn't know just when the final explosion would come, but we knew it was inevitable.

How things reached this stage, or just when the situation really began to get serious, is difficult for a bystander—even one as close to the case as I naturally was—to know exactly.

My own impression is that they never quite belonged together. They were completely opposite types, with different emotional needs and conflicting temperaments.

Mother probably never should have been married to a comedian —particularly one who enjoys being an iconoclast. And Father never should have been married to anyone as shy and sensitive as my mother.

Father has many admirable qualities that go into the making of a good husband. He has always liked his home, he loves his children, and most of his interests keep him pretty close to his family.

But at the same time I can see where he would be a very difficult person for the average woman to cope with around the house. He's moody, eccentric and just old-fashioned enough to believe that the husband should be boss.

Also, he has a decidedly masculine point of view on most subjects. His views, for instance, on some of the minor courtesies, like opening a car door for a lady, or lighting her cigarette, or helping her into a dining room chair, were always certain to infuriate Mother. He didn't refuse to do these things, but his reluctant way of doing them was indicative of how he felt, and feels, about what he calls "phony chivalry." He firmly believes that this type of thing should have gone out when women got the franchise and started demanding equal rights.

"The trouble with you women is you want to have your cake and eat it, too," he used to tell Mother. "You want to be treated like equals and yet you expect special privileges. That was all right when women were supposed to be helpless creatures. But they're not helpless any more. If a girl can go out and play eight sets of hard tennis in the hot sun, it's a little difficult to believe that she's so helpless that she can't light her own cigarettes or sit down by herself."

"Well, I think those little things are important," Mother would reply indignantly. And then she might point out some fellow she had met at a recent party—a man who looked very handsome in a tuxedo, and who had been extremely attentive to her, and who had impeccable manners.

"That'll get him a lot," Father would scoff. "I'll bet he hasn't got a dime."

"Maybe not," Mother would say, "but at least he knows how a gentleman should act. That's important, too."

"Well, if I were a girl," Father would say, "I would think it would be more important to have a husband who wasn't out chasing every pretty girl he sees, and who didn't come home drunk, and who could support me. I'd be willing to pull out my own chairs if I could have a guy like that."

In spite of their differences it seems to me that until I was about sixteen years old they managed not to be too unhappy as man and wife. For what Mother lacked in the way of being a good straight man for Father, she made up for by remaining extremely pretty and youthful looking, and by being a good mother and charming hostess.

The actual turning point, when they changed from being a couple who merely had a lot of arguments (as what couple doesn't?) into a man and wife who appeared to be acting out parts in a very bad melodrama, seemed to be a trip they took to Honolulu in 1937.

Father had wanted to take Miriam and me with them, but Mother managed to convince him that it would do them both good to get away completely from household problems and noisy children for a while. So at the last moment Father decided to leave us behind.

But the trip did neither of them any good. Father had a miserable time, and he could hardly wait to get back to California.

"The whole place reeks of gardenias," he reported upon his return. "Every time I turned around, someone was putting one of those damned leis around my neck, or handing me a pineapple. And that beach I've heard so much about—it's hardly wide enough to lie down on. I spent the whole two weeks in my room at the Royal Hawaiian, reading."

I could believe it. His face was paler than when he left.

Honolulu isn't his type of resort under any circumstances, but he later confessed to me that the real reason he despised the place so much was because he had been angry at himself for having left Miriam and me at home.

While they were in Honolulu, Mother was upset because she claimed Father insulted their host, Duke Kohonomoko, at dinner one night. The Duke had served poi, as a special treat, but after one taste of it, Father shoved his plate away and said he didn't like to eat wet cement. The Duke thought it extremely amusing, but Mother, who was quite impressed by the island food and quaint customs, felt that Father had hurt the Duke's feelings, and insisted that he apologize.

"I apologize," Father told the Duke. "It doesn't taste like wet cement. It tastes like rat poison."

Father's quirks about spending money irritated Mother, too. One thing, especially, never failed to get a rise out of Mother. When he'd take her out to dinner to a place like Chasen's or Romanoff's, he'd nearly always insist on parking his car on the street instead of giving it to the parking lot attendant at the front entrance of the restaurant. This way he could leave his hat and coat in the locked car, and not have to tip either the parking lot attendant or the hat check girl.

Here again, it wasn't the actual money involved that mattered. "It's the principle of the thing," Father would insist uncompromisingly, as he circled the block trying to find a parking space. "I feel that when I give my business to a restaurant and pay those fancy prices, the least the proprietor can do is allow me to hang up my hat for nothing and park my car."

But Mother felt it was conduct not befitting a man of his position in the movie colony, and they probably wouldn't speak all through dinner.

The other major issue grew out of the fact that they simply didn't enjoy doing the same things together any more.

Mother, with her background as a dancer in vaudeville, enjoyed going to nightclubs and getting out on the dance floor. Father would take her dancing occasionally, but he'd do so much grumbling about it that Mother would claim she could have just as good a time by staying home—particularly since he would usually limit his dancing to what he called "one quick swing around the floor."

After many years of this, Mother finally decided that if Father were a better ballroom dancer, he might not be so reluctant to get out on a dance floor. So with the help of the Arthur Murrays, who were close friends of theirs, she finally persuaded Father to submit to a few lessons. The Murrays were very generous about giving our whole family free lessons, and to make the proposition even more attractive to Father, they would bring their instructors to our house.

Father was quite serious about it for the first few lessons, and he even learned to do a couple of fairly intricate rhumba and tango steps. But he began to lose interest when he discovered that the more his dancing improved, the more insistent Mother was becoming that he take her out and practice what he had learned.

Father was content to stay home in the evenings, with his books, phonograph, guitar and pool table. Pool is the only game he can play well, and when he was home he liked to shoot me a few frames after dinner. Then he'd often read or play the guitar for a couple of hours. To say that Mother didn't enjoy this sort of an evening is an understatement.

"If I have to listen to your father play one more piece on the guitar," Mother would say to me after dinner, "I think I'll go out of my mind."

Father had become very serious about his guitar playing late in life. Dissatisfied with playing by ear, he wanted to learn to read notes. He started taking lessons. He practiced scales and classical pieces for two and three hours a day. After he had mastered the rudiments, he began studying Rachmaninoff's *Prelude in C Sharp Minor*. This is an exceptionally difficult piece to play on the guitar, which anyone who has heard Father's rendition will realize. But Father was very proud of the fact that his teacher thought he was even good enough to attempt such a difficult piece, and one night, after months of practicing the *Prelude* without an audience, he played it for the family.

"Well, aren't you going to say anything?" Father asked Mother, after he had struggled through the *Prelude* to its final note.

There was a long silence, and then Mother said, "Why don't you go back to playing by ear? You used to sound much better before you knew what you were doing."

However, his enthusiasm for the guitar as a serious instrument was far from dampened. And when Andre Segovia came to town to play a recital at the Los Angeles Philharmonic, Father was in the front row, listening in ecstasy. I think he was more impressed with Segovia than with anyone he had ever seen or heard before in his life. He just couldn't get over how a man could sit on a small stool, in the center of a huge stage, and hold an audience in the palm of his hand with only a guitar. After the performance he went backstage, introduced himself to Segovia, and invited him out to the house to dinner.

At first Segovia was reluctant to accept, apparently feeling that he might be asked to play. Father didn't say he wouldn't ask him to play, but his counter-offer was just as appealing.

"I promise you won't have to hear me play. Where could you get a better offer than that?"

On the night Segovia dined at our house, Father couldn't resist the temptation to try to get him to play. He didn't actually ask him, but after dinner he walked into the living room with a guitar under each arm and sat down beside Segovia on the couch. Segovia knew what Father was driving at, but he had a sly sense of humor, and for a couple of hours he pretended not to notice that his host had brought the instruments into the room. Finally, Father handed one of the guitars to Segovia, and said, "Would you mind holding this for me for a while? I'm exhausted from holding both of them."

Father then launched into his version of the *Prelude*. This piqued Segovia's interest. He was so delighted that anyone else would attempt to play the classics on the guitar that he joined in and started strumming a few chords himself. But after a few minutes of this, he handed Father's prized Gibson back to him and said, "You can't play good music on this thing. It's got steel strings. It cuts my fingers to pieces."

The next day Father threw away his pick and steel strings, and bought a guitar with gut strings. But unfortunately Segovia was already on his way back to Madrid.

Also present the night Segovia came to dinner was Max Gordon, who had never heard of Segovia before he was introduced to him. He couldn't quite figure out how Segovia earned a living with just a guitar, and immediately started grilling him on the subject.

"Well, it is very simple," said Segovia, making one of the great understatements of all time. "I just sit on the stage and play Bach and Beethoven on my guitar, and people pay to come in and hear me play."

"But where do you play?" persisted Gordon. "How many people want to hear that long-haired stuff?"

"I keep busy," said Segovia. "One night I maybe play at Carnegie Hall, another night at the Paris Conservatory of Music, another

243

night in Leipzig, and another night at the Royal Albert Hall in London."

Gordon thought it over for a moment, then turned to Father and exclaimed, "My God, Marx—it's just one-night stands with a banjo!"

Father was also rediscovering Gilbert and Sullivan in the later years of his marriage. He had seen a couple of stage performances of *The Mikado* and *Pinafore* during his life, but until Norman Krasna introduced him to Gilbert and Sullivan again, by way of the Victor Recording Company, it hadn't really appealed to him.

Now he was going overboard on the subject. He bought all the D'Oyly Carte recordings, and whenever he and my mother didn't have anything specifically to do in the evenings, he would sit in front of the phonograph, with the Gilbert and Sullivan librettos on his lap, and sing along with the records. When he wasn't listening to the operettas on the phonograph, he'd be playing the songs from them on the guitar, or reading every biography of Gilbert and Sullivan he could get his hands on, or discussing, with great seriousness, the intimate details of their lives.

Mother thought that this was a pretty foolish way for a grown man to be acting. She had never been overly fond of the operettas, but now that they were becoming the number one reason why Father wouldn't leave the house in the evenings, she couldn't even bear to hear the names of Gilbert and Sullivan mentioned. And the subject was on Father's tongue constantly.

"Did you know that Gilbert wasn't speaking to Sullivan during the last few years of their collaboration?" Father might ask Mother at the dinner table.

"To tell you the truth, I've never given it much thought," Mother would say.

"Well, it's true," Father would go on. "Gilbert got so he hated Sullivan. He used to walk to Sullivan's apartment, and shove the completed libretto for their next play under the door. Then Sullivan would write the music, and send the whole thing back to Gilbert. They couldn't stand to see each other."

244

"I don't blame them," Mother would reply. "I can't stand either of them any more myself."

If Father suggested to Mother that she sit in the playroom with him after dinner, and listen to Gilbert and Sullivan, she'd start thinking up excuses to get out of the house.

"No, thanks," Mother would say. "I think I'll go to a movie by myself, if you're going to listen to *that* again."

After she'd go out, Father would shake his head sadly and say, "Your Mother either hates music or me. I can't figure out which. Maybe it's both."

Mother wasn't a baseball fan, either, and Father was—an avid one. During the summer he attended most of the Hollywood Stars' night games, whether Mother accompanied him or not. Usually she'd find something else to do on those evenings. Her attitude about baseball used to annoy Father, although he claimed the way she felt was typical of nearly the whole female sex.

"There are a few sensible girls who are real ball fans," says Father, "but the average girl just pretends she likes baseball while she's trying to hook a fellow. Once the preacher says, 'I now pronounce you man and wife,' she'll never set foot in a ball park again."

With Mother enjoying so few of the things Father enjoyed, there was a natural tendency on her part to start looking for new friends—friends whose interests were more like her own. She didn't dislike Father's friends; they just bored her a little bit. After all, they liked Gilbert and Sullivan and baseball, too.

I watched my parents drifting farther and farther apart, until I entered the Coast Guard early in 1942. I was away when they made the decision to get a divorce.

A few months later I received the following letter from Father:

Your mother moved out today, and the whole thing was kind of sad. I was sorry to see her go, for I am still fond of her, but obviously this uncomfortable set-up couldn't continue.

I said good-bye to her before she drove off in her car. It was one of those awkward, half-serious, half-comic moments, and I didn't

245

know quite what to say. I put my hand out and said, "Well, it was nice knowing you, and if you're ever in the neighborhood again, drop in." Your mother seemed to think that was a funny line—so for once in my life I got a laugh when I wasn't trying for one.

The house is pretty quiet now with just Miriam and me rattling around in fourteen rooms. Well, it's better than fourteen people rattling around in two rooms. I'll let things drift along—anyway, for the present.

CHAPTER 25

WITH ANOTHER WORLD WAR in full swing, and only an "A" gasoline ration card, Father did not consider himself to be in an enviable position. In addition to everything else, he was out of work.

The Marx Brothers' last picture for MGM, *The Big Store*, had been released in 1941. Early in 1942 the Marx Brothers officially announced that, after more than thirty years as a team, they were disbanding for good.

Harpo wanted to retire. Chico had taken a band out on the road and was smashing all kinds of records. And Father, who'd never really enjoyed making pictures, except when he was working for Thalberg, was ready to get out of the movie business entirely.

But he'd had a taste of radio, and he liked that.

Father considered radio a "very soft racket," compared with making pictures, or acting in a show. In radio, there were no lines to memorize, no costumes or makeup to put on, and very few back-breaking rehearsals. Writers handed you a script, and you simply stood in front of a microphone, wearing your own comfortable street clothes, and read off the jokes.

The one trouble with radio was that you not only had to have a sponsor, but you also had to keep a sponsor. And you had to have a formula that not only would fit your personality, but one that would appeal to a mass audience of people, a good percentage of whom had probably never seen you in pictures or in Broadway shows.

And so far Father's luck had not been too good on either of these counts.

The "Flywheel, Shyster and Flywheel" program had got big laughs from studio audiences, but it had lost its only sponsor after twenty-six weeks on the air in 1934. And in 1939 Father's hopes for becoming an important radio personality were given another shot in the arm, when he and Chico landed a job on the Kellogg Show, sponsored by the corn flakes company. This was a big, ambitious, hour-long variety show that had a large roster of other stars performing on it regularly. In addition to Father and Chico, there were Cary Grant, Basil Rathbone, Madeleine Carroll, Lawrence Tibbett, Carole Lombard, and each week a couple of big-name guest stars as well.

The Kellogg people had a lot of money to spend, and they were determined to give radio listeners the best entertainment ever heard over the ether waves. There were serious sketches, comedy, good music and sophisticated dialogue. Father and Chico did a "two-spot" together and also performed any place else on the show where they were needed. Father's favorite stint on the show was a husband-and-wife sketch he did every week with Madeleine Carroll, in which they discussed their daughter, Olive. These sketches were written by television producer Mannie Manheim, and they were Father's favorite pieces of material, because they were not only hilariously funny, but also completely away from anything else he had ever done before in his life. "Who's Olive?" became sort of a catch phrase around the country.

Father felt that he had at last found his proper niche in radio. The Kellogg people liked the show, too, for it was beginning to get a very high rating. But as the situation in Europe became increasingly worse, and America started participating in lend-lease, certain shortages in the corn market began to develop. Products no longer had to be oversold to the public. As a result, the Kellogg Company decided that it was foolish to spend all the money on advertising, and they canceled the show.

In 1941 and '42, Father guest-starred regularly on the Rudy Val-

248

lee Sealtest show. He also made a number of guest appearances on other programs. He never had any trouble getting that kind of job. Writers liked to suggest him as a guest because he was a big help when it came to punching up their scripts, and having him on the program therefore made their work easier.

But Father was fed up with guest shots. He wanted a show of his own that would stay on the air indefinitely and not lose its sponsor after the first thirteen or twenty-six weeks. Unfortunately, there weren't many sponsors around who were dying to have Groucho Marx star on a radio program.

This was made pretty clear to Father with the success of a show called "The Life of Riley," starring William Bendix. Originally this show had been Father's idea. Early in the war, he and his writer friend Irving Brecher had written the audition script with the intention of selling it as a Groucho Marx vehicle. Not the Groucho Marx character of stage and screen, but Groucho the family man, the father who gets pushed around by his wife and children: himself at home (or so he thought).

However, with Father playing the leading character on the audition transcription, the show just couldn't be sold. So Father gave up the idea in disgust, and told Brecher to do anything he wanted with it. He wasn't even interested in holding on to the fifty per cent he was entitled to as one of the writers. A few months later, Brecher turned the father in the series into an Irishman, made another audition record with William Bendix, and a sponsor bought it almost immediately.

"I'm certainly in demand these days," Father told Brecher when the latter informed him that "Riley" had been sold with Bendix as its star. "Why, you know something—a fellow could make a fortune in this business if he played his cards right. All he'd have to do is go around promising sponsors that he has a show that Groucho Marx won't be on. Why, they'd snap up everything he wrote, just like that!"

It was a disappointment to Father, but what could he do? He'd just have to sit back and wait for an offer. Certainly he'd get some kind of an offer eventually. Of course, if he lost his next sponsor, (provided he could get one) that would be something else again.

But meanwhile he was content to bide his time during 1942, doing occasional guest shots, playing a great many Army and Navy camps and hospitals, and in general fighting the Battle of Beverly Hills.

Father's biggest problem was transportation. He had an office in a Beverly Hills office building which he liked to go to every day. He also had to do the marketing, since he was now the woman of the house as well as the breadwinner. Being the woman of the house suited him fine, because there is nothing he enjoys more than doing the marketing. But unfortunately his only means of transportation was a Cadillac that consumed more gasoline a week than the ration board allowed him for a month. And Father isn't the type who'd trade on the black market, or try to get anything out of the ration board that he wasn't entitled to.

To get around this problem and still remain loyal to Uncle Sam, Father bought himself a bicycle with a basket affixed to the handlebars. And thenceforth he pedaled to and from Beverly Hills. He was admittedly a little too old for this sort of thing, but as he said at the time, "I regret that I only have one life to give for my country." This had a familiar ring to it. I think he had read it somewhere.

Father conformed to a rigid schedule during the war years. After an eight-thirty breakfast, he'd go directly to his study and read all the war news and latest magazines while he was shaving with an an electric razor. Father hasn't used an ordinary safety razor since the first electric shaver came out on the market and he discovered that not only could he throw away his soap and old razor blades for good, but, more important, he could also read while he was shaving. "Of course, I get five o'clock shadow by around one in the afternoon," says Father, "but look how well informed it keeps me."

Reading and shaving simultaneously is a feat very few men can pull off, but because Father has always had so much reading to do, he forced himself to master it. Otherwise he would never be able to devour the deluge of newspapers, books and magazines that arrives at his home through the mails every week.

After he had whittled down his beard and read where Walter Lippmann had said that it would only be a question of time before the Russian armies would engulf the Nazis in a huge pincer, Father would call up his secretary and dictate a few letters over the telephone. Then, dressed in shorts, sweatshirt and a beret, he would get out his bicycle and pedal down to Beverly Hills, with Duke, his police dog, trotting beside him. He and Father soon became a familiar sight. And if you've ever seen Father in a beret, you'll know what I mean by the word "sight."

Father's office was on the second floor of a building that had no elevator, and by the time he arrived there, he'd frequently be so tired out from the bicycle trip that he wouldn't have the energy left to climb the stairs. When this was the case, he'd remain on the sidewalk and whistle up to Rachel Linden, his secretary, who would open the office window and lower his letters needing signature down to him by means of a basket affixed to a long rope. He'd stand there for possibly twenty minutes, nonchalantly conducting his business affairs from the sidewalk, signing letters and perhaps even dictating a few more, which he'd have to shout up to Rachel. Then, his business for the day finished, he would go and haggle with the butcher and the grocer for a while, and after that, with his bicycle basket full of groceries, he'd hop on his bike and ride back home.

For a good many months, his business activities had dwindled down to little more than the routine which I just described. I was still away in the Coast Guard, but I could keep track of Father's activities from the many letters he wrote me describing his experiences during the war:

DEAR ART:

After many years, I've finally had my maiden voyage on a local bus, and it was quite an experience. I sat on a stone wall across from Schwab's Pharmacy waiting for it. A Negro dishwasher from

The Bit of Sweden sat next to me on the bus and quickly told me that she had been married, but that her husband had run away from her, and that she was now living alone. She added that she wouldn't object to getting married again, if the right man came along and if he was old enough not to get snatched away from her by Uncle Sam. She kind of looked at me when she said it, and I think I know what she was driving at. Another woman on the other side of me—about fifty and with very phony blond hair—quickly let me know that she was not accustomed to riding on buses; that she was doing it for a lark; that her daughter went to UCLA and that she had a fine big car in the garage at home. I made many friends on my little trip and we promised to write each other often, but you know how these bus friendships are—out of sight, out of mind. The chances are we'll never see or hear from each other again. The rest of the trip was pretty smooth going. We ran over a cat at Rexford Drive, but apparently that's not an unusual incident, for nobody seemed to think anything of it—except the cat.

I am short-waving a show to the men in foreign lands Friday night. Luckily it won't be heard in this country so nothing I say can be used against me.

Artur Rubinstein was at my house last night. He is a very cute guy, around sixty, and still likes to look the frails over. But he wouldn't play the piano for me. He said that he's working in a movie and that he had to get up at six in the morning. He said that he was so nervous thinking about it that he wouldn't sleep all night. We wound up with Iturbi playing. The trouble with Iturbi is that he now imagines that he's a hot pianist and wants to devote most of his time to playing boogie-woogie instead of the three B's and Mozart.

Butter has completely disappeared from Beverly Hills, but I find that yellow vaseline gives almost the same effect. It can also be used on your hair and in this way it's far superior to butter, which makes a very poor pomade. Also there are no coupons required for vase-

252

line. Last night I polished the piano with vaseline and it looked very nice, although it's still badly out of tune. Arthur Schwartz was outraged that I would permit Iturbi to play on such a piano; so was Harry Ruby; in fact, everyone seemed to object but Iturbi, who, as I said before, hammers hell out of boogie-woogie.

Life is very quiet and serene. Sitting up in my study, it doesn't seem possible that there is a war going on. Speaking of the war, I decided to outsmart the Westside Grocery Store and various dairies, who have virtually stopped delivering butter. I went to Sears Roebuck, chuckling as I walked in about how clever I was. I had decided to buy a butter churn. I would make my own butter. No one could outsmart foxy Groucho. I planked down six bucks and dreamed of the days in the near future when I would be sitting back with a house full of butter.

Arriving home, I told the cook about it. The cook, being an ex-farm girl, disillusioned me quickly. She said, "Mr. Marx, in order to have butter, you have to have sour cream, and sour cream isn't sold any more." So if you know a sailor along the coast who would like to buy a butter churn at a reasonable price, you might slip him my address.

We are looking forward to seeing you and would like to get a picture of you in your sailor suit—just as England has photographs of Admiral Lord Nelson and America has pictures of John Paul Jones.

I took Duke out yesterday, and around the corner he encountered a good-sized chow and promptly proceeded to eat him. He had the mutt by the throat and I had a hell of a time separating them. I hit Duke with the bicycle, but with the chow's throat in his mouth, Duke was wise enough to keep circling and it was hard for me to get between them. I finally found a big club in the lot and beat hell out of him. I am afraid his running days are over. I can't take him out any more. He wants to fight with every dog, and

I will get in legal trouble. So in the future he will have to remain in the back yard. I honestly believe he will die of a broken heart if I go biking and leave him home, but there is no choice.

I had kind of an offer to write on the next Bob Hope picture, but I'm still a year away from that kind of a job. I have a couple of radio deals on the fire that look very hot and I'm in no hurry to take anything else. It's strange, but both these deals are with concerns that peddle alcohol—one is a brewery, and the other is a whisky distillery. I guess they figure that only a drunk would listen to me on the air. If I had a radio deal tied up, I'd really prefer it for the fall instead of for the spring, but my theatrical career is so frail at the moment that I'll grab at anything—no matter how lowly, as they say in Pinafore.

I am still doing nothing, just waiting to hear from the Blue Ribbon Brewery. I have consumed thousands of gallons of their beer since I auditioned for them, and I am so water-logged I can hardly walk. I don't know why I drink this beer—it's probably some superstitious hunch that they'll get wind of it and put me down as a faithful and loyal servant. As a matter of fact, they want the show and have okayed it, but before they can actually make the deal, they have to get a decision out of Washington as to whether or not Eastern beer can be transported and sold on the West Coast. You see, there is some talk that with the transportation problem being what it is, only West Coast beer will be sold out here. And if that is the case, Pabst wouldn't want to advertise.

Love and kisses from
Dr. Hackenbush

Apparently all that beer-drinking did pay off, for the Pabst deal, that saw Father starring in a half-hour, coast-to-coast, weekly variety show, became a reality in early 1943.

So Father had two things to celebrate: not only was he among the employed, but he was getting rid of me. I was to be married to

254

Irene Kahn on one of my leaves home, and there was a good chance that he would never have to give me free room and board again.

Actually, when I first mentioned the subject, it came as quite a shock to him that a very low-salaried petty officer would dare to take on the responsibilities of marriage. "What do you want to get married for now?" he said. "You're already in the service. It won't do you any good. You might as well stay single."

But when I stood firm, he said, "Okay, but just don't have any babies for a while. I don't think the Pabst people would have hired me if they thought I was old enough to be a grandfather. And just remember, once you get married, you're on your own. Don't come to me for any money."

The only reason I mention my marriage is because I think the merging of the Marxes and the Kahns is rather interesting from the long-arm-of-coincidence standpoint.

Irene's father, who died shortly before we entered the war, was Gus Kahn, one of this country's most famous popular song lyricists. The recent movie, *I'll See You in My Dreams*, was the story of his and my mother-in-law's life.

Way back in the pre-World War I days, Gus Kahn had written the lyrics for *Cinderella Girl*, the vaudeville show I mentioned earlier as being the first one in which all the Marx Brothers worked together as a team. And before that, Irene's mother, Grace Kahn, had once journeyed from Chicago to Grand Rapids to get my father to plug a song for her. Grace was a song-plugger for the Remick Music Company, and she offered my father twenty-five dollars to sing one of her firm's songs in his act. She told me about her first meeting with Father. She knocked on his dressing room door and when the clean-shaven youth, who eventually became my father, opened the door and found out what she wanted, he invited her in. "Sit down," he said. "Have a cigar." He offered her one of the cheap stogies he was smoking in those days, and when she refused it, he said, "Well, would you rather take a shower instead?"

255

Twenty-five years later, the Marxes and the Kahns had become famous in their respective fields. And the Kahns moved into a house directly behind ours in Beverly Hills. They had a swimming pool, and we didn't, so naturally I struck up an acquaintance with their younger set. Irene looked good in a bathing suit. One thing led to another. And before you knew it, Irene and I were standing in front of a rabbi in Grace Kahn's living room, in February of 1943, getting married.*

Father and Mother arrived together for the occasion, and Father, just to show Mother that he hadn't changed any since their wedding, made funny remarks all through the ceremony and finally succeeded in breaking up the bride and our assorted guests and relatives.

And when the ceremony was over, Father walked up to the rabbi, shook his hand, and said, "Is it true that you fellows breed like rabbis?"

Father spent the next year or so trying to make a success of the Pabst Show, entertaining servicemen, and insulting everybody in general.

Because of the help shortage, Father started doing his own gardening. One day he was out by the sidewalk, weeding a flower bed, when a dignified looking lady in a Cadillac pulled to the curb. She was obviously in search of a gardener herself, and Father must have looked like a likely prospect.

"Oh, gardener—how much do you get a month?" she called.

"Oh, I don't get paid in dollars," said Father. "The lady of the house just lets me sleep with her."

As was the custom in those days, most of the important radio shows emanated from various service camps around the country. The Pabst Show was no exception.

Father was willing to do anything to make the enlisted men happy, but he was a violent opponent of the officer caste system.

* *In bathing suits?* GROUCHO

"I think I insulted more officers than any other living American," claims Father proudly.

Father had nothing against any of the officers personally. It simply bored him to sit around with the brass and their wives, and whenever a general or an admiral requested him to do a special show just for the officers, Father would turn him down.

"Why should I just entertain you?" he said to one four-star general. "You can go off the base and have a good time for yourself any time you want. Those poor enlisted men can never get off, unless you give them permission."

Since I was stationed at the Coast Guard Base in Alameda, California, and later in the Philippine Islands, I again had no way of knowing what Father was up to, except through his letters. Unfortunately, I destroyed most of them because lugging a bunch of letters around with me got to be too impractical in the service. However, I do have one last letter which pretty well explains what he was doing in the fall of 1943:

DEAR ARTHUR:

I received a letter from you this morning and a general complaint that you get practically no mail. I don't understand this as I write to you at least three times a week. Either you are drunk or I am hitting the bottle or maybe my letters are so unimpressive that you don't even remember them.

We previewed last night with Dotty Lamour and had a lot of fun. The previews are always more fun than the actual shows anyway. Since the chips are not down, everyone is at ease and the audience is aware of it. We leave tomorrow morning for March Field, where we'll again get shoved around by the brass until midnight.

I don't know whether I told you but I met your old collaborator Charlie Isaacs at CBS last week, and he is being shipped to sea. They are unquestionably going to grab off the fathers in the draft pretty soon, and we will lose Artie Stander. I believe he is by far our best writer and I am trying to persuade him to puncture his ear

257

drums. It's a fine state of affairs if I have to puncture all the ear drums of our writers in order for them to continue grinding out wheezes for the brewery.

How about a furlough? Don't you ever get enough time off to fly down here? I would pay your fare and you could live in your old room or you could live at the Kahns' or you could sleep in the window of the English Bakery. Since your kisser slightly resembles a fruit cake, you'd look great.

Do you really have to wait until the Admiral gives you permission to leave? Can't you just walk up to him, as they do in the movies, and say, "Look here, old boy, who's running this show? When I say I want to fly down to Beverly Hills for a few days, that's exactly what I mean." I wouldn't let old Mutton Chops start pushing you around so early in the war. Once you let those captains and admirals get the upper hand, there's no holding them.

Anyway, see what you can do.

Love and kisses,

HUGO Z. HACKENBUSH.

In February of 1944, Father traveled with the show to Milwaukee, to celebrate the hundredth anniversary of the Pabst Brewing Company. Among those on hand for the occasion was Edward Pabst, whose deceased father had founded the brewery and left it to him. By this time Edward, who was almost eighty, was just a figurehead in the company, having been bought out by larger interests, but because of his name he was slated to make the main address on the evening of the Centennial Celebration. About an hour before he was supposed to make his speech, Mr. Pabst confessed to Father that he was so nervous he didn't think he'd be able to go through with it. To calm him down, Father took Pabst to a nearby bar, where they both ordered beer.

"Miller's High Life," Father told the bartender.

"I'll have the same," said old man Pabst.

Father isn't sure whether or not this incident had anything to do with the fact that the Pabst people didn't pick up his option, a few weeks later, and that they replaced him with Danny Kaye. Father suspects not. But, anyway, he's always been very proud of the fact that he managed to get Mr. Pabst a little bit tipsy on Miller's High Life on the hundredth anniversary of the brewery his father had founded.

When Father first found out that the brewery was dropping him, he phoned Nate Perlstein, one of the Pabst executives, and said, "Wouldn't you reconsider if I went around the country and collected all the empty bottles of yours I could find?"

Having failed to establish any new endurance record with one sponsor, and having no more prospective sponsors on the horizon, Father devoted the remainder of the war to doing more camp shows and hospital appearances and raising money for worthwhile causes.

On one of these expeditions, Father took out a small troupe consisting of himself, Harry Ruby, Joe Carioca, the guitar player, and Faye MacKenzie, who'd been on the Pabst Show. They put on shows in hospitals up and down New England and through the Midwest.

One day the four of them found themselves in the Union Depot in St. Louis, with an hour to kill between trains. While they were waiting on the platform, a streamliner drawn by a very flashy-looking diesel engine pulled into the station. Father, for some unaccountable reason, suddenly became interested in finding out what the inside of such an engine looked like, and he shouted up to the engineer in the cab, asking him if he would let them go through the engine.

When the engineer said it was against regulations, Father said, "We're doing camp shows. This is my cast and we're pretty good. Would you let us go through if we put on a show for you first? If you liked it, that is."

The engineer didn't say yes, but he didn't say no, either. However, Father felt this was an encouraging sign, so he and his companions got out their musical instruments and did a show right there on the station platform. Joe Carioca played a number of hot guitar solos, Faye MacKenzie sang a ballad, and Father sang "Dr. Hackenbush."

At the completion of the performance, Father turned to the engineer and said, "Well, was it good enough to let us go through the engine?"

"No, but I'll let you go through the coach," replied the engineer.

In addition to putting on shows in the hospitals, Father was exceptionally good at just walking through the wards and cheering up despondent, wounded GIs with conversation. When he's not in one of his grumpy moods, in which case he'll barely say "hello" to a person, he has a rare talent for drawing out people and making them talk about themselves. I had always been somewhat aware of this, but it didn't really occur to me exactly how expert he was at it until I went along with him once during the war on a tour of some of the GI hospitals around San Francisco.

He had no cast of entertainers with him. He didn't even bring his guitar. He simply walked through the wards, stopping at each bed to talk to its occupant.

"Where are you from?" he would ask.

"Racine, Wisconsin."

"I played the Orpheum Theater there before you were born," Father would say. "Tell me—does Ed Hofheimer's restaurant near the theater still have such wonderful potato pancakes?"

No matter what home town a GI might mention, Father could truthfully say that he'd been there in his vaudeville days, and he'd always be able to recall some landmark of the place that you'd think only a native would know about. Naturally, this approach struck a responsive note in the service men he met, and soon each one would be rambling on about his home, his job, his girl friend, or practically anything else except his immediate troubles.

Father would throw in a few funny anecdotes now and then, too, or maybe a couple of jokes; but I think what the men enjoyed most was the chance to reminisce.

In the course of Father's wartime travels—I think it was on a Victory Bond tour with a number of other stars—he wound up on the front steps of the White House, talking with Eleanor Roosevelt. This was a great treat for Father, who had been a liberal and staunch Democrat since the days of Woodrow Wilson. He'd voted for Al Smith, he was a loyal Roosevelt supporter, and he felt that Eleanor was one of the greatest women of all time.

In the midst of Father's conversation with Eleanor Roosevelt, the official U. S. Marine Band started banging out a couple of very loud Sousa marches on the White House lawn. Father hates military band music, and after he listened to a few bars, he turned to Mrs. Roosevelt and said, "Now I know why you travel so much."

By the spring of 1945, Father's personal life was about to undergo another change. Romance was in the air and Miriam was on the verge of losing her position as head hostess of Father's house which, incidentally, was no longer the same one I was brought up in.

Father had sold his fourteen-room house in Beverly Hills shortly after I was shipped overseas. He figured he'd never need such a large home again. After all, he didn't need a room for me, since I was already married and wasn't planning to return to his domicile following the war, and Miriam was about to embark on a college career in the East and would only be around in the summers for a while. Besides, his income wasn't what it had been when he was working, and what was the use of spending a lot of money to maintain a large establishment? Who could tell? He might never get another job again.

So Father had bought a much smaller house in Westwood Village, and there he planned, once Miriam went off to college in 1945, to spend his "declining years" as a lonely bachelor—all but forgotten by the brewery for whom he had toiled away for such a short time.

Father, if the truth be known, was kind of looking forward to the life of an elderly recluse, and he certainly had no intentions of getting married again. He'd had a number of brief romances since he and my mother had split up, but Father was a little wary of getting involved seriously for a second time, and he had always managed to sidestep nimbly at just the right moment.

But as Father firmly believed—or at any rate, he does now—man does not control his own destiny.*

Father kept saying in his letters to me in 1945 that he was not going to get married a second time, but I kind of suspected from his frequent references to a young lady named Kay Gorcey that he would, and that it would only be a question of time. And I was right.

The date they chose for the marriage ceremony was July 21—my birthday. I'm not sure now, it's been so long, but I think this was supposed to be some sort of a tribute to a wandering son.

After I had been out of the Coast Guard for a couple of years, our family relations and titles became quite confused.

A daughter named Melinda was born to Father and Kay in 1946. And a boy named Steve was born to Irene and me in 1947. That made Melinda my half-sister, Steve's aunt, and Irene's sister-in-law, and Melinda wasn't even a year old yet.

Ours had been a rather unconventional family all along, and Father was still seeing to it that it remained that way.

* You're damn right he doesn't. It's the women who control it. GROUCHO

CHAPTER **26**

FATHER HAS always maintained that there is a great element of luck in show business, and he cites his success in "You Bet Your Life" as the prime example.

"You Bet Your Life" was broadcast for the first time in October of 1947, and it's been on the air ever since. But until the first show had been aired, and the reactions started pouring in, Father was extremely skeptical that there would be an audience for it, or even that he could be good on that type of show.

Father, in fact, had been pretty despondent about his entire career ever since he had been yanked off the Pabst Show so unceremoniously. It had seemed to him that the Pabst Show had been going along fine. Audiences liked it, and it was getting a higher rating by the week. He couldn't understand why the sponsors were dissatisfied with it and wanted to replace him with Danny Kaye.

By the time the war was over and he still hadn't landed another show, Father had pretty well talked himself into believing that he might never become an important radio star, or even an unimportant one.

At any rate, it looked as if it might be months yet—maybe even years—before he'd get another chance to prove himself on radio. Sponsors were pretty wary of comedians who had flopped a number of times before. They'd rather take their chances with some of the young blood coming up, if they were going to gamble, and who could blame them?

In the meantime, mainly to keep himself from disappearing completely from the public eye, but also because Chico was running out of money again, Father consented to make one last Marx Brothers picture. So he and his brothers formed an independent producing company with David Loew, and Father took his trusty frock coat out of mothballs and started painting on the phony black mustache once again.

The picture was called *A Night in Casablanca*, and it was a satire on Humphrey Bogart's *Casablanca*. Warner Brothers Studio made the latter, and when they heard of the Marx Brothers' plans to release a picture with a similar title, they claimed the name "Casablanca" belonged to them and threatened legal action.

Father immediately sat down and wrote the legal department of Warner Brothers the following letter:

DEAR SIRS:

Apparently there is more than one way of conquering a city and holding it as your own. For example, up to the time that we contemplated making a picture, I had no idea that the city of Casablanca belonged to Warner Brothers.

However, it was only a few days after our announcement appeared that we received a long, ominous, legal document, warning us not to use the name "Casablanca."

It seems that in 1471, Ferdinand Balboa Warner, the great-great-grandfather of Harry and Jack Warner, while looking for a short cut to the city of Burbank, had stumbled on the shores of Africa and, raising his alpenstock, which he later turned in for a hundred shares of the common, he named it Casablanca.

I just can't understand Warner Brothers' attitude. Even if they plan on re-releasing the picture, I am sure that the average movie fan could learn to distinguish between Ingrid Bergman and Harpo. I don't know whether I could, but I certainly would like to try.

So they say that they own Casablanca and that no one else can use that name without their permission. What about Warner Brothers—do they own that, too? They probably have the right to use the name Warner, but what about Brothers? Professionally, we were brothers long before they were. When Vitaphone was still a gleam in the inventor's eye, we were touring the sticks as the Marx Brothers, and even before us, there had been other brothers —the Smith Brothers; the Brothers Karamazov; Dan Brouthers, an outfielder with Detroit; and "Brother, can you spare a dime?"

We now come to the Burbank Studio. This is what the Warner Brothers call their place. Old man Burbank, who crossed all those fruits and vegetables, is dead. But who knows—perhaps Burbank's survivors aren't too happy over the fact that a plant that grinds out pictures settled in their town, appropriated Burbank's name and uses it as a front for their films.

It is even possible that the Burbank family is prouder of the potato produced by the old man than they are of the fact that from this town emerged Casablanca or even Gold Diggers of 1931.

This all seems to add up to a pretty bitter tirade, but I don't mean it to. I love Warners—some of my best friends are Warner Brothers. It is even possible that I am doing them an injustice and that they themselves know nothing at all about this dog-in-the-Wanger attitude. As a matter of fact, I have a hunch that this attempt to prevent us from using the title is the scheme of some ferret-faced shyster serving an apprenticeship in your legal department. I know the type—hot out of law school, hungry for success and too ambitious to follow the natural laws of promotion.

Well, he won't get away with it. We'll fight him to the highest court! No pasty-faced legal adventurer is going to cause bad blood between the Warners and the Marxes. We are all brothers under the skin and we'll remain friends till the last reel of A Night in Casablanca goes tumbling over the spool.

In due time, thanks to Father's fine grasp of the law, Warner Brothers withdrew their legal action, and the picture was released under its original title. But after Father saw the finished version, he was convinced that the Marx Brothers really had run their race, so they broke up as a team again.

265

In spite of *A Night in Casablanca*, Father got an offer soon afterwards to star in a picture without his brothers—this time from song writer Sam Coslow, who had turned independent producer to make a musical called *Copacabana*.

This was Father's first solo attempt at picture making, and he considered it quite a challenge. It was what he had always wanted to do—play the part of a normal human being who spoke funny lines but who didn't wear a grotesque, phony mustache.

He did wear a mustache, however—a real one, which he had been grooming for quite some time. At first, no one in the family approved of his wearing a mustache in every-day life, but Father said he would never shave it off, and he never did after that. He claimed that he couldn't appear in a picture without some kind of an identifying mark, after having worn a phony mustache for thirty years. Audiences would find it hard to get used to such a complete change. A real mustache would serve the same purpose as the phony one, and yet it wouldn't give the illusion that he was a slap-stick comic.

That was his story. Radio and television producer Mannie Manheim gave me an entirely different reason why Father, after all those years, suddenly wanted to wear a mustache full time.

It seems that a couple of months before he did *Copacabana*, Father was in New York to do a guest show on the Al Jolson radio program, which Manheim was writing with Charlie Isaacs. One day Father, Jolson, Oscar Levant and Manheim were walking down a New York side street, killing some time between rehearsals, when they came to a theater where *A Night at the Opera* was playing a rerun.

Several people were emerging from the theater just as Father and his party were walking under the marquee, and they recognized Jolson and Levant at once and rushed up to them and asked them for autographs. But these same people failed to recognize Father, who was the star of the picture they had just seen. After getting Jolson and Levant's autographs, they hurried away without giving Father a second glance.

As I've pointed out all through this book, Father could be pretty indifferent to the adulation of fans. In fact, he had always preferred not to be recognized. But to be completely ignored by the fans, at a time when his career was more or less on the downgrade anyway, was too eloquent a reminder of what life would be like when he was all washed up and people wouldn't want his autograph whether they recognized him or not.

The ham in Father suddenly came to the fore. And according to Manny Manheim, he did a big, slow burn. Moreover, he also must have made up his mind on the spot that as long as he was still some kind of a marquee name, he might as well make it easier for strangers to know who he was. At any rate, he started cultivating a mustache from that day on, and now he can complain along with the rest of the stars whenever he gets pestered by autograph hunters.

Copacabana, real mustache and all, did not do for Father what *It Happened One Night* did for Clark Gable. If Father thought he was going to get away from the old Groucho character, which he hated, simply by shedding Harpo and Chico, and getting rid of the painted mustache, he was mistaken. *Copacabana* was a Marx Brothers picture without Harpo and Chico, and not anything Father was especially proud of. Soon after its release, it, too, was playing second- and third-run neighborhood theaters, and before long Father was again on the prowl for another sponsor or independent producer he could bankrupt with his sharp wit.

Father's fortunes finally sank so low that he even agreed to audition for a quiz show—"Take It or Leave It." Eversharp needed someone to fill the vacancy created when Phil Baker walked off the program.

Father couldn't stand to listen to most quiz shows. He felt that they were entirely too hypocritical. "I could never be one of those kindly quiz masters, who asks people questions and then gives them the answers," he told me at the time. But because he considered "Take It or Leave It" the best of a bad lot, and at least it had a ready-made following, Father decided to take a whack at it.

I saw the audition he did for that show and, considering that he wouldn't help any of the contestants get the correct answers, nor would he even give them subtle hints, I think he gave an entertaining performance. But the sponsor hired comedian Gary Moore instead.

"A fine thing," commented Father. "I'm not even good enough any more to replace an elderly accordion player."

By the spring of 1947 it had been exactly ten years since Father had had anything even remotely resembling the hits that A Night at the Opera and A Day at the Races were. Financially, he wasn't too badly off. He had enough money salted away to last him the rest of his life, if he lived modestly. It was his ego that had been hit the hardest.

"I just don't understand it," he used to tell me. "I think I'm as good a comedian as Benny and Hope and the rest of those guys. As a matter of fact, I was once much bigger on the stage than they've ever been. And yet I lose every sponsor I get, and they go on year after year with the same sponsors. What's wrong with me that I can't click on radio?"

Then one day in April the phone rang, and it was Mannie Manheim calling. "Want to do a spot on the Walgreen Show?" he asked Father.

The Walgreen Show was an hour-long, star-studded radio extravaganza that the drug-store people put on once a year. The show was going to be transcribed and broadcast at a later date, and Mannie Manheim and his collaborator, Charlie Isaacs, had been assigned to write and produce it.

A steady job would have been better, but Father was in no frame of mind to turn anything down. He jumped at the opportunity.

There were a great many other stars on the show, including Bob Hope and Art Linkletter. Hope's part ran all through the program, but Father wasn't scheduled to make his first entrance to do a "two spot" with Hope until about the halfway mark. Because there were so many other names in the line-up, and because, on the night of the actual performance, all the spots were running longer than they were supposed to, Father had to wait about thirty minutes longer than he had expected, in order to get on. Meanwhile, Bob Hope had been in front of the mike most of the time, killing the audience.

The sketch that Father was to do concerned a radio station that Bob Hope was running in the middle of the Sahara Desert. And Father was playing a traveling salesman who was calling on Hope.

Hope's first line in the script was: "Why, Groucho Marx! What are you doing way out here in the Sahara Desert?"

Father was supposed to announce that he was a traveling salesman, but he was so annoyed that he'd been cooling his heels in the wings for so long that he ignored the answer that had been written for him, and instead replied: "Desert, hell! I've been standing in a drafty corridor for forty-five minutes."

This succeeded in breaking up both Hope and the audience. Crazed with success and in a reckless mood anyway, Father literally dropped his script from that moment on and started bombarding Hope with ad libs with the relentlessness of a panzer attack.

Hope, a pretty fair ad libber himself quickly entered into the spirit of the thing, and before Mannie Manheim or Charlie Isaacs could figure out how to stop them, the two comics had made an absolute shambles of their carefully prepared show. The spot ran twenty-five minutes overlength, and much of it would never have passed the censors. Among a great many other off-color remarks, Father and Hope, all through the spot, had made frequent references to a notorious Los Angeles madam of a few years back.

Luckily for the sponsor, who had invested thousands of dollars in the program, it was transcribed and the censorable material could be cut out. "But it was practically an impossibility to edit the spot and make it sound like anything," Mannie Manheim confessed to me some weeks later.

He and Charlie Isaacs still have nightmares when they think

of what Father did to them that evening. But they'll also tell you that in twenty years of radio they had never before heard such a hilarious routine.

Luck enters the picture, because if a man named John Guedel had not been in the studio that night to hear the best ad libbing performance of Father's career, "You Bet Your Life" might never have come into being.

Today, at the age of thirty-nine, Guedel is probably the most successful producer and packager of audience-participation-type shows in the business. But in 1947, his chief claims to fame were that he had originated "People Are Funny" and "House Party," and made a star out of Art Linkletter.

Father had never met or even heard of Guedel until that night, and chances are their paths never would have crossed if Linkletter hadn't been working with an unusual number of props on the Walgreen Show and needed an assistant to hand him the props during the broadcast. Guedel, being somewhat of a ham, anyway, volunteered for the job. But usually he wasn't in the habit of accompanying Linkletter to every show on which he was slated to make a guest appearance.

However, he was there, and on this occasion he saw and heard Father doing what he could do best, and he was so impressed that he sought out Father in his dressing room after the performance, and said, "Tell me something, Groucho—how come you don't have a show of your own? Wouldn't you like one?"

"Very funny," said Father. "Who's writing your material these days?"

"I'm not being funny," said Guedel soberly. "I mean it."

"Well, if you must know," replied Father, "I haven't got a sponsor. And when I get one, I can't keep one."

"You want to know why?" volunteered Guedel. "I can tell you."

"Yeah—why?" said Father, slightly irritated that a young punk who wasn't even born when he was a headliner in vaudeville should be telling him what was wrong with his comedy.

270

"Very simple," replied Guedel glibly. "On all the shows I've ever heard you on, you were tied down to a script. In my opinion, you never quite came off on a script show. Lots of people can read lines better than you. But nobody can touch you when it comes to ad libbing. You should be doing a show without a script, so you could utilize the thing you do best."

Three days later Guedel dropped by Father's house, with the original format for "You Bet Your Life"—a page and a half of hunt-and-peck typing, explaining how such a program would operate.

Father wasn't too impressed with it. "I can see where it might give me a chance to do some ad libbing," he said, after reading it over hastily, "but as far as I can see, it's still just another quiz show. There are hundreds of these audience-participation shows on the air, all presided over by jolly emcees who double up with laughter at their own bad jokes, and who can't wait to give a contestant the right answer. Personally, I think they're pretty sickening, and I wouldn't be surprised if the radio audience doesn't tire of them pretty soon, too."

"But this one is different," said Guedel.

"What's different about it? It's a quiz show, isn't it?"

"Yes, but the quiz is only a gimmick so you can ad lib. If you'll look it over again, you'll notice that there are very few actual quiz questions on the program. The rest is devoted to you interviewing them."

"I'm still pretty skeptical," said Father. "I don't know whether or not the audience will accept me in one of these things. Whether I've been a success on the air or not, I'm still supposed to be a sophisticated comic. I don't know if I can do the glad-hand bit, and be sincere."

"You tried out for 'Take It or Leave It,' " said Guedel, "and that was a quiz show."

"Yeah, and you see what happened. I didn't get the job."

"Well, this is a better format for you than 'Take It or Leave It.' "

"I don't know," said Father. "Give me a few days to think it over."

Father had already decided to try it. "What can I lose?" he asked me. "No one else is beating any paths to my door with any better ideas. If we get a sponsor, okay; if we don't, the hell with it. All I'll be out is the couple of hours it took me to make an audition record. I've got nothing else to do anyway. And who can tell? Maybe this guy Guedel knows what he's doing after all. He seems to have been pretty successful with Linkletter."

So he and Guedel formed a fifty-fifty partnership, and after a few conferences on the type of contestants and interviews they should have on the program, they set a date to make the audition record at NBC, rounded up a studio audience, and transcribed their first "You Bet Your Life."

However, before he agreed to go through with it, Father had insisted on two conditions: (1) The quiz would have to be completely honest. He would not help, or even give hints to, any contestant who was stuck for the right answer. "Either they know it, or they don't," said Father. "If we're going to have a quiz show, let's make it a real quiz show." And (2) the show would always have to be done by the transcription method, even if a sponsor bought it.

Father felt that it would be foolish—if not downright dangerous —to put an ad lib show on the air "live." Who could tell from looking at a contestant beforehand whether this was the type person who would let an unsavory remark slip out on the show and shock thirty or forty million listeners, the FCC, and a jittery sponsor?

And for that matter, who could tell what Father might say? He had, and still has, a notoriously bad reputation for letting remarks slip out that he afterwards regrets. His tongue is simply faster than his mind, and though he has often wished that it wasn't, there's not much he can do about it.

Once, not too long ago, a friend of Father's who is a movie director invited him and me out to the studio, to watch him shoot

272

his latest picture. The actor who was playing the lead is one of the biggest names in Hollywood, and though Father had never met him previously, he had heard considerable talk to the effect that the man's masculinity was a little bit in doubt.

When the director introduced them, they shook hands, and evidently the actor had a very powerful handshake. Pulling back his hand as though it were injured, Father said, "Say—you don't shake hands like a pansy!"

Apparently the full meaning of the remark completely escaped the actor, for instead of getting insulted, he threw back his head and laughed heartily. But Father was so embarrassed and ashamed of himself that if you had handed him a knife at that moment, he would gladly have slit his throat.

And yet if Father made a conscious effort to curb his tongue, he'd probably tighten up so during his interviews on "You Bet Your Life" that he might never say anything funny. Not only that, he was supposed to be an ad lib expert, and very fast on the uptake. That was part of what they were selling. How would it look if, before each remark he made, he sat there for forty or fifty seconds, trying to decide whether or not it would be wise to say the thing that had just come into his mind?

But if they put the whole show on wax, and were able to edit the questionable material later, Father could feel as free and easy before the mike as he would if he were conducting the interviews in his own living room.

I don't know how free and easy Father actually felt the night he made the audition for "You Bet Your Life." I wasn't there. But if I'm to judge by the jumpy way he acts before a broadcast today—and the insomnia he usually has the preceding night—I would imagine that he was pretty nervous when he faced his first pair of contestants—a bachelor and an old maid, I believe. I say "I believe" because no one connected with the show seems to know for sure. Father, in fact, can barely remember who was on his program last week.

I remember, however, that Father wasn't particularly elated

about the results of the audition when I asked him how it went the next day.

"It went all right—if anyone's interested in listening to a washed-up comedian grilling a group of contestants from the audience," he said unenthusiastically. "Personally I have no faith in the whole thing. I don't see why any sponsor would ever buy it."

However, there was one good reason why a sponsor might go for it, which Father had apparently overlooked. "You Bet Your Life" was being offered at bargain rates. A sponsor could buy it for five thousand dollars per week, not including air time. This was about one quarter of the budget for the average script show that had any kind of a name personality in it. The tremendous difference in cost was due to the fact that there were no major running expenses, except Father's salary, and he had agreed to take considerably less than the twenty-five hundred dollars a week he had received from Pabst. There was no one else in the cast, and they didn't need high-priced writers to write quiz questions.

Nevertheless, none of the big sponsors were interested. And it wasn't until about a month before the fall radio season was about to start that Father and Guedel received word from Gummo that there was definite interest in the show by Allen Gellman, president of the Illinois Watch Case Company.

"Who are they?" asked Father. "I've never heard of them."

"They make the cases for the Elgin Watch Company," explained Gummo. "They have a product called Elgin-American Compacts they want to exploit. They've never been on the air before."

"No, and if I know old Groucho, they won't be on for long, either," replied Father with his usual optimism.

When Father and Guedel started negotiating with Elgin-American, they discovered, to their horror, that Gellman wanted the show for an even cheaper price than it had originally been offered. He insisted that Father and Guedel contribute some of the prize money for the contestants out of their own salaries. Furthermore, air time on the two major networks, NBC and CBS, was too expensive for Gellman's blood. The show would have to be aired over ABC—a nationwide network, but one that was finding it difficult to capture listeners from the other two.

It wasn't a very good deal, but after thinking it over, Father and Guedel decided that it was better than no show at all. So they accepted the deal on Gellman's terms, and neither they nor Gellman ever regretted it.

The show started to catch on almost immediately. First reactions were amazingly good the country over, from Vine Street to Maine. And oddly enough, the show seemed to appeal to nearly every type of person—not just quiz and audience-participation show fans, but the people who liked sophisticated comedy. All of the radio critics but one raved about it. The lone dissenter was John Crosby who wrote, after the show had been on the air six weeks, that it was a shame that a comedian of Father's proven talents had to stoop to doing a lowly quiz show. He said that Father was not good on "You Bet Your Life," that it didn't fit him, and that he sounded too insincere when he was interviewing the contestants and handing out the money.

Perhaps Father was a little out of his element in the beginning. I know he confessed to me that he felt slightly uncomfortable doing it—especially since he thought it wasn't the kind of show his friends and the people he respected could be expected to go for. But after a few months, he became adjusted to the new surroundings, and started to sound as if he had been doing quiz shows all his life. His adjustment to it was helped considerably by the fact that even his most intellectual friends thought the show was great. And after about six months, even John Crosby swung around the other way and admitted that perhaps he had been a little too hasty in condemning the show.

Father was astounded by the success of "You Bet Your Life." "I don't understand it," he used to say to me. "This certainly proves I know nothing about show business. We get a sponsor not because he thinks the show is any good, or because he thinks

I'm a great comedian, but because it's the cheapest show he can buy. And what happens? It sweeps the country and I turn out to a bigger name than I ever was on Broadway."

Not only was the show a success from the standpoint of the radio audience liking it, but Elgin-American Compacts, which were given away to contestants on the program, were selling so fast that the factory couldn't keep up with the orders. Elgin-American literally wasn't equipped to handle such a sudden rush of business, and by the time early spring came, the product was completely sold out. As a result, Gellman jerked the show off the air four weeks before the regular season was supposed to end.

He said it was foolish to spend any more money on advertising that fiscal year, since he had nothing left to sell. However, it wasn't much of a blow to Father, because Gellman had already bought the show for the following season. Gellman, in fact, was so grateful that he sent Father a solid gold watch. And Father was so grateful that he wrote Gellman the following letter:

DEAR MR. G:

You could have knocked me over with a compact when one of your hirelings arrived here last week with a solid gold watch in his hands. My previous sponsors sold gasoline, corn flakes and beer. These, needless to say, have their value, but how would a man look walking around with a bottle of beer tied to his wrist?

The watch is a thing of beauty and will be a joy forever, and I would have thanked you sooner, but I purposely waited a week, for I wanted to be sure that the lousy thing would run.

Sincerely,
GROUCHO MARX

CHAPTER 27

IN 1953, around the time Dean Martin and Jerry Lewis invaded the British Isles, a group of English critics were discussing, over the BBC, what constituted a "great comedian."

One of the critics on the panel said that a comedian could never be considered great, no matter how funny he was, if his comedy didn't have an ingredient called "heart."

"With one exception," piped up another member of the panel. "I think Groucho Marx is a great comedian and he has no heart at all."

This story was told to me by movie producer Victor Saville, who is a native Englishman, and who had just returned to Hollywood from a visit to his homeland. "Isn't it amazing," Saville went on, "that so many people got that impression of your father before he started doing 'You Bet Your Life.' People recognized the fact that he was terribly funny, but at the same time they thought he was a little bit cold and heartless. Anyone who knows him personally knows this isn't true, and the masses who see him every week realize it today. But 'You Bet Your Life' hasn't been seen in England yet, so they still have the other impression over there."

Corny as it may seem, the lack of heart or warmth or whatever you want to call it in father's comedy was probably one of the main reasons why he was never able to capture a mass radio audience before he started doing "You Bet Your Life." And it was John Guedel who was responsible for changing Father's radio character into one towards whom audiences felt sympathetic. It has always been his theory that, if it came down to a choice, it was far better to be not so funny and be a person the audience likes than to be the funniest man who ever lived and have the audience not give a damn about you as a person.

With this in mind, Guedel took Father aside about ten minutes before they were to do their first show for Elgin-American, and said, "Now, Groucho, when you go out on the stage to do your warm-up, the first thing I want you to do is tell the studio audience a story. It doesn't have to be full of big laughs. Just be sure that you're the object of ridicule—to show the audience that you can laugh at yourself. That'll make them like you, they'll want to laugh all the more when you say something funny during the show. And that feeling will carry right over the air waves too."

As he finished his words of advice, Guedel suddenly realized that it was pretty nervy of him to be telling a man who'd been in show business thirty-five years how to get an audience to like him. It would probably be taken as an insult.

"I'm sorry," he quickly added. "Don't pay any attention to what I said. Just go out there and do what you feel like doing. I have no right to be telling you how to get an audience to like you. You were bigger in show business once than I'll ever be."

"Don't apologize," snapped Father. "I'm going to take your advice. I've lost every sponsor I've ever had. All your shows have been successful."

Father went out and told several stories about his daughter Melinda during the warm-up, and he found it to be such a successful formula that he's been doing it ever since. One of the stories he tells today concerns the time Melinda, who was then six years old, walked up to him and said, in all seriousness, "Daddy—are you dead?"

"Not that I know of," replied Father. "Why do you ask?"

"Well, I thought all people died when they got old," said Melinda, "and you look very old to me."

Father has had Melinda appear in person on the program several times, and they have sung duets together, quite successfully.

278

Fifteen years ago Father would have cringed at this sort of thing, and even now he can't stand to see other people's children perform. But in Melinda's case he's willing to make an exception, since (a) the public seems to like it, and (b) he thinks Melinda is very talented.

Of course, there are other reasons, too, why Father has become such a likable personality on the air. I think one of the things that has a lot to do with his popularity is the fact that he's now dealing with average people. His jokes are motivated by situations in real people's lives—not phony characters dreamed up by gag men. He can be funny on the air in the same way he's funny at home—commenting on life itself. His humor around the house was always as sympathetic and warm as it was amusing—as when he was playing the downtrodden father.

Furthermore, if a contestant is good, Father is willing to let him or her do most of the talking. The audience gets a big kick, for example, out of watching Father trying in vain to get back into the conversation with a housewife who won't stop talking. And the audience also seems to love it when Father, with his reputation for fast talk and cutting remarks, gets squelched himself by a remark from someone who is not supposed to be a comedian.

Naturally, it took more than audience sympathy alone to make Father a success on radio. The show itself had to be basically sound. And John Guedel deserves most of the credit for this, too, for in addition to originating "You Bet Your Life," he was the one who was convinced it would be a good vehicle for Father, and he stuck to his conviction even when Father believed the idea was practically worthless.

In the fall of 1949, "You Bet Your Life" moved from the ABC network to the Columbia Broadcasting System. There it continued to gain in popularity, and that year it won the Peabody Award for the best comedy show on the air—the only time, incidentally, that a quiz program has won this highly coveted award.

By the following spring, the National Broadcasting Company was fighting desperately to take the show away from CBS. Gummo was handling the deal, and the negotiations wound up in his home in Beverly Hills one evening. Father sat in the parlor, with representatives from NBC in a room on his left, and representatives from CBS in a room on his right.

Gummo trod back and forth between the rival factions, getting each to outbid the other, and alternately reporting the latest results to Father, who sat there with a smug expression, puffing on a two-dollar cigar. After several hours of high-tension dickering, the National Broadcasting Company succeeded in purchasing "You Bet Your Life" in a deal involving millions of dollars. Under this arrangement, which was one of the biggest deals of that sort ever negotiated, NBC owned the show outright, and Father would get paid for his services whether he had a sponsor or not. It was up to the network to see that the show had a sponsor, which wasn't much of a problem.

Many sponsors, including Elgin-American Compacts, wanted the show, but unfortunately it had become such an expensive property that Elgin-American could no longer afford to pay for it. So when "You Bet Your Life" went off the air for the summer, its first sponsor had to let it go, and the De Soto–Plymouth Dealers of America picked up the tab immediately.

That fall—1950—"You Bet Your Life" was televised for the first time. And luckily for Father, it also turned out to be a natural for television, which was in its infancy at the time the show came into being. In those days, television was something that most comedians who were already a success on radio didn't want to contemplate, for in the majority of cases, radio shows weren't adaptable to the new medium. You couldn't, for example, just set up television cameras in a radio studio and shoot the Jack Benny or Bob Hope shows as they were. Putting on a television program was like putting on a whole stage show once a week. Scenery and production values became important, and actors could no longer merely read off their lines. And this meant that most of the radio comedians would have to get entirely new programs if they expected to click on television.

But "You Bet Your Life" didn't have to undergo any but the most trivial changes—like getting an attractive backdrop behind Father. Father could keep right on doing what he had always done—sitting on a high stool at a desk, with the quiz and interview questions typed out in a notebook in front of him, and talking and joking with the contestants.

Nobody expected a quiz master to commit questions and answers to memory, and since the contestants didn't have any lines to learn either, and no scenery was necessary, it would be comparatively easy to set up movie cameras in the studio and simply photograph the radio show exactly as it was. In that way, "You Bet Your Life" could be on both mediums, without Father having to do any more work, and listeners could have their choice of hearing the show on radio or seeing it on television.

When Father and John Guedel announced that this was how they were going to handle the television problem, many people said that television audiences wouldn't accept a program that was nothing more than a photographed radio show. But they were wrong. "You Bet Your Life" was an overnight success on television. And at no time since then has it been out of the first five top shows in the Hooper and Nielsen ratings.

Father, needless to say, was sublimely happy, for not only had he succeeded in conquering his old nemesis, radio, by winning the 1949 Peabody Award for the best comedy show, but he was also a hit on television, getting his picture on the cover of *Time* Magazine for the second time in his life.

Looking back over his seven years on "You Bet Your Life," Father believes that the main reason the show made it to the top is because of its format. It contains something for two different types of audiences—quiz fans and devotees of comedy.

Father feels that another extremely important factor involved in the show's success is this business of taping the radio program and filming the television program, which he had insisted on from the beginning.

First of all, it has saved Father many a moment that would have been extremely embarrassing—and bad for the show—had the performance been actually going out on the air at the time it was being done for the studio audience. Father has several reels of censorable material that has been cut out of his television program over the past four years. Most of the off-color remarks weren't intended that way by the contestants responsible for making them. And a good many of them couldn't actually be called off-color at all. What made them sound dirty might have been just the way they fell into a particular conversation.

A good example of this occurred on the program one evening when Father was interrogating a traveling salesman, and he asked the man to relate his most embarrassing experience.

The salesman promptly launched into a detailed account of a harrowing escape he had once made from a hotel fire.

The blaze had started in the middle of the night, and was out of control by the time the salesman awoke and realized his life was in danger. All exits were blocked by flames and the firemen were raising the hook and ladder to his room window.

Being nude, the salesman looked around for some clothing, but in his excitement, all he could find was a pair of trousers belonging to his three hundred-pound roommate, who was still out on the town. He stepped into the ill-fitting pants and headed for the ladder that by now was up against the window sill.

Once he got on the ladder he found himself in the position of having to hang on for dear life with one hand, and at the same time hold his trousers up with the other. He managed to negotiate a few rungs of the ladder in this fashion, and then, just when he thought he could get all the way down without mishap, he felt himself losing his balance and had to grab for the ladder with the hand that formerly had been holding up his trousers.

"It was highly embarrassing," the salesman contestant concluded to Father. "The pants fell down to my ankles, and the crowd down below could see my whole predicament."

I wasn't at the broadcast that night, but I've heard from people who were there that that line got the longest and loudest laugh in the history of NBC.

Occasionally, Father himself will be an accomplice in the crime by unwittingly asking too direct a question during the interview.

On one program Father was questioning a young bride of two days, and he was trying to find out all about the wedding ceremony and how she and the groom celebrated afterward. But Father's choice of words was unfortunate. "Tell me," he asked, "what did you and your husband do on your wedding night?"

The bride told him exactly what she did on her wedding night, and in rather blunt language, at that.

But considering that "You Bet Your Life" has been on the air for seven years, there haven't been too many shocking statements made on the show. At least not as many as Father had thought there would be when he first suggested that they transcribe the show instead of doing it live.

As it turned out, however, Father discovered another much more important advantage to taping and photographing the show, which he hadn't foreseen in the beginning. That advantage comes from being able to edit all the material before sending it out over the air. This is especially helpful in this type of show, because no matter how carefully contestants are screened before they are chosen, a certain number of fairly dull people inevitably wind up on the program.

The interviews, when Father's actually performing, run longer than they are on the air. That way, when a dud contestant turns up—one who's too frightened to say more than "yes" or "no" to Father's questions, for instance—that spot can be cut down to its barest essentials—what's your name? where are you from? what's your occupation? and then into the quiz. And Director Bob Dwan, who edits the show, can let another interview, that's more interesting, run a little longer.

In the early days of the show, Guedel was so anxious to insure the success of the program that he insisted that Father interview four sets of couples. And from that the best three were chosen and kept in the final version. But after a few months they decided that this was an unnecessary precaution, and they settled for the way they're doing it now.

The show's high batting average is the main reason why there are so many skeptics who believe that Father rehearses every contestant before he puts him or her in front of the cameras. They claim it couldn't be an ad lib show for the very fact that there are so few poor contestants and dull spots on it. What they don't realize is that by doing an ad lib show for forty-five minutes, it's comparatively easy to get a solid half hour out of it for the broadcast.

Most of the contestants are chosen from the studio audience, as they have been ever since the show came into being. Before the performance, George Fenneman, the announcer, might ask all the housewives in the studio to raise their hands. He'll pick the ones that he thinks are the most likely, and send them to the back of the house. There they'll be screened by Guedel's staff, consisting of Bob Dwan, Bernie Smith, and Ed Mills. The staff will choose the two they like the best, and send them to the stage, where Fenneman leaves the final decision up to the studio audience. This he does by giving each housewife a short stint at the mike, to see who has the best personality. Fenneman will say to one, "Pretend you're a door-to-door salesman, and you've stopped at my house and you want to sell me a cow. What would you say?" And to the other he might say, "Pretend you're a reporter, and I'm the city editor, and you're reporting a fire to me over the phone."

After the two housewives are put through their paces, Fenneman will stand them side by side and ask the audience to clap for the one they like the best. The housewife who gets the most applause is the one who is put on the show. And I know this is on the up and up, because I've seen Father awfully disappointed when the prettier of the two wasn't selected by the audience.

Occasionally, Guedel might want a personality on the show who isn't likely to turn up in the average studio audience—an

284

admiral or a politician or a famous athlete. In this case he has no choice but to send out an invitation and put the man on the show. They couldn't very well expect a dignified admiral or anyone else of any prestige to stand up on the stage and be chosen by a show of hands.

In the cases of unknown people with unusual occupations—a private detective, for example—they'll generally send out invitations to two different detectives, asking them both to come down to the show. When this happens, the audience will again be called upon to decide which of the two they want for a contestant.

Father and Guedel shy away from using the type of person known as "professional quiz-goers." These are the people who go from one audience-participation show to another, hoping to get on the program and frequently succeeding. A lot of them even live on the prizes they win, but they're not good to have on a program because they're such extroverts that they give the whole show an air of artificiality. Very often, they will have been rehearsing (on their own) for days in advance, and might even have worked up a little routine that they can use if they get on the show.

Guedel's staff is very good at spotting these people, but sometimes they slip through by using phony names, and even disguising themselves. Then all the wise guys will see the program and say, "We knew it all the time—the Groucho Marx show is rehearsed."

Despite this talk, Father never sees a contestant until George Fenneman brings the first couple out of the wings for the opening spot. Until about twenty minutes before the show, you can find Father in the Brown Derby, eating dinner, and signing autographs. And when he goes over to NBC, he'll stay in his dressing room, getting made up until show time.

However, Father does know beforehand the type of contestants who are going to be on the show. He couldn't be expected to go out on the stage and ad lib without knowing anything about the people he is going to interview. He's not that good, and doesn't claim to be. If, for example, a prizefighter is going to be on the program, Father will have a few prizefighter jokes written in his notebook alongside the regular interview questions. He doesn't like to rely on the prepared jokes, because almost always the real ad libs get the biggest laughs. But he does have to have a certain amount of material prepared as a necessary protection against the contestant who is a real dud. If Father's interview questions fail to prompt the contestant into answers that he can bounce laughs off, then he'll be forced to use the prepared jokes to keep the spot from dying completely. And the same thing applies if Father is having an off night, and he's not as quick or funny as usual.

Another thing that makes some people believe the show is rehearsed is that every so often a contestant will come up with a perfect feed line for one of Father's remarks. With some exceptions, this is no accident, but it's also not a case of the contestant being rehearsed. It's due to the way the interview questions are written. The staff tries to think of questions that can only lead to certain answers. That way Father can more or less tell beforehand what the contestant's reply will be, and he'll have comeback lines for as many as three or four likely answers on the tip of his tongue. But the writers have become so skilled at preparing these questions that it sometimes gives the illusion that a contestant has been rehearsed, when it actually isn't so.

On rare occasions, Guedel will come across someone who he believes will make an unusually good contestant on the show. He might hear of such a person through a friend, he might receive a letter from the person himself, asking to be put on the program and stating his background, or he might find him through one of his other audience-participation programs—"People Are Funny" or "House Party." When this happens, Guedel will issue the prospective contestant a special invitation, thus insuring him a place on the program.

In the case of the Mexican song-and-dance boy, Gonzales Gonzales, who created such a sensation on "You Bet Your Life," and later got a picture commitment out of it from John Wayne, Guedel discovered him when he turned up as a contestant on "People Are Funny." Gonzales Gonzales, until he did his stint on "You Bet

Your Life," was strictly an amateur. He had theatrical ambitions, to be sure, as many people do who want to be contestants, but the closest he had come to working in show business was when he had driven a truck for a small radio station in New Mexico.

Father has never helped a contestant with the answer, and he never will. If a contestant gets any help from the audience, the question is thrown out and a new one is asked, even though the contestant might have known the correct answer without any assistance. Furthermore, Father never knows what the jackpot question is until George Fenneman hands it to him a few seconds before it is asked.

There have been many times when Father wished he could help someone with the answer, for it breaks his heart when a very needy person comes up before him for the jackpot question, and then stumbles on something comparatively easy. Very few of the questions could actually be called easy, but some of them are harder than others. I've seen a college professor miss the big question one week, and on the following week, when there is an entirely different question, a scrubwoman might come up with the answer without batting an eye.

One of the contestants Father was really pulling for was a young man named Sergeant Joseph Rodriguez, a Congressional Medal of Honor winner from San Bernardino, California.

In the interview it turned out that Rodriguez had single-handedly captured a strategic Chinese Red gun emplacement on a Korean hillside. He and his comrades had been ordered to take the hill, but by the time they were halfway up the incline, Rodriguez discovered that he was the only remaining member of the platoon. The rest had been killed. Instead of retreating, Rodriguez continued up the hill, bombarded the gun emplacement with hand grenades, and, when he was completely out of grenades, ran back down the hill to get more ammunition. He then ran up the hill again, and finished wiping out the Reds and the gun emplacement.

Most assuredly, it was a feat deserving of the Medal of Honor, and practically anything else the boy could be given to make his

287

life easier. Father hoped and prayed the soldier would win the four thousand five hundred dollar jackpot question—especially after the rest of the interview revealed that Rodriguez was now practically broke.

Rodriguez got off to a promising start, by answering all the preliminary questions and running his bankroll up to about three hundred and twenty dollars plus fifty more for hitting the secret word. This entitled him to try for the jackpot question, which was: "During World War II, Hitler and Mussolini had a favorite meeting place where they met and discussed strategy. For four thousand five hundred dollars, what is the name of this place?"

It wasn't a very difficult question for anyone who knew that it was Brenner Pass, but Rodriguez and his partner just didn't happen to know it. Father could tell this the moment he asked the question, and if ever there was a time when he wished that there was such a thing as mental telepathy, this was it. But he couldn't do anything about it, and he had to sit there and look impartial, even though he was rooting with all his heart for Rodriguez to win.

Father took quite a ribbing about this from his friends, many of whom accused him of being callous, cold-blooded, and even unpatriotic.

"You're the most heartless man I've ever met," Norman Krasna said to Father at the luncheon table the day after the Rodriguez show was broadcast. "Do you realize what that man did for his country? Not only did he go up the hill once in the face of enemy fire, but he ran all the way down again and then up a second time. And now he's broke and hasn't got anything to eat. How could you conceivably let that man get away from the program without giving him the four thousand five hundred bucks? You should have helped him get the answer."

"I can't help how many times he ran up the hill," replied Father. "If he ran up the hill a dozen times, I still wouldn't have given him the answer. Our quiz is not based on how many times a person runs up a hill. Besides, how could I have given him the answer in front of thirty million people?"

288

"Don't tell me that," concluded Krasna. "You could have thought of something if you had really wanted to. But you didn't want to, because you're a cold potato, and I'm not so sure now I even want to play golf with you this afternoon."

In spite of Krasna and a few others with similar views, Father feels that it's more important to preserve the show's integrity than it is to frame the quiz so that an exceptionally needy and deserving person wins the big money. And he also believes that the average home listener prefers it that way, too.

"Once you make an exception," claims Father, "it starts to become a habit. Pretty soon you're making a lot of exceptions and the whole quiz gets to be rigged, and you lose all your listeners. The people at home aren't interested in charity. They want to see a quiz where everyone has an even chance."

After Father had been on the air a few months for De Soto–Plymouth, he got the notion one day that he'd like to own one of those small, sporty English cars that were becoming all the rage in Hollywood. He intended to keep his Cadillac too, but he wanted a lighter, easier-to-handle car for driving in city traffic.

At the time, he didn't have a De Soto or Plymouth to his name. Not that he didn't think his sponsor made fine cars, but because he had been driving Cadillacs for a good many years, and he saw no reason why he should make a change simply because he was working for a rival company. And besides, De Soto–Plymouth hadn't offered to give him a car for nothing, so he figured they couldn't care much about what kind of an automobile he did drive.

Father was more naïve in the ways of sponsors than he should have been. He started looking around for a lightweight car to buy, and soon came upon a dealer who offered to knock a thousand dollars off the purchase price of an English Sunbeam, provided Father would pose for a few publicity stills standing beside the car.

Thinking nothing of it, Father agreed to the man's terms, posed for the pictures, and started riding around town in a very sporty convertible Sunbeam. He liked the car quite well, for a little car, and he even boasted to his brother Gummo about the good buy he had made.

"Are you crazy?" exclaimed Gummo. "You can't work for De Soto–Plymouth and advertise another car. That's in violation of your contract. It's bad enough that you don't even own one of their products."

"I'll own one when they give me one," Father said.

Nevertheless, he had to give the Sunbeam back. He didn't like it well enough to pay the full retail price to keep it. But he still wanted another light car, so he bought a convertible Ford.

De Soto–Plymouth couldn't complain about this. It was perfectly ethical for him to drive any kind of car he wanted, just as long as he didn't accept money for exploiting it.

He drove the Ford for about three months, all the while stoutly maintaining to his friends that he was a free man in a free country, that he was technically employed by NBC, and was therefore under no obligation to drive either a De Soto or a Plymouth. But underneath this bold front he was beginning to feel more and more ashamed of himself for being such an ingrate to the people who were actually paying his salary. He got so that when he was out on the street in his Ford or Cadillac he couldn't bear to look strangers in the eye.

Then one day, at the height of the noon rush hour, Father stalled his Ford right in the center of the intersection of Beverly Drive and Wilshire Boulevard. What was worse, he couldn't get the motor started again, no matter how hard he tried. But what was even worse than *that*, he had the top down, and everyone who drove by recognized him and was shouting, "Why don't you get a De Soto—like you tell everybody else to do?"

Within twenty-four hours, he had traded his Ford and Cadillac in on two De Sotos.*

* *At a slight discount.* Groucho

290

CHAPTER 28

FOLLOWING his divorce from Kay in 1951, Father continued to live in his sixteen-room house in Beverly Hills. It's a rambling Mediterranean-style house complete with swimming pool, Inclinator, and four television sets.

When he married Kay, Father was living in the small house he purchased during the war. When Kay became pregnant, Father bought a little larger house on a hillside overlooking the Sunset Strip. When Melinda reached the toddler stage, the hillside home was no longer practical, for there was no place for a little girl to play, except in the street.

In view of these developments, Father started looking around for another place to live, and he soon found the present huge house he's living in today. Even before he and Kay were divorced, it was really more house than they needed. But Father just couldn't resist buying a place that had nearly an acre of ground, twenty-four fruit trees, and a regulation-size pool table that the owners had offered to throw in along with the carpets and drapes.

After the divorce, it was definitely too much house for him, and he began talking of selling it and buying a bungalow in which he could live without having to negotiate any stairs. He had disliked walking up and down stairs even when he was young. Now that he was getting on in years, he'd frequently spend the whole day in his study on the second floor, even though he preferred to be outside in the garden, rather than walk down the stairs and then up again later.

So he and a real estate agent started combing every inch of Beverly Hills, in search of a bungalow that would meet all his specifications. But he couldn't find one to his liking.

Finally, when I was over at his house one day, I noticed that the "For Sale" sign was down, and I asked him if he had sold it.

"No, and I'm not going to," he said. "I don't want any of those cracker boxes I've been looking at. I'm going to stay right here where I can be comfortable."

"But what about the stairs?" I asked.

"I've taken care of that," he said. "I've bought an Inclinator."

And he led me to the back staircase and proudly showed me the strange-looking chair device that was affixed to the wall on a track that ran up to the second floor. "Greatest thing I've ever owned," Father went on enthusiastically. "All you have to do is sit down on this seat, press this button, and before you know it you're upstairs. No home should be without one—not even a bungalow."

With the stair-climbing problem out of the way, Father had no more qualms about living by himself in such a tremendous house. Besides, he wasn't really alone. He had Matty and Sarah, his two faithful servants, to look after his every need. Sarah is in charge of the upstairs and also doubles in foot-scratching, "at which she has no peer," says Father.

And Matty, up to the time she died last year, did the cooking and also took care of putting the Inclinator back in working order whenever it broke down. It's not in the habit of breaking down often, but, being mechanical, it does occasionally. But Matty was on to all its little eccentricities and could generally get it running again without Father having to call in a mechanic.

Recently, the Inclinator broke down over a long holiday weekend, and Father couldn't get a mechanic to come out and fix it. "I don't know what I'm going to do," he said sadly. "Matty was the only one around here who knew how to get it running again. I may have to hold a séance and see what I can find out from her."

With no one living in the house who can repair the Inclinator, Father's foremost concern is to see that it doesn't break down at all. But this is a pretty difficult assignment for anyone who has an

292

eight-year-old daughter and two grandchildren who seem to think that an Inclinator is a wonderful plaything.

"Hey, you kids, get away from that Inclinator," Father will roar out as soon as he sees any of them heading for it. "That's no toy for your enjoyment. Now go on outside and play."

Later, he'll say wearily, "I'm too old to be starting all over again with children. Children are for young people. My nerves can't take it any more."

Actually he loves having children around, and he spends a good deal of time entertaining Melinda and her friends.

After two marriages, Father seemed determined to remain a bachelor, and for a time he apparently enjoyed being single. He plunged diligently into his housekeeping chores. Keeping the household functioning smoothly had always been one of Father's major interests, and his devotion to this job often amazed Sarah, his housekeeper.

One day Sarah informed him that the washing machine had broken down and said that the repairman had recommended that he turn it in on a new model. This was agreeable with Father, but first he had to find out for himself if the new model was all it was cracked up to be. So he took a basket of dirty clothes down to one of those self-service laundry places—one that featured the particular make washing machine he was interested in buying—and spent the afternoon doing the wash.

"I guess I should have stayed home and sent Sarah," recalls Father. "All the housewives there recognized me and looked at me as if to say, 'How do you like that guy? A big television star, and he's too cheap to hire a laundress.' Not only that, but when I finished the laundry, I picked up the wrong basket of clothes by mistake, and an indignant housewife accused me of trying to steal her husband's shirts."

As a bachelor he has had some unique romantic experiences too.

A couple of years ago, Father had occasion to escort Deborah Kerr to a large party. This was the first time Father had ever taken her out, and he didn't have any idea where she lived because he hadn't picked her up at her home. She had come down to his broadcast in a cab, watched the show, and they had proceeded to the party from NBC.

Around midnight the party, which was in Beverly Hills, began to break up, and Father asked Deborah Kerr where she lived.

"Pacific Palisades," she answered.

"Pacific Palisades?" Father was shocked. Pacific Palisades was a good fifteen-minute jaunt from Beverly Hills, a thirty-minute round trip, and he'd be damned if he'd go that far for anyone—even Deborah Kerr.

Climbing up onto a chair, Father commanded the attention of the other guests, and yelled, "Anyone for Pacific Palisades?"

Another time, Father found himself in the company of a very pretty model who was a terrific bore. He took her to Chasen's, where all through dinner he got nothing but monosyllabic answers out of her. After dinner, when they were back in his car, he asked her how she would like to spend the rest of the evening.

"I know what I'm simply dying to do," the model exclaimed. "They're having a Charleston contest at Ocean House. What do you say we enter it?"

"Never before in the history of courtship has a girl found herself back on her own doorstep so quickly," reported Father the next day. "I was home with the *New Yorker* by ten after nine."

Father was a pretty choosy Don Juan, considering that frequently he couldn't even be bothered with finding a date for himself. "See if you can dig up a girl for me, too," were his final instructions when making dinner arrangements with Irwin Allen one afternoon. "Someone who looks like Marilyn Monroe and talks like George S. Kaufman."

Allen couldn't promise to deliver anyone meeting those specifications, but he did think he could find an attractive girl who'd be willing to double date with Father. On the night of their date, however, Father was pretty disappointed when he got his first glimpse of the girl the writer had brought for him. According to Father, she was about forty, not very attractive, and awfully tired looking.

294

Taking Allen aside, Father said to him, "For God's sakes, is that the best you can do for me? Where'd you get her?"

"She's very nice," explained Allen. "She's a widow. Her husband used to be a friend of mine before he died."

"He's not dead," said Father, glancing at the widow again. "He's just hiding!"

Father played the field for quite some time, but early in 1954 he started dating just one girl—Eden Hartford. In the summer, after practically every Hollywood columnist had reported that he and Eden were secretly married, I phoned to ask him if the rumors were true.

"No," he said emphatically, "but I am contemplating marriage. Do you give your consent?"

"Of course," I replied. "Have you set the date?"

"Now just a minute, my boy," countered Father. "Don't be so nosey. Just remember—when I married your mother, I didn't consult you."

I asked him no more about it.

Then, one morning in July, I picked up the Los Angeles Times and read that Father and Eden had been married by a justice of the peace in Sun Valley, Idaho. An hour later a messenger delivered a telegram to my home. It read:

IF YOU'VE HEARD ABOUT THIS, PLEASE REFUND THE PRICE OF THE TELEGRAM. LOVE FROM US BOTH. GROUCHO

Eden is a tall, attractive brunette, with a quiet manner and an easy-going temperament. She was once a model, and has had a few parts in pictures, but today she has no aspirations for either a modeling or a theatrical career. Her main interest is painting. Until recently, she was studying under Sueo Serisawa, one of Southern California's best known artists, and she's considered to be an extremely promising amateur.

"But promising or not, I'm never going to do any posing for her," claims Father. "I made that clear before we got married."

295

Father has changed remarkably little during his lifetime—or at least since I've known him.

He's still the devoted father he was when he used to tell me a joked-up version of Little Red Riding Hood when I was barely old enough to understand the story as told conventionally. Of course, he doesn't tell it to me any more. But Melinda is privileged to hear one of his bedtime stories every night that she spends at his house. And she appreciates his story-telling talent, too. One night, when Father was about to go out to dinner, Melinda rushed up to him in tears. "What's the matter?" he asked.

"You promised me Little Red Riding Hood," she cried.

"Well, I haven't got time tonight," he said. "Get Sarah to tell it to you."

"I don't like the way she tells it," complained Melinda. "You tell it better."

"Ridiculous," said Father. "It's the same story no matter who tells it. Why is mine any better?"

"Because you put more food in Red Riding Hood's basket," said Melinda.

Father still expects his children to play straight man for him. Melinda got hardened to this sort of thing quickly.

"Daddy, will you tie my shoe?" she asked him one day. "It's too loose."

"Too loose? He was a painter," said Father.

"Will you tie my shoe, please?" persisted Melinda. "It's too loose."

"Too loose?" exclaimed Father. "Didn't John Huston just make a picture about him?"

"Daddy," said Melinda patiently. "I know you want to be funny, but will you please tie my shoe first, so I can go out and play with the kids?"

Father is still insecure about money. When there is a parking space available around the corner from Chasen's, he still prefers to take advantage of it, and during the daytime he'll occasionally wear a beret, because he can fold it up and put it in his pocket instead of handing it over to a hatcheck girl.

But he's not insecure to the degree he once was when he was still worrying about what he was going to live on when he was completely washed up. Last year, in fact, he finally put a swimming pool in his back yard—even though he has never cared very much about swimming and likes it even less today. How he happened to spend seven thousand five hundred dollars for this luxury has always amused me.

My wife and I and our family live in the Pacific Palisades, and Father is always complaining that he doesn't get to see enough of his grandchildren, Steve and Andy, because we live so far out. But if he wouldn't drive out there with Deborah Kerr in the car, you can be sure he wouldn't make the trip very often just to see his grandchildren, especially since he has a small child of his own in his house a good deal of the time.

One hot day, a couple of summers ago, my family and I were invited to go swimming at Sol Siegel's house in Beverly Hills. Siegel, who is a movie producer, lives directly behind Father's house, and Melinda was welcome to use his pool whenever she felt like taking a swim.

This arrangement suited Father, until the day Irene and I took our children swimming at the Siegels'. On that afternoon, just before we arrived at the Siegels', Father, who was out cruising around in his De Soto, spotted our car and yelled, "Where are you going?"

I told him we were going swimming at the Siegels'. "A fine thing," said Father indignantly. "You bring Steve and Andy all the way into town to go to a stranger's house, and you never bring them to my house during the day."

"We wouldn't have brought them in if we weren't going swimming," I explained to him. "We can't go swimming on the grass in your back yard."

Two days later, while I was dropping a book off at Father's house, I noticed a steam shovel in the back yard. Father said in a disgruntled tone, "I'm putting a pool in, so when you take the kids into town next summer, you can bring them to my house instead of the Siegels'. It's a hell of a note when I have to pay seven thousand five hundred for a swimming pool in order to see my own grandchildren."

Father uses the pool, too, but only if the temperature rises above a hundred. On most days he's still content to get his recreation by taking a brisk walk around the block or inspecting his orchard. Or if he's in an exceptionally good mood, he might take Melinda to the Griffith Park Zoo or the Beverly Playland Amusement Park, where he'll sit on a bench reading a magazine, while his daughter goes on all the rides.

Father never lets himself get caught without a magazine. He keeps one on the front seat of his automobile at all times, so that if he ever gets stuck with some time to kill—even if it's just a prolonged traffic jam—he can put the time to good advantage.

Father is still reading and shaving simultaneously, too. And he still indulges in what has always been one of his favorite pastimes —proselytizing. When he reads something he considers particularly worth while, he'll first give you a verbal summary of it, and then he'll hound you for days until you read it yourself. He's very dogmatic in his views, and Heaven help you if you don't agree with him about the merits of a book, a movie, a certain restaurant, a joke, or even a particular line of thinking. Unless you're one of the few people whose mentality he really respects, he'll take it as a personal affront if you disagree with him about anything, and he's likely to get quite angry and upset about it.

He still does a lot of the marketing for the household, and he's still insisting that no bogus pumpernickel or rye bread be smuggled in. He still eats lunch at the Hillcrest Comedians' Round Table a couple of times a week, and he still reverts to the "World Telegram golf swing" on the rare occasion whenever anybody can lure him out onto the course.

He still sees the same people socially he's always seen, and when they come to his house to dinner, he still insists that they be there promptly by seven o'clock, otherwise "we're going ahead and eat without you."

His relationship with his brothers is the same as it's always been. He sees Gummo perhaps the most frequently, because the latter handles his business affairs and they share the same office in Beverly Hills. He sees Harpo almost as often. They live within a few blocks of each other and generally exchange dinner invitations a couple of times a week. They also meet at the Hillcrest lunch table and when Father brings Melinda over to Harpo's house to play with his children.

But Chico is still as elusive as ever, and it would take the combined forces of the Pinkerton Agency to keep track of his activities, and a roulette wheel, or at the very a least, a gin game to attract him over to dinner.

Zeppo dissolved his theatrical agency in 1949, and he can be found managing his plant in West Los Angeles, which manufactures airplane parts under government contract. And Chico is usually on the road, playing nightclub engagements, either solo or teamed with Harpo. Together they are a very successful and much sought-after team in the nightclubs, but Harpo is like Father in many ways, and he's not crazy about traveling around the country just to make money.

In so far as his practical jokes are concerned, Father has mellowed considerably in the last few years. He just isn't the prankster he used to be, though he will still insult somebody if a good opportunity arises, and if the person is important enough. In 1952, Father and a number of other Hollywood luminaries journeyed to Mexico City to participate in a movie festival, and, incidentally, to help cement Pan-American relations. Shortly after they arrived in the Mexican capital, Father and his companions were herded into an auditorium where a Mexican official greeted them with a warm welcoming speech. After that, he explained what their itinerary would be for the following day.

Miguel Aleman was president of Mexico at the time, and the official concluded his speech by saying, "And tomorrow afternoon at four o'clock you will come with me to a reception to meet President Aleman."

Father stood up and said, "What assurance can you give me that Aleman will still be President by tomorrow afternoon at four o'clock?"

Not long ago, at a tremendous party given by Edward G. Robinson, Father was elbowing his way through a rather crowded living room, when an elderly lady who was seated regally in a chair, pointed her finger at him and said, "Come here—you. I want to talk to you."

Father hadn't been introduced to her, and he didn't know who she was, but he didn't like to be spoken to in that manner, and he approached her belligerently.

"Who are you to speak to anyone in that tone?" he growled. "You've got a nerve."

"I'm Mrs. Vanderbilt," she said.

"Oh, I know you," said Father. "They named some alley in New York after you."

When he was telling me about the incident, Father said, "When I was a young boy, I used to think that if you were very nice to very rich people they would take a shine to you and give you fabulous presents, like a Cadillac * or a house on the French Riviera. But as I journeyed through life I discovered that rich people give you nothing—that's why they're so rich. So now I insult them all I want."

The word "moderation" still guides Father's every move, and it's one of the reasons, I'm sure, why he's in such excellent health today. Except for the fact that he still gets "a grippy feeling" now and then, or "a half a cold," which is the same thing, he's in perfect physical shape. He's only been in a hospital twice in his life—once for an appendectomy many years ago, and more recently he had to undergo some minor surgery at the Cedars of Lebanon Hospital in Los Angeles.

* De Soto. GROUCHO

300

Upon showing Father to his room the day he was admitted, the floor nurse, a rather prim, middle-aged woman, handed him a white sleeping gown and told him to get into it. She then bustled out of the room, and when she returned a few minutes later, she found him standing in the middle of the room with the sleeping gown on over his suit.

"You're supposed to take your clothes off first," she said.

"I won't take mine off unless you take yours off," said Father, firmly.

Mannie Manheim phoned Father the day after the operation and asked him why he had chosen to go to the Cedars of Lebanon.

"Because it's so handy to Forest Lawn," replied Father.

But aside from that one operation, Father has stood the test of time extraordinarily well. Norman Krasna calls him the Rock of Gibraltar because he never seems to change. He can go through the most terrible mental anguish and come out of it apparently unaffected. And along with all his success, he's had plenty of mental anguish. He's been through two world wars, a stock market crash that wiped out his life's savings, two divorces that saw his family broken up the same number of times, and several lean periods when it appeared that he really was "washed up" in show business.

"He's an amazing man," Krasna once told me. "Someone else might have wound up on a psychoanalyst's couch five times a week, but not your father. He just keeps rolling along. He looks as young now as he did when I first met him."

And Father is content to just keep rolling along. He's enjoying his present age, for he has found that there are many advantages to growing old. "For one thing, I can keep seated when a young girl comes into the room and nobody expects me to stand up," claims Father. "And secondly, I don't have to worry about the state of the world, and about whether or not the right candidate gets into office, and what unscrupulous senator is witch-hunting who. Let the young people carry the ball for a change. I'm just going to sit back and take life easy. And I'm all prepared for any eventuality—I've got two cans of sardines and a bottle of distilled water in my basement."

And as I said in the beginning, Father hasn't the slightest interest in looking backward.

One day, he and I were sitting having a drink in the men's grill at Hillcrest Country Club, when Clarence Meyers, who is in his late sixties and one of the club's oldest members, joined us.

During the conversation, Meyers looked at me, and then, turning back to Father, said, "Wouldn't you like to be his age and starting all over again?"

"I can't think of a more revolting idea," answered Father. "I've been through life once, and that's enough for me. I'm perfectly happy right where I am. I hope to live for many years, but if I knocked off tomorrow, I wouldn't have any kick coming. No sir, I wouldn't go through the whole damn thing again for all the money in the world."

"Not even for a million dollars?" asked Meyers.

"Well, maybe for a million dollars," answered Father, after giving the question some thought, "but it would have to be all tax free!"

INDEX

309

ABOUT THE AUTHOR

LIKE HIS NOVEL of 1951, The Ordeal of Willie Brown, which satirized the foibles of the amateur tennis world, Arthur Marx's second book is based on personal experience—in this case, thirty-three years of it as the subject's son.

Born in New York City in 1921, he spent his early years accompanying his parents around vaudeville circuits in this country and abroad. When he was eight, he moved to California where his father and several relations began making Marx Brothers movies. He attended the University of Southern California, applied himself with special zeal to tennis and won the National Freshman Intercollegiate title. After a brief span as a tournament player, he worked as an advertising copy writer, a radio writer, and later on as a movie writer. He now devotes all his time to writing magazine articles and books. He has sold humorous articles to Collier's, Esquire, Redbook, Cosmopolitan and other magazines. During the Second World War he served a three-and-a-half year stint in the Coast Guard, fifteen months of it in the South Pacific. He and his wife Irene have two sons, three-year-old Andy and seven-year-old Steven—the latter a disappointment to his grandfather because his name is not Amos. Mr. Marx lives in Pacific Palisades, California, and is currently at work on a novel.